The Mummy Unwrapped

To my wife and best friend, Celia;
to Kharis, the Mummy, wherever he is;
and
in loving memory of Peggy Moran Koster
(October 23, 1918–October 24, 2002)

The Mummy Unwrapped

Scenes Left on Universal's Cutting Room Floor

THOMAS M. FERAMISCO

with a foreword by
PEGGY MORAN KOSTER

McFarland & Company, Inc., Publishers
Jefferson, North Carolina, and London

The present work is a reprint of the illustrated case bound edition of The Mummy Unwrapped: Scenes Left on Universal's Cutting Room Floor, *first published in 2003 by McFarland.*

LIBRARY OF CONGRESS CATALOGUING-IN-PUBLICATION DATA

Feramisco, Thomas M.
    The mummy unwrapped : scenes left on Universal's cutting room floor / Thomas M. Feramisco; with a foreword by Peggy Moran Koster.
        p.   cm.
    Includes bibliographical references and index.

    ISBN-13: 978-0-7864-3734-4
    softcover : 50# alkaline paper ∞

    1. Mummy films—United States—History and criticism.
    I. Title.
PN1995.9.M83F47   2008
791.43'675 — dc21   2002012544

British Library cataloguing data are available

©2003 Thomas M. Feramisco. All rights reserved

No part of this book may be reproduced or transmitted in any form or by any means, electronic or mechanical, including photocopying or recording, or by any information storage and retrieval system, without permission in writing from the publisher.

On the front cover: Mummy ©2002 Superstock; Reel ©2002 PhotoSpin

Manufactured in the United States of America

McFarland & Company, Inc., Publishers
    Box 611, Jefferson, North Carolina 28640
        www.mcfarlandpub.com

Acknowledgments

During the course of this undertaking, there were many who provided invaluable contributions that helped make this book a reality.

I'm indebted to my wife, Celia, not only for her patience and encouragement, but for her masterful editing abilities and for saying "I do" to her favorite Universal monster — me.

A special thanks to Ron Borst of Hollywood Movie Posters for providing me with the precious copies of many rare Mummy scripts.

I also owe a special debt to everyone from Universal Publishing Rights. It was an indescribable joy working without red tape.

A very special thank you to one of the sweetest ladies I've ever had the great pleasure to call my friend, Peggy Moran Koster. Peggy was gracious enough to invite me into her home and her heart. She took me on a guided tour through her many incredible photo albums, and answered all my questions regarding *The Mummy's Hand* and her days at Universal.

I owe special thanks to another lovely Universal contract player of the '40s. Elyse Knox generously shared her *Mummy's Tomb* memories with me and described what it was like being carried off into the night by a fully bandaged Lon Chaney, Jr.

My long hours of research could never have been so successful without the help of those at the Margaret Herrick Library at the Academy of Motion Picture Arts and Science in Beverly Hills, California. They are the most professional staff of librarians I have ever known.

Further thanks go out to two real pros, Universal experts Tom Weaver and Michael Fitzgerald, for taking the time to answer all my questions, significant or not.

Thanks, Mom and Dad, for not only introducing me to *Creature Features*, but for having the good sense to abandon any hope of ever getting me to bed at a decent hour.

And finally, a posthumous thank you to Martin Kosleck for taking the time to answer my letter and for making *The Mummy's Curse* special, every time I watch it!

Contents

Acknowledgments   v
Foreword (by Peggy Moran Koster)   viii
Preface   1

Chapter 1	*The Mummy's Hand*	5
Chapter 2	*The Mummy's Tomb*	35
Chapter 3	*The Mummy's Ghost*	55
Chapter 4	*"The Mummy's Return"*	85
Chapter 5	*The Mummy's Curse*	99
Chapter 6	The Heroes Who Saved the Day	133
Chapter 7	The Heroines Who Were Whisked Away	149
Chapter 8	Who Were the High Priests?	161
Chapter 9	Getting to Know the Victims	181
Chapter 10	The Mummies	195
Chapter 11	Behind the Scenes	205

Appendix: More Mummies   217
Bibliography   223
Index   227

Foreword

by Peggy Moran Koster

I made movies such a long time ago that I almost forgot I ever did! They started showing my films on television, and much to my surprise, I started to receive fan mail. I never could have imagined these old films would be so beloved. I never thought many of the films I made were very memorable. They were all "B" pictures. I would get a new script every two or three weeks, memorize it and make the film. Then I would get another script and do the whole process all over again. They worked us contract players very hard.

I didn't make many horror pictures, but people seem to remember them. I was in *The Mummy's Hand* and another film called *Horror Island*. I remember *The Mummy's Hand* because I would bring the script home and my mother would read with me to help me learn my lines. But I couldn't practice my screams because of what the neighbors would think. I never met the actor who played the Mummy, Tom Tyler, without his makeup. He had to be at the studio at about 4:00 A.M., so by the time I got there, he was all made up, and it was hard for him to talk. When the time came for him to creep up on me, I had no trouble screaming at all! It certainly was an experience I'll never forget.

Preface

I wasn't around when Universal sold its first package of horror titles to television back in 1957. Twelve years later would prove to be a true year of miracles. Men walked on the Moon. The New York Mets won the World Series. And my parents introduced me to WNEW Channel 5's *Creature Features* Saturday nights at 8:30.

All throughout the 1970s, these wonderful Universal horrors aired repeatedly on television. Since VCRs were not yet household items, I was armed with my trusty cassette recorder, making audio copies of these ghoulish goodies, many of which I still have today. With my tape recorder rolling, I watched in awe whenever these films appeared on *Tales of Terror*, *Jeepers Creepers*, *Fright Night*, *Mystery Theater*, even *Spaced Out Films*. However, it was *Creature Features* that blazed the trail.

My foray into the genre began one cold winter night with *The Invisible Man*. My family gathered in the den in time to catch the airplane circling the globe. The words "A Universal Picture" appeared, then came the rest of the film and a love affair that has continued to this day.

In the weeks that followed, *Dracula* bid us welcome, *Frankenstein* created a living being and the mummy of Imhotep got a new lease on life after 3,700 years. They were all magnificent spectacles and all welcome guests in my home. As strange as it may sound, my brother and I made it through the dreary days of winter without losing so much as a wink of sleep. These monsters didn't really scare us. They were fun.

Spring finally arrived. However, all the baseball games, sunshine and family barbecues couldn't begin to dilute the terror I was about to experience by *the* film

I was waiting to see, *The Mummy's Hand*. The film opened with the words "A Universal Picture," this time circling an art-deco globe, complete with shimmering stars and upbeat music. And as the sun faded away in the New York sky, so did any hope of a good night sleep. The first half of the film was cake, and then came the crunch, clutching hands, howling jackals and especially the Mummy's shadow on the tent wall. This kid was scared!

Everyone has special childhood memories they treasure, hopefully, with the same fondness I have for these wonderful films. As time went on, the terror I felt while watching *The Mummy's Hand* for the first time evolved into a special affection. For those of us who are more fortunate, a small piece of our childhood can survive and prosper into a genuine passion that accompanies us throughout our adult lives. For me, that passion is the Universal horror and horror-related films from Hollywood's golden age, especially the Mummy movies.

He not only walked in the shadows and swamps of Universal's famed back lot, but he also walked in the shadows of the Frankenstein Monster, Dracula, the Wolf Man and even the A-budgeted Invisible Man films. Kharis, the Mummy, certainly deserved a better rap. His four films never received the budgets or the fanfare they deserved. The price tags on these films were cheap, even by B-picture standards. And yet, this ancient specter from Egypt's darkest catacombs has not only survived three centuries of must and mold, he has become more popular today than when he was first called upon to distract war-weary audiences, over half a century ago.

All throughout the early and mid–1930s, Universal Pictures established itself as the premier studio of cinemacabre. In fact, horror was what kept the corporation from bankruptcy. Then, out of the fog came a horror worse than anything seen on theater screens—a very effective British ban on horror films. It seemed that the front page news and international threat of war was enough to give the British a good case of insomnia. Ever fearful of a lack of box office receipts abroad, Universal's horror output came to a screeching halt. From late 1936 to the end of 1938, the closest the studio came to producing a horror film was the "Crime Club" series and *Night Key* starring Boris Karloff. But a new day was about to dawn. The Regina Theater in Los Angeles obtained inexpensive prints of *Dracula*, *Frankenstein* and *The Son of Kong*, ran them as a triple-feature and proceeded to clean up.

Upon hearing the news, Universal quickly reissued *Dracula* and *Frankenstein*. The films did so well playing together that some U.S. cities reported grossing more than they did during the first release of the two films seven years earlier. Realizing that horror was their bread and butter, Universal, now under new management and no longer apprehensive about the English ban, quickly began production on *Son of Frankenstein*, the third and most elaborate of the Frankenstein series.

However, the cameras did not roll smoothly during the next year and a half. All the horror and horror-related films released during 1939 and early 1940 ran over budget and were considered "problem films." They included *Son of Frankenstein*, *The House of Fear*, *Tower of London*, *The Invisible Man Returns* and *Black Friday*. The Universal brass knew that moviegoers would plunk down their cash at the box office regardless of what the films cost to produce. So by the spring of 1940, a new law was established. Tight shooting schedules and even tighter budgets were the new mandate. Sadly, the first horror film to feel the pinch was *The Mummy's Hand*. Its final cost was—ready for this?—$84,000! Even that was $4,000 over budget. Peanuts, even back then.

The Mummy's Hand had a meager budget that did not allow time or money for necessary retakes. In the end, there were continuity errors due to inconsistent editing, and overdubbed dialogue to repair the damage caused by last-minute scene snipping.

But most genre loyalists are willing to overlook these shortcomings, and today *The Mummy's Hand* and its sequels remain some of Universal's most popular horror efforts.

Few people know what changes occurred between the first and final drafts of the scripts, and their bewilderment has evolved into an insatiable appetite to find out.

The Mummy Unwrapped will take a close look at what Universal's classic series of the 1940s *might* have been. It will reveal scenes that were edited out of *The Mummy's Hand* only days before the film was released to theaters. It will treat readers to dialogue that was filmed and then cut down to almost nothing. And it will compare and contrast the original story of "The Mummy's Return" to the final shooting script of what was later renamed *The Mummy's Curse*.

The Mummy's Hand

> "TERROR that waited 3000 years ... stalks the Earth again!"
> — Trailer for *The Mummy's Hand*

Cast: Dick Foran *(Steve Banning)*; Peggy Moran *(Marta Solvani)*; Wallace Ford *(Babe Jenson)*; Eduardo Ciannelli *(The High Priest)*; George Zucco *(Andoheb)*; Cecil Kellaway *(Mr. Solvani)*; Charles Trowbridge *(Dr. Petrie)*; Tom Tyler *(The Mummy)*; Siegfried Arno *(The Beggar)*; Eddie Foster *(Egyptian)*; Harry Stubbs *(Bartender)*; Michael Mark *(Bazaar Owner)*; Mara Tartar *(Girl)*; Leon Belasco *(Ali)*; Frank Lackteen *(Old Priest 1)*; Murdock MacQuarrie *(Old Priest 2)*. **Crew:** Ben Pivar *(Produced by)*; Christy Cabanne *(Directed by)*; Griffin Jay, Maxwell Shane *(Screenplay)*; Griffin Jay *(Original Story)*; Elwood Bredell *(Director of Photography)*; Jack Otterson *(Art Director)*; Ralph M. DeLacy *(Associate)*; Philip Cahn *(Film Editor)*; Hans J. Salter *(Musical Director)*; Bernard B. Brown *(Sound Supervisor)*; Charles Carroll *(Technician)*; Vera West *(Gowns)*; Russell A. Gausman *(Set Decorations)*; Jack P. Pierce *(Makeup)*.

A mysterious Egyptian (George Zucco) arrives at the Temple of Karnak. Two priests (Frank Lackteen and Murdock MacQuarrie) escort him to a large altar and leave him with a very old High Priest (Eduardo Ciannelli). The High Priest escorts the Egyptian to a small pool of swirling vapor. As the High Priest begins to tell his visitor why he was summoned, the vapor dissolves. "Look deep into the waters of Kar." We see visions of ancient Egypt in the pool.

The High Priest tells his story: Over 3,000 years ago, Princess Ananka died.

She was the forbidden lover of Kharis, a Prince of the Royal House. Very much in love, Kharis "refused to believe she was lost to him, forever." He broke into the altar room of Isis to steal the secret of eternal life, tana leaves. Kharis was discovered by guards while attempting to restore his beloved to life. As punishment for this sacrilegious act, Kharis was sentenced to be buried alive with his tongue torn from his mouth to prevent him from uttering any further blasphemy that would offend the great god Amon-Ra. Kharis inevitably wound up (pun intended) in a cave on the other side of the mountain, guarding a secret passageway which led straight to Ananka's sacred resting place.

At this point, the High Priest informs the Egyptian that Kharis never really died. Kharis has been kept alive through the centuries by a steady intake of fluid from three tana leaves administered "once each night, during the cycle of the full moon." The High Priest warns that should any archaeologists too smart for their own good happen along, the fluid from nine leaves would restore movement to the Mummy, enabling him to do away with any nosy intruders.

The High Priest warns that it is imperative the dose never exceeds nine leaves. This "overdose" would make the Mummy uncontrollable, and would put the Egyptian's life at risk. The Egyptian takes his vows right before the High Priest collapses and dies.

Meanwhile, at the Cairo bazaar, American archaeologist Steve Banning (Dick Foran) and his sidekick Babe Jenson (Wallace Ford) purchase a vase. This is not an ordinary vase, according to Dr. Petrie (Charles Trowbridge) of the Cairo Museum. Petrie claims that the ancient pottery could lead to Ananka's Tomb. Steve, Babe and Petrie anxiously share this discovery with a leading authority on the subject, Prof. Andoheb, who unbeknownst to them is also the Egyptian from the temple. Despite Andoheb denouncing the vase as a fake, the trio decides to set out on their own to search for Ananka's tomb. Obstacles continue via cablegram as they are denied financial funding by Steve's boss back at the Scripps Museum in New York:

> Your presumed Princess Ananka discovery affords us great amusement. Not interested in financing further desert vacation for you. Should you return to New York will hold position open in bone washing department.
> Regards
> Dr. Lyons
> Scripps Museum of Manhattan

It sounds like they may just be better off in Egypt after all.

Andoheb instructs another disciple of Karnak, a beggar (Siegfried Arno), to follow them. The beggar learns that Steve and Babe find an investor in a gullible, kind-hearted magician named Solvani (Cecil Kellaway), who is currently headlining at the Egyptian Theater. The beggar informs Andoheb that the group now has the capital they need to begin their dig. Andoheb makes one last attempt to keep them from entering the forbidden valley by visiting Solvani's assistant, his no-nonsense daughter, Marta (Peggy Moran). Andoheb fools Marta into believing

1. The Mummy's Hand

that the would-be expedition is bogus, and that her father is being swindled. When Dad returns a bit looped, she is convinced. Marta and her revolver make a beeline right for Steve and Babe, as she demands that they return her father's money. When the duo explains the money is already spent, she calls their bluff and invites herself to tag along on the expedition.

Steve, Babe, Petrie, Solvani, Marta and several native diggers set out to find the Tomb of Ananka. What they fail to realize is that Andoheb and the beggar know exactly where the group is headed and are several steps ahead of them.

A few coins and beads are all the expedition turns up until Babe accidentally dynamites the side of a hill and exposes the seal of the Seven Jackals. Against warnings from the superstitious natives, the party enters the cave. Ananka is nowhere in sight. Instead, they discover a different mummy, Ananka's eternal guardian, Kharis (Tom Tyler). Later that night, when Petrie is alone in the cave examining the Mummy, Andoheb pays a visit. As shocked as Petrie is to see his Cairo Museum colleague, he hasn't seen anything yet. Andoheb places the dormant Mummy's wrist in Petrie's hand and says, "As a scientist, you are very unobserving, Dr. Petrie." Petrie can hardly believe his senses as he detects a faint pulse. Andoheb removes a small vial from his robe and pours its content into the Mummy's mouth. Within a few seconds, the potency of the tana fluid quickens the Mummy's pulse. Petrie reacts in shock upon realizing the creature has been restored to life. Shock quickly turns to horror as the monster's hand tightens around Petrie's wrist. Despite the terrified doctor's screams, the Mummy slowly sits up and strangles Petrie to death.

Steve and Babe are jolted by the scream and rush into the cave. When they arrive, they find Petrie dead on the floor and the Mummy nowhere in sight.

Andoheb instructs the beggar to plant vials of the tana fluid in the tents of the defilers and he commands the Mummy to kill wherever he finds the fluid. After Kharis knocks off native guide Ali (Leon Belasco), Andoheb orders Kharis to kidnap Marta. It seems Andoheb is so smitten with Marta, that his new plan (courtesy of an ample supply of tana fluid) is to spend eternity with his new metaphorical bride, just so long as Kharis doesn't drink all of the fluid first.

After Andoheb sends the obedient Mummy out to kill again, he hears a shot fired by Babe outside of the temple. Andoheb literally leaves Marta at the altar to investigate and has a confrontation with Babe that proves fatal. Andoheb falls down arguably the tallest flight of steps anyone has ever seen, leaving the full brazier of tana fluid boiling away in the temple.

By now, Steve has discovered the secret tunnel that leads from Kharis' cave to the temple of Karnak. He makes his way through to rescue Marta. The only problem is that Kharis is shuffling along right behind him. When Steve tries to free Marta, Kharis shows up and heads right for the tana fluid. Steve tries to block the Mummy's path, but the monster sends him hurdling across the room. It's a close call. Kharis reaches the dangerous excess of fluid. He lifts the cup to his mouth, but Babe arrives in the nick of time and shoots it out of his hand, splattering tana fluid onto the floor. The desperate Mummy gets down on the floor in a final attempt to salvage as much of the liquid as he can. Steve smashes the flaming brazier on top of Kharis and the Mummy goes up in flames. In the end, the victors prepare to return to America with the jewels of Ananka intact.

The Mummy's Hand is a very neat 67 minutes of good quality fun, despite the fact that we are not introduced to the Mummy until the final half-hour of the picture. After the film entices the audience with an atmospheric opening reel, it gives us a taste of almost every other genre that Universal was known for in the '40s— comedy, romance and action in the form of a barroom brawl. But as soon as the expedition gets underway and the Mummy is discovered, horror fans quickly realize the wait was well worth it. The film opens by teaching us the secret that has kept Ananka's guardian alive for over 3,000 years. More importantly, we learn who Kharis and Ananka are, and we gain an appreciation for the devotion that Kharis has for his princess.

The film does not contain the same romantic aura as 1932's *The Mummy*; however, *The Mummy's Hand* is certainly not devoid of romance entirely. Kharis must have had some idea of the consequences he would face if he were to get caught trying to restore Ananka to life. Amon-Ra must have had a soft spot for Kharis and Ananka. Even though Kharis' penalty was to be buried alive, the great god ordained that Kharis would stand guard over Ananka's tomb for eternity and protect her from the forbidden eyes and plundering hands of infidels. If one cared to sift beneath the surface, it really *is* romantic. In fact, if the rest of the players were not so likable, one might have hoped to see old Kharis do away with all of them and get the girl.

Ten minutes into the film, we meet archaeologist Steve Banning and his friend Babe Jenson, portrayed by Dick Foran and Wallace Ford, respectively. Their jovial and easygoing screen dispositions make it possible to forget that this is a horror movie. Two minutes into their screen time, we quickly see what makes them tick. The serious-minded Steve tends to correct Babe's grammar, and after nearly two bone-dry months of hard luck in Egypt, Babe, Steve's happy-go-lucky sidekick, is ready to pack it in while Steve insists on persevering. Steve is interested in a vase, which he believes is an important archaeological link to the past. Babe, on the other hand, purchases a small wind-up doll that reminds him of a Brooklyn girl named Poopsie. Despite how different these two men are, they remain loyal to each other. Whatever obstacles the writers have penned for them, we remain by their side every step of the way. They are denied funding twice before convincing Solvani to finance their dig. Once they finally secure the funds, they survive a barroom brawl which proves to be a day at the beach compared to their confrontation with Solvani's skeptical daughter who pays them a visit toting a sidearm. Eventually, the pair wins her over.

This is what makes *The Mummy's Hand* so enjoyable and several notches above its sequels. By sticking with Steve and Babe from the moment they purchase the vase at the Cairo Bazaar, to finally breaking the seal of the Seven Jackals, we almost feel as though we've become part of the expedition. Thus, we've given the film *our* loyalty by staying with it until the last reel.

1. *The Mummy's Hand*

This is more than we can say about the loyalty between the scriptwriters and the editor.

Throughout the entire script, many lines of dialogue and several scenes have been shortened in order to keep the pace. This was a very common practice at Universal during the quick, "shoot 'em in two weeks" programmer days.

The first major cut or difference between the final edited version of the film and the completed screenplay occurs immediately after Andoheb takes his sacred vow. In the film, the High Priest, seated in his throne, dies. Andoheb solemnly bows his head and the scene fades out. In the script, Andoheb is about to practice his new duties as the High Priest of Karnak:

> HIGH PRIEST: *(very quietly)* Oh, mighty gods of Egypt, receive my soul and judge me not harshly. By the signs of his birth you have chosen my successor. May you find him worthy... (*His eyes flutter and his body relaxes in death.*)
>
> CLOSE SHOT—EGYPTIAN
>
> *The body of the old High Priest barely IN.*
>
> EGYPTIAN: *(fanatically)* In my hands is the power of life and death. I swear that no unbeliever shall desecrate the tombs of our ancient dead—and live! (*One hand grasps the medallion about his neck. As the CAMERA PANS, he picks up a small vial, moves to the copper pot, tips it and the liquid pours into the vial.*)
>
> EGYPTIAN: *(as if memorizing)* Three leaves a night to keep the heart beating—nine leaves to give him life!
>
> *As the HOWL of a jackal COMES INTO SCENE, the Egyptian straightens up, listening. Then he moves toward the door to Ananka's tomb, CAMERA PANNING with him. He pushes open the door leading to the outer chamber, holding the vial in front of him. Door swings closed.*
>
> SKY SHOT—NIGHT (L.S.)
>
> *The full moon is half obscured by the broken clouds. OVER SCENE COMES the remote HOWL of a jackal.*
>
> FADE OUT.

In the script, Kharis was about to receive his first feeding by the new disciple of Karnak. In the film, we don't see Andoheb feed the fluid to the Mummy in this scene, but it would have made a good opening act better. Why such an atmospheric scene was deleted is really not known; however, when cast and crew are assembled for 18-hour work days and have but two weeks to get the film in the can, it's doubtful that this scene was ever filmed at all.

Fade in to the hustle and bustle of the Cairo Bazaar. The film introduces our two heroes. As they pass the beggar, Steve gives him a coin, then continues on. Steve then spends 75 of his last 84 bucks on a vase that can't hold water. But he's sure it's old enough to hold something, maybe a secret. Babe thinks his partner has spent too much time under the hot Egyptian sun. As the two begin to exit, Babe looks at his newfound good-luck charm, a small dancing doll, and sarcastically remarks, "Good luck? Poopsie, you're just an eight-ball with hips."

In the film, the scene dissolves to the Cairo Museum, but in the original script, the beggar utters a grim warning that we never got to hear:

> *He (Babe) shakes his head and follows Steve. As they leave the bazaar, PAN with them as they pass the beggar who again takes up his chant:*
>
> BEGGAR: *Alms! Alms for the poor unfortunate!*
>
> *Babe looks at his box and frowns.*
>
> CLOSE SHOT — BOX OF SAND
>
> *A few small coins lie on the edge of the box.*
>
> BACK TO SCENE
>
> *Babe bends over and scoops up two of the small coins.*
>
> BABE: *(explaining to beggar)* Just forgot my change!
>
> *He hurriedly puts the coins into his pocket and EXITS SCENE after Steve. CAMERA MOVES into a CLOSE SHOT of the beggar, who looks after Babe grimly. He smoothes the sand with one hand and then draws a series of lines in it.*
>
> BEGGAR: *(to boy beside him)* You see, my son? The sands of the desert reveal all. The tall one is an archaeologist, one-who-digs-for-the-tombs-of-the-dead. But failure has been his reward — as it should be, for only death and destruction can come to those who disturb the shrines of our forefathers! (*His eyes narrow as he looks after the two Americans, and a cruel expression grows on his face.*)

In the film, the beggar's appearance *looks* sinister enough. So much so that any excess of dialogue would have only diluted this mystique. The content of his scripted conversation also spoon-feeds the viewer facts that they are capable of figuring out themselves. At this point we are not certain exactly what the beggar has up his sleeve. However, time and another reel of film allow further facts to surface.

Following a couple of quick stock shots, again from *The Mummy*, we dissolve to Dr. Petrie's office. The discussion regarding Steve's vase is also considerably longer in the script:

> *INT. DR. PETRIE'S OFFICE — DAY*
>
> *The broken vase in a man's hand. Hieroglyphics can be seen, the marking interrupted by the missing pieces.*

1. The Mummy's Hand

DR. PETRIE'S VOICE: *Amazing! An absolutely amazing bit of luck!*

CAMERA PULLS BACK TO MED. SHOT, REVEALING *the vase in Dr. Petrie's hand. He is a middle-aged English professorial gentleman. Steve and Babe face him interestedly.*

STEVE: *(tensely)* Then you think it's authentic, Dr. Petrie?

DR. PETRIE: *It's an unequivocally authentic relic.*

BABE: See — what did I tell you? It ain't worth a plugged nickel!

STEVE: *(happily)* Babe — it's authentic!

BABE: That's what I said.

STEVE: It's real.

BABE: Yeah… *(double take)* Huh?

Dr. Petrie is examining the vase closely.

DR. PETRIE: These appear to be the hieroglyphics of the Seventeenth Dynasty. Don't you think so?

STEVE: *(nodding)* That makes the vase three thousand years old.

BABE: Three thousand years! It's a good thing you found a vase instead of an egg!

CLOSE SHOT — VASE

In Dr. Petrie's hand. Just under the broken out section are two hieroglyphics.

DR. PETRIE'S VOICE: *(excitedly)* Banning! You see these two hieroglyphics?

STEVE'S VOICE: *(his finger COMES IN and touches them)* Translated — they form two letters of our alphabet — "A N."

MED. SHOT — DR. PETRIE

DR. PETRIE: There was only one person of any importance identified with the Seventeenth Dynasty whose name began with those two letters.

STEVE: A — N — Ananka!

DR. PETRIE: *(nodding)* Ananka!

BABE: Who's that — a tootsie?

STEVE: One of the richest Egyptian princesses who ever lived! *(excitedly, to Dr. Petrie)* No one has ever discovered Ananka's tomb.

DR. PETRIE: Nor even the slightest clue to its location. *(holding up vase)* But I think you've found one —

STEVE: I can hardly believe it! We've got to be right.

The two men look closely again at the vase.

The next two shots are the only part of the scene that survived the final cut:

CLOSE SHOT — VASE

DR. PETRIE'S VOICE: This curving line must mean a hill or a mountain.

> These markings... *(his finger indicates them)* translated, give us another name.
>
> STEVE'S VOICE: The Hill of the Seven Jackals! *(excitedly)* That cross at the base of the hill ... that must indicate Ananka's tomb!
>
> *MED. GROUP SHOT*
>
> STEVE: *(continuing)* If that's true and we find it ... *(breaks off, thrilled by the possibilities)*
>
> DR. PETRIE: Your place in archaeological history would be assured, Banning ... As important to find as the tomb of Tutankahman.
>
> BABE: *(interested)* That sounds good! Say whereabouts is this Hill of the Seven Jackasses?

In the film, Steve suddenly blurts out, "This square at the base of the hill must indicate Ananka's tomb." With the scene shortened like it was, his response seems to come out of left field. Viewers get the distinct feeling they've missed something. Could he tell immediately that this vase would lead him right to the tomb of Ananka? The scene was understandably shortened, otherwise it would have approached four minutes instead of the 30 seconds that viewers are familiar with. At this rate, poor Kharis, already 3,000 years old, would be approaching 4,000 before getting any screen time. Once again, had time and budget permitted, more care could have been put into the editing.

Again, on paper, the scene continues. But in the film, the next and final line from Dr. Petrie, "We'll go in and ask Prof. Andoheb," has very clearly been dubbed. This was lifted from the more lengthy footage that would have appeared later in the scene, but was cut. Thus, it brings the scene to an abrupt end. Here is what the continuing banter would have been in its entirety:

> STEVE: Don't mind Babe. His interest in archaeology is strictly as an amateur. He jumped ship to go along with me on the ill-fated Scripps' Expedition.
>
> BABE: Yeah. I don't go much for grave digging. But one thing—it sure keeps me in training—for the W.P.A.
>
> *Dr. Petrie smiles and moves to a map on the wall. CAMERA PANS the other two over.*
>
> DR. PETRIE: The Hill of the Seven Jackals—about here, in the Mountains of the Moon.
>
> STEVE: I don't wonder the tomb's never been found. That's about the wildest, most isolated spot in Egypt. *(anxiously)* Would the museum finance an expedition to search for the tomb?
>
> DR. PETRIE: I see no reason why it shouldn't. We'll go right in and see Professor Andoheb.

> BABE: Who's the guy? I never heard of him.
>
> DR. PETRIE: He's head of the museum.
>
> STEVE: And the greatest of all authorities on Egyptology. *(excitedly)* If he says this vase is authentic — we're in!
>
> BABE: Say! Then what's holdin' us up? Let's meet the Prof!
>
> DR. PETRIE: *(carrying vase)* This way, gentlemen.

In conclusion, it appears that this entire scene *was* shot; however, all but 30 seconds wound up in the trash. The decision to scrap it was probably made because a good deal of this information is repeated only a minute or so later in Andoheb's office.

Reading through old screenplays always unearths a wealth of information. It not only uncovers scenes that did not survive scissors, but it often reveals who was more adept at memorizing their lines. Dialogue rarely, if ever, makes it to the screen exactly word-for-word as indicated in the script. This is especially true in B-pictures due to the tight time constraints. In *The Mummy's Hand*, Peggy Moran and George Zucco come the closest, with Cecil Kellaway following. This is not to say that Dick Foran and Wallace Ford fell short in learning their lines. Comedy and comic relief have always been most successful when spontaneous, and these two pulled it off quite well.

Director Christy Cabanne has more than his share of comedies on his resume. Cabanne's screen credits contain close to 200 features from nearly every genre and date back to 1910. Yet *The Mummy's Hand* is his horror film debut. And a fine job he does. Once we get past Andoheb's initiation into the priesthood, Cabanne keeps the mood light during the early reels by keeping us entertained with magic tricks, a barroom brawl and the wholesome face of Peggy Moran.

Once the Mummy is discovered, Cabanne lowers the boom. *The Mummy's Hand* contains more chills than any of the sequels, despite the Mummy's lack of screen time. Cabanne spices up the scene where we are first introduced to Kharis and makes it far more memorable on film than in the script, which left a great deal of room for improvement. This is mostly due to Babe's humor, which would have diluted the scene had it remained as originally written in the script:

> *INT. KHARIS CAVE — DAY — FULL SHOT*
>
> *A flashlight in the hands of Steve moves quickly about the cave, stopping momentarily among the urns and jars. It finally settles upon the mummy case of Kharis standing upright against the wall directly opposite the entrance.*
>
> *Steve moves up to the case, closely followed by the others.*
>
> STEVE: *(indicating case)* Give me a hand.
>
> *He hands the flashlight to Dr. Petrie, who keeps it trained upon the case. Steve and Babe remove the top carefully. Dr. Petrie plays the flashlight up and down the figure of Kharis, bound from head to foot in his bandages.*

> BABE: *(more awed than ever)* A mummy! He's dead!
>
> STEVE: You didn't expect him to be alive, did you?
>
> SOLVANI: *(peering into case)* But is that all there is? Where's the treasure? ...The gold and stuff?
>
> BABE: *(looking around)* Nothin' here! Looks like this mummy must've been on relief!
>
> CLOSE SHOT—MARTA
>
> *She stares at the Mummy and tears come to her eyes. She turns and leaves the cave abruptly, CAMERA PANNING.*

Cabanne comes through in grand fashion, turning that ordinary page of dialogue into a true goose-pimple experience. As the musical strains of Frank Skinner gradually build, we see the horror on everyone's face before the camera pans across, giving us our first look at the frightening figure of Kharis. The film continues with dialogue that was not in the script:

> STEVE: That isn't Princess Ananka. It's a man!
>
> DR. PETRIE: And in the finest state of preservation of any mummy I've ever seen.
>
> SOLVANI: But is that all there is? Where's the treasure? ...The gold and jewels?

Cabanne effortlessly weaves elements of horror and suspense with Babe's humor, which continues at an unobtrusive level throughout the film. Babe makes more than one reference to the howling "jackasses" instead of the jackals, and how they give him "goose pimples on top of [his] goose pimples." Also, Babe nearly swallows a stone when Solvani tries in vain to teach him a simple magic trick. None of this humor interferes with the suspense of the picture. It doesn't even come close, not only due to the nocturnal prowling of Kharis, but also to the mastermind behind it all—George Zucco's foreboding Prof. Andoheb.

If anyone can upstage a Universal monster, it's George Zucco. Whether scowling menacingly or smiling broadly, Zucco emits an aura of evil that is unparalleled in the history of Hollywood villainy. When Andoheb discreetly warns a startled Dr. Petrie in Kharis' cave that "some things should be left alone," the result is one of the most frightening scenes in the entire Mummy series.

When the Mummy strangles Dr. Petrie, his screams bring Steve and Babe running into the cave to investigate. But by the time they arrive, Kharis and Andoheb are gone and Petrie is on the floor, dead. Steve and Babe are left bewildered; however, the expedition goes on as if Petrie's untimely demise didn't amount to the tiniest ripple. A mere two scenes later, Solvani is joking with Babe, attempting to teach him a magic trick. This seems a bit unexpected from a group of characters we have, by now, grown to like. In the screenplay, our friends react much more solemnly to the death of their colleague. In an earlier draft, there is even a brief burial scene which will be mentioned later in this chapter.

The deleted scene that follows would have demonstrated greater compassion for their deceased colleague. In the final print, Dr. Petrie is rarely even mentioned again after his murder, but in the script, Petrie's murder has Solvani and Marta rattled enough to start packing:

> FADE IN:
>
> INT. TENT— DAY— MED. CLOSE SHOT
>
> *Solvani and Steve are alone in the tent, which is practically empty with the exception of a few personal effects lying around. Steve is sitting on a box, using the back of a book as a writing pad. He has just finished signing a piece of paper. He folds this and hands it to Solvani.*
>
> SOLVANI: *(indicating folded paper)* You didn't have to do this…
>
> STEVE: I wanted to.*(hesitates)* It's probably better that you and Marta are leaving—after what happened to Dr. Petrie.
>
> SOLVANI: Any idea what did happen?
>
> STEVE: *(shaking his head)* Those natives could have sneaked back and taken revenge for his opening the tomb.
>
> SOLVANI: It could have been a heart attack.
>
> STEVE: I hardly think so. There were those gray streaks across his throat. They might indicate a struggle.
>
> SOLVANI: That wouldn't explain the disappearance of the Mummy.
>
> STEVE: Unless the natives took it.
>
> SOLVANI: *(earnestly)* You ought to return with us, Steve. Maybe there is a curse on that tomb.
>
> STEVE: No. I've got to try to find out what happened to Petrie … and I'm still convinced we're on the right track of Ananka's tomb.
>
> SOLVANI: Well…
>
> *He sticks his hand out. Steve takes it.*
>
> STEVE: You're sure your booking office will cable your passage to New York?
>
> *Solvani nods, Steve shakes his hand.*
>
> STEVE: Good luck. Let me hear from you.
>
> *He turns and goes out. Solvani looks down at the paper in his hand and shakes his head, sentimentally.*
>
> EXT. EXCAVATION— DAY— FULL SHOT
>
> *Two pack mules stand near the tents. Ali and Babe are adjusting the baggage as Marta stands close by. Steve comes out of tent.*

CLOSER SHOT

As Steve comes up to group.

BABE: *(cinching a strap)* All set.

MARTA: I'll tell Pop.

She exits SCENE. CAMREA MOVES IN to a CLOSE SHOT of Babe and Steve.

BABE: Too bad it worked out like this. *(seeing Steve's look)* I mean about you and Marta.

STEVE: What are you gabbing about?

BABE: Playin' dumb, huh? Well, I been watching the way you look at her and I ain't cock-eyed.

STEVE: Shut up or I'll send you back to town with them.

MED. CLOSE SHOT — EXT. HILL

Hidden by brush, the Egyptian beggar is looking down. Andoheb appears behind him.

BEGGAR: The girl and her father are leaving. The others stay.

Andoheb nods.

BEGGAR: They must not return to Cairo, master. They may tell other unbelievers who will come here to search for the tomb.

ANDOHEB: They will not reach Cairo. The old man will die.

BEGGAR: And the girl?

ANDOHEB: *(as he looks off)* I have other plans...

BEGGAR: *(shocked surprise)* But, master —

Andoheb looks at the beggar sharply. The beggar backs off and Andoheb continues to look down with a malignant smile.

INT. TENT — MED. CLOSE SHOT

Marta is picking up a few odds and ends as Solvani comes close to her.

SOLVANI: *Marta...*

She turns, arrested by the tone of his voice.

SOLVANI: *(continuing)* I've always seen eye to eye with you, honey. But this time you're dead wrong.

MARTA: What do you mean?

Solvani hands her the paper. As she reads it aloud, her brow knits.

INSERT — SHEET OF PAPER

Marta's voice comes over:

MARTA'S VOICE: *(reading)* I hereby promise to repay at any time in the future when I am able, the entire sum of two-thousand dollars advanced

1. The Mummy's Hand

by you to finance the Ananka Expedition. This has no bearing on your share of the proceeds. You will still receive one third of whatever we discover. Signed, Steve Banning.

CLOSE UP—MARTA

As she finishes reading, Solvani's VOICE COMES OVER.

SOLVANI'S VOICE: He doesn't care anything about the money or the jewels he might find ... his interest is entirely the advancement of human knowledge. And the way you've treated him—

CLOSE SHOT—SOLVANI AND MARTA

As Marta looks up.

SOLVANI: I think you owe him an apology.

MARTA: *(biting her lip)* You wait right here.

She goes out quickly, CAMERA PANNING with her.

EXT. TENT—MED. CLOSE SHOT AT ENTRANCE

As Marta comes through. CAMERA PANS with her as she walks hurriedly in to Steve. Babe and Ali can be seen on the far side of the mules, cinching straps, rearranging luggage.

MARTA: *(holding out paper to Steve)* You can't do this to us!

STEVE: *(taken aback)* What do you mean? I only thought—

MARTA: *(interrupting)* Well, you thought wrong. If you can give up everything for this work—we can give up a little, too.

Steve regards her in surprise.

MARTA: *(continuing)* The natives have left you flat. Would an old man and a girl be of any help?

STEVE: *(puzzled)* Help? *(eagerly)* You're not going?

MARTA: I wouldn't blame you for wanting me to.

STEVE: Marta—

He takes her by the arm and is about to say something else, as Babe saunters by, giving him a knowing look.

BABE: *(grinning)* We can get you unpacked in two shakes of a lamb! Come on Ali!

He walks right on by, circles around the mules, back to the position from which he started. Babe grins as he comes into Ali. They start unpacking and Babe peeks over top of mule, as Marta and Steve come close together, but are almost hidden by the mule's body.

FADE OUT.

It's easy to understand why this scene was cut. We finally see Kharis in action and then suddenly three or four minutes are invested to see if Solvani and Marta are going to leave or stay. Too much talking in between Mummy murders caused later Mummy films (such as Hammer's *The Curse of the Mummy's Tomb*) to suffer.

While Solvani and Marta are trying to figure out if they're coming or going, we get a peek at a riff taking place between Andoheb and the beggar, who are spying on the expedition from some distance away. Andoheb's "plan for Marta" is first mentioned in this deleted scene and is met with resistance from his underling. Of course we can only surmise what the beggar already seems to know. One look at the curvy heroine and it isn't too difficult to imagine what's on Andoheb's mind. The disagreement, such as it is, suggests trouble in the ranks and the possibility that their plans may begin to unravel.

The cut scene would have provided the Egyptian guide, Ali, with a bit more screen time. His already chilling death sequence would have packed a bigger wallop if we were given a chance to get to know him better. Poor Ali, who never even set foot inside the cave of Kharis, became the Mummy's second and final victim of the film.

However, according to publicity still number 1078-67 and several pages of the script that were deleted from the film, the body count continues.

In the film, after Kharis takes Marta from her tent, he brings her to Andoheb, who is waiting for them back in the temple. As the Mummy places the unconscious heroine on the slab, Andoheb gives Kharis further instructions; "You will return at once to the tombs of our ancient dead." It is apparent, even in this LONG SHOT, that Andoheb's mouth is not moving. We also see him turn his head to his left (right for the viewer) as if he has been distracted. And he was. The two priests who escorted him into the temple during the film's opening sequence reappear and quickly object to Andoheb's desecration. Unfortunately, the editor's scissors have once again robbed us of seeing what would have easily been one of the highlights of the film. The following scene appears as it was originally written:

> INT. CIRCULAR CHAMBER — MED. SHOT (OVERHEAD)
>
> *The two old priests come quickly down the stairs.*
>
> MED. CLOSE SHOT — AT ENTRANCE
>
> ANDOHEB: *(to priests)* Return to the temple. Only the High Priest may enter Ananka's tomb. You know that.
>
> FIRST OLD PRIEST: *(angrily)* We know, too, you are defiling the tomb.
>
> SECOND OLD PRIEST: You must destroy the girl. This is sacrilege. The wrath of Isis will fall on our heads!
>
> ANDOHEB: I will make her my immortal High Priestess.
>
> FIRST OLD PRIEST: We will not allow this unholy act.
>
> ANDOHEB: I am [the] High Priest of Karnak. *(he turns)* Kharis!
>
> *Kharis comes up to him. He looks at Kharis intently, then at the old priests, who are cowering back against the stairs.*
>
> INT. CIRCULAR CHAMBER — MED. SHOT — ANOTHER ANGLE

1. The Mummy's Hand 19

"You are defiling the tomb," says one of the temple priests (Murdock MacQuarrie, lower right), as he and another priest (Frank Lacteen) confront Andoheb (George Zucco, left). They are almost his last words as the Mummy (Tom Tyler) puts the squeeze on him in this scene that was filmed, then discarded from *The Mummy's Hand* (Universal, 1940).

> *Kharis advances toward the two old priests, who back in terror up the stairs. They turn and try to run. Kharis follows. Halfway up the stairs, Kharis reaches a hand out toward the priest nearest him. The priest loses his balance and falls sideways to the floor of the chamber. CAMERA FOLLOWS Kharis as he goes after the other priest, who reaches the top landing. There Kharis grasps him by the waist, holds him overhead and deliberately dashes him toward the floor. CAMERA STAYS on Kharis a moment, and we HEAR the SCREAM of the priest and an abrupt ending. CAMERA immediately PANS to Andoheb, who smiles slightly up at Kharis.*
>
> ANGLE SHOT— FROM BEHIND ANDOHEB
>
> HEADING UPWARD *on Kharis at top landing.*
>
> ANDOHEB: You will return at once to the tents of the white men. You will find more of the fluid there. Go while the moon is yet high in the heavens…for your power to move wanes with the moon. Go!

> *Mummy GRUNTS in eagerness and turns and goes through the upper doorway.*
>
> INT. JUST OUTSIDE ENTRANCE TO ANANKA'S Tomb — MED. SHOT
> *Andoheb in the f.g. turns, looks toward Marta lying in the background and starts toward her.*

One can only imagine the words coming to life and Kharis' lurching movements as he menacingly pursues his latest victims. And one can ponder the Skinner-Salter library of endless music cues and play the themes over in the mind, envisioning what scores might have been used. Unfortunately, we'll have to be content with what our imaginations can provide as we read pages of dialogue and direction long absent. This scene, which would have run about a minute and a half, is clearly the most fantastic find discovered in the *Mummy's Hand* scrap heap. Such a truly chilling sequence would have not only added to Kharis' screen time, but would have doubled the Mummy's body count (from two to four).

In the film, when Andoheb gives Kharis his latest instructions from within Ananka's tomb, more continuity errors can be found due to this edit. After a quick cut-away to Kharis, and then back to Andoheb, a close look at the High Priest indicates he is not standing in the same room. He is standing at the lower doorway within the circular chamber. According to the script and the publicity still, this is where Kharis has just killed the two old priests. After this slick bit of editing, one has to assume that this exciting double Mummy murder was indeed shot, then edited out.

The two old priests would have been the Mummy's last victims before Steve and Babe finally put an end to the mayhem, at least in this film.

The reason for this cut might have been that the interruption of the two old priests momentarily sidetrack the immediate business at hand. But, most likely, the scene was deleted because a retake was needed and there was simply not enough time to get it done. Whatever the reason, it's our loss.

The final sequence of the film shows Steve and Marta back at the Cairo bazaar, this time arm-in-arm. As Steve picks up another vase from the same peddler, no-nonsense Marta takes it from his hand and gives it back, not chancing a repeat of the same ordeal. "We're going back to America — remember?" Wait. The closing scene is longer in the script, with credit for discovering Ananka's tomb being dispersed to everyone present, even the girl Babe bought his Poopsie doll from:

> *As Babe's VOICE is HEARD, calling, they turn.*
>
> BABE'S VOICE: Steve! Hey, Steve!
>
> *Babe hurries in, his left arm in a sling, with an envelope in his right hand, followed by a perspiring Solvani.*
>
> STEVE: You get everything set at the boat?
>
> SOLVANI: The jewels of Ananka are safely stowed away in the ship's strongbox.

1. The Mummy's Hand 21

BABE: Here's a cable for you.

As he reads it, Steve bursts into laughter.

BABE: What's cookin' boss?

Steve hands cable to Babe who reads it out loud.

BABE: *(reading)* That job in the bone washing department is no longer open. Stop. I'm taking it myself. Stop. You're getting my job. Best regards. Dr. Lyons.

Babe grabs Steve's hand.

BABE: I always knew you'd do it!

Marta and Solvani ad-lib congratulations. The Egyptian girl who sold Babe the doll enters to see what's cooking.

STEVE: *(arm around Marta)* We've got Babe to thank for everything.

BABE: *(seeing the Egyptian girl)* Babe, nothin'! You can thank little Egypt here! If she hadn't sold me this good luck doll — *(his hand goes to his breast pocket — fumbles)* I could have sworn —

SOLVANI: *(drawing dancing doll out of Babe's neck)* Is this what you were looking for?

INSERT — DOLL with a hole in its tummy.

BABE'S VOICE: Yeah! If it hadn't been for Poopsie in my pocket, that monkey's bullet would've gone right through me!

BACK TO SCENE

Babe sees the Egyptian girl is fascinated by Solvani's trick.

BABE: Oh, you like that trick, huh? Well, I'll show you one that's really a mystifier!

He picks up a round stone carving from counter, passes it over his mouth. Suddenly his eyes bulge, his hands come down, and he starts to choke and gesture for help. The thing's stuck in his mouth again! But the others deliberately walk away this time, laughing at him. CAMERA MOVES IN to a CLOSE UP as he stands there foolishly choking with the stone in his mouth.

FADE OUT.

THE END

A Universal Picture

After going through hell for his friend, would it have been too much for writers Griffin Jay and Maxwell Shane to let Babe walk off with the Egyptian girl? At least the silly ending of Babe possibly choking to death was left out, preserving some of his dignity.

One would have to agree that most of the changes from script to film were made for the better, contributing to the fact that decades later, Universal's horror films of the '30s and '40s remain overwhelmingly popular. Should any of this footage, by some miracle, be unearthed one day, it would certainly be regarded by film buffs as greater than the discovery of Ananka herself. Personally, I think there's a greater chance of Kharis returning to seek vengeance on Universal Studio heads!

All the previously mentioned scenes were presumably filmed and then edited out. An even earlier draft of the screenplay, dated May 6, 1940, includes scenes, ideas and even names of key characters that were changed or left on the drawing board.

By the time production began on *The Mummy's Hand* in late May 1940, some of the earlier thoughts that writers Jay and Shane transferred to paper were already ancient history. It is still fascinating to the dedicated legion of fans to explore what *might* have been. These changes include:

- The long staircase outside the temple of Karnak behind the credit titles was originally intended to be a panoramic view of Egypt that included the Sphinx, the great pyramids at Giza and the Nile River.
- Many scenes from the first few pages of this earlier draft bear similarities to *Dracula* and 1932's *The Mummy*. It is surprising that writers Jay and Shane even considered putting them on paper. A horse-drawn carriage with a bat flying next to it moves through a landscape shrouded in fog; a stone stairway is covered in spider webs; large rats and insects scurry through the dirt and dust. Bela Lugosi would have felt right at home:

> *FULL SHOT — NIGHT (STOCK)*
>
> *A train roars into a station and stops with a hissing of steam. OVER THE SHOT a title:*
>
> *EGYPT 1931*
>
> *MED. SHOT*
>
> *At side of coach, on which are the words: CAIRO EXPRESS. Natives cluster about the passengers as they alight. CAMERA MOVES FORWARD through the crowd and picks up the figure of a small Egyptian, just as he is alighting. He is attired in European clothing. His eyes are hidden behind thick glasses, and his upturned coat collar and down turned hat brim tend to disguise him. He carries a leather portfolio. As baggage hawkers approach him, he quickly sidesteps and pushes his way through the crowd.*
>
> *DISSOLVE TO:*
>
> *EXT. MOUNTAIN ROAD — NIGHT (F.S.)*
>
> *A carriage drawn by two horses moves along it. The landscape is clouded with fog.*
>
> *SHOT OF HORSES (M.S.)*
>
> *Directly above the horses a bat flies along with them.*
>
> *INT. CARRIAGE — MED. SHOT — NIGHT (PROCESS)*

1. The Mummy's Hand

> *The Egyptian who stepped from the train stares grimly ahead, as the carriage bounces over the rocky road.*
>
> EXT. MOUNTAINS — NIGHT (M.S.)
>
> *The Temple of Karnak is SEEN in the distance. Carriage moves toward it over a narrow, rocky ledge.*
>
> *When the Egyptian arrives at the temple, he is escorted up a long curving stone stairway, covered by spider webs.*
>
> AT WINDOW (C.S.)
>
> *Bats fly about.*
>
> FLOOR (C.S.)
>
> *A rat scurries along.*
>
> CORNER (C.S.)
>
> *A bug moves through the dirt and dust.*
>
> CLOSE SHOT — LITTLE EGYPTIAN
>
> *As he moves forward, his eyes darting from side to side.*

If this were any closer to *Dracula*, we would soon learn the Egyptian's name is really Renfield and the actor behind the glasses is Dwight Frye!

- According to *Variety*, the flashback footage of ancient Egypt was supposed to be tinted green.
- After Andoheb is sworn in as the new High Priest of Karnak, the story continues in the Cairo Bazaar nine years later. The title reads; CAIRO — 1940. The final release print of the film never identifies the year Andoheb takes his vows. It isn't until we catch a glimpse of Solvani's contract from Steve Banning that we see the date (May 12, 1940).
- Steve's last name was originally Allen before it was changed to Banning.
- After being denied funding via cablegram by the Scripps Museum, Steve fires back with a cable of his own:

> INT. CABLE OFFICE — CLOSE UP — CABLEGRAM
>
> **Steve:** *(raging)* I'll show him! *(turns abruptly to the desk, behind which a clerk is working) (shouts)* Take a cable!
>
> *Startled, the clerk drops papers in his hands and jumps up, blinking. Steve, realizing he has been shouting, swallows, then repeats quietly...*
>
> **Steve:** *(cont'd)* Take a cable.
>
> *Clerk nods and takes up the pencil and blank.*
>
> **Steve:** *(dictating)* Dr. Lyons, Scripps Museum of Manhattan, New York City. Received your very amusing cable just ten minutes after obtaining other financing for Princess Ananka expedition...

BABE: Heh! We ain't got no other financing!

STEVE: Well, he doesn't know it! *(continues dictating)* Stop. Too bad Scripps Museum will not share in greatest discovery of the decade. Stop. Regards. I hope you choke!

CLERK: *(reading over what he has dictated)* You have here twenty-nine words. If you cut out the last four words you can send this at a cheaper twenty-five-word rate.

STEVE: The last four words?...

CLERK: *(reading)* I — hope — you — choke.

STEVE: *(abruptly)* Cut out the first twenty-five and send the last four!

The clerk looks up, surprised.

STEVE: *(cont'd)* Oh, and send it "collect." *(to Babe, still puzzling over wire)* Come on, Babe.

He starts out.

- When one door closes, another opens, in this case, the door to the local Egyptian watering hole. This is where the Breen office did a little objecting to the boys' behavior, at least their drinking.

"This is the 'casual drinking' that Breen is screaming about," was handwritten on the script next to Babe's request for a double Scotch.

- The words "machine gun?" were also handwritten on the side of the page where Marta shows up at the Cairo Hotel to confront Steve and Babe. Does this note suggest that one of the films' creatives considered having Marta actually tote a machine gun through the streets of Cairo?
- In the desert, Babe is working with an electric drill. Next to this line is another handwritten note; "power drill?" Without a portable source of electricity, they just had to use old-fashioned picks and shovels.
- Steve remarks how all the symbols that protect the soul after death have been removed from Kharis' coffin. This line was lifted practically word-for-word from *The Mummy*, eight years earlier.
- When Andoheb suddenly appears in the cave, he informs a startled Dr. Petrie as to the correct use of tana leaves:

ANDOHEB: *(indicating leaves)* You know what these are?

DR. PETRIE: I — I believe they are tana leaves. Used for embalming.

ANDOHEB: *(slightly mocking)* Indeed? You know the name, Doctor — but not the purpose.

DR. PETRIE: Wh — what's that?

ANDOHEB: To preserve life, Doctor. Never for embalming.

- We know the ill-fated Dr. Petrie became Kharis' first victim. We also know

1. *The Mummy's Hand*   25

a scene was filmed, then cut, where Solvani and Marta pack to leave due to Petrie's death. However, one scene that never went before the cameras was a brief burial sequence. Steve and Ali bury Petrie's body:

> *EXT. VALLEY — MED. CLOSE SHOT — DAY*
>
> *Ali finishes patting a mound of dirt — Dr. Petrie's grave. Steve nods and Ali leaves. Steve straightens the rude cross, as Babe comes IN.*
>
> **BABE:** Pretty lonely spot for the old guy.
>
> **STEVE:** I think he would have liked being buried here — the Egypt to which he devoted his life.

• Ali had no idea that he only had until the next full moon to live. His death scene is one of the best-staged and frightening scenes in the entire Mummy series. That night as the jackals howl and the others are inside the cave, Ali stands guard at the camp. Hearing a noise from inside one of the tents, he enters but finds no one. As the chilling Skinner score increases in tempo, Ali notices a small vial on the table.

Just as Ali picks up the vial, he hears the tent flap open. He looks up and sees the horrible living corpse of Kharis. Ali, far too terrified to move, quickly becomes an easy victim. Again, this earlier script draft cribs a bit from the 1932 film where Bramwell Fletcher's character, upon seeing the living Mummy, literally dies laughing:

> *MED. SHOT*
>
> *Ali suddenly begins to laugh in hysteria. The Mummy jumps for him and one horrible hand reaches for his throat. The creature crouches over him. Ali's hysterical laughter ceases. Kharis straightens up with the vial in his hand. He glances quickly about him, then in a frenzy he begins to smash everything in the tent. His instinct to destroy seems completely without direction. Then he turns and runs from the tent.*
>
> *EXT. VALLEY — MED. SHOT — NIGHT*
>
> *Kharis disappears into the shadows and mist.*

It isn't likely a 3,000-year-old mummy could run, even in the movies. In fact, he can barely walk even after the required nine-leaf dosage. Perhaps Amon-Ra miscalculated the dose of the fluid. To get Kharis running he would need the fluid from a lot more than just nine tana leaves.

• Later, the prowling Mummy slowly creeps toward the camp for a follow-up dose of tana fluid. Solvani and Marta try to get some sleep as Steve and Babe stand guard and anxiously await the rising sun. Steve is visibly on edge while Babe tries to amuse himself with a game of mumblety-peg:

EXT. TENTS — NIGHT — MED. SHOT

Babe lies upon the ground, playing mumblety-peg with a hunting knife. Steve puts another small log on the fire. Both men wear guns strapped to their legs. As a jackal's HOWL is HEARD, Babe jumps with a start.

STEVE: Those jackals give me goose pimples. They howled like that just before Dr. Petrie was killed.

BABE: They give me goose pimples on top of my goose pimples.

He tries the mumblety-peg shot off his left ear to the ground, and as the jackal howls again, he misses.

BABE: Agh! It made me miss! Wish we had a cribbage board. Ever play cribbage?

STEVE: *(looks toward tent, worried)* No.

BABE: I had an uncle once who was the cribbage champ of Queensborough. Went kinda batty about puttin' those pegs in the little holes. Ended up in a tragedy.

STEVE: *(not paying attention)* It did?

BABE: *(really talking to give himself courage)* Yep. One day my uncle is sitting out on the porch, dreamin' about a cribbage game ... when a man with a wooden leg came stomping down the street. Well, there's a hole in the sidewalk where the W.P.A. ain't quite finished, and before he knows what's happening, my uncle is surrounded by cops and screaming people.

STEVE: For the love of Mike — why?

BABE: Well, it seems before he knew what he was doing ... that cribbage-playing uncle of mine had grabbed that man by his wooden leg and jammed it down into the hole in the sidewalk — and hollered — "game!"

STEVE: *(laughing)* Keep it up, Babe. It'll pass the time, anyhow.

Steve moves toward the tents and peers in.

INT. STEVE'S TENT — NIGHT — FULL SHOT

Marta and Solvani are asleep. Steve drops the flap across the camera.

EXT. TENTS — NIGHT — MED. SHOT

Steve comes back up to Babe, who is playing again.

STEVE: They're all right.

...But not for long. Kharis sneaks into the tent and, after emptying the file of tana fluid, attempts to strangle Solvani. Fortunately for the magician, the monster makes off with Marta before finishing the job. Steve and Babe give chase but, instead of pursuing the Mummy into the cave as in the film, they lose him, not to mention each other, in the dark:

1. The Mummy's Hand

> *MED. SHOT*
>
> STEVE: *(calling)* Babe! Babe! *(The sound echoes with a hollow ring through the valley.) (louder)* Babe!
>
> BABE'S VOICE: *(faintly)* Yes!
>
> STEVE: Where are you?
>
> *Steve waits a moment and then Babe comes up to him.*
>
> BABE: Not a trace. You....
>
> *Steve nods his head.*
>
> BABE: *(cont'd)* I tell you, Steve — we ought to beat it to town for help.
>
> STEVE: And leave Marta here? Not for a minute!
>
> *Babe looks at him for a second.*
>
> BABE: *(quietly)* Okay, Steve — but we can't do anymore here till daylight. We better go back and have a look at Pop, too.

After the beggar attempts to let some of the air out of Steve and Babe via an Egyptian bow and arrow, he is gunned down by Steve. Recognizing a medallion around the dead Egyptian's neck, Steve examines it and finds the same diagram that was on the vase, except for a secret passage leading from Kharis' cave. While Steve heads for the cave, Babe attempts to find the temple.

After chopping relentlessly in vain at the wall of the cave, Steve returns to check on Solvani, who is lying on a cot outside one of the tents. The script continues:

> SOLVANI: *Anything?*
>
> STEVE: *(shaking his head)* I've chopped half the cave down looking for that tunnel.
>
> SOLVANI: *(pleadingly)* Marta ... we've got to find her.... *(breaking)* Was my fault ... my fault ... she didn't want to come....
>
> STEVE: *(pressing him back on cot)* Now, Pop.... Relax. We'll find her. *(indicates medallion)* I left my enlarging glass in the tent. Might pick up something I can't see myself.
>
> *Solvani falls back on the cot, breathing hard, sobbing. Steve goes to the tent.*
>
> *EXT. SLOPE — AMONG ROCKS — CLOSE SHOT*
>
> *The Mummy looks stealthily down at the tent, moves slowly forward.*

- The next several scenes, which lead up to the climax, bear no resemblance to the final film at all. Kharis is depicted as a somewhat athletic monster, displaying much more mobility now than he did earlier. One would never guess he was dormant for over 3,000 years:

INT. STEVE'S TENT — NIGHT — MED. SHOT

Steve goes to the stand, picks up the little vial, and eyes it speculatively. The shadow of the Mummy can be SEEN through the rear wall. Steve suddenly removes the stopper from the vial and smells it.

STEVE: Tana leaves!

At a slight SOUND, he looks up and sees the shadow. Quickly, he crashes the vial to the floor. Almost in the same motion, he puts his hand over the single candle and extinguishes it.

EXT. REAR OF TENTS — NIGHT — MED. SHOT

The Mummy is looking through the slit in the tent. He seems to realize the vial has been smashed. With a little inhuman WHINE, he turns and runs waveringly FROM THE SCENE.

MED. SHOT — ANOTHER ANGLE — TENT

Steve, his gun in hand, comes about the tent. In the B.G. the Mummy is running toward the excavation. Steve starts to shoot, and then stops. He follows the creature.

EXT. CLIFF — NIGHT — MED. SHOT

The Mummy comes to the entrance of the cave. He stops and glances behind him.

CLOSE SHOT — STEVE

His eyes widen with horror at seeing him for the first time.

MED. SHOT — CAVE ENTRANCE

The Mummy disappears inside the cave. A second later Steve comes into SCENE and also enters the cave.

INT. KHARIS CAVE — NIGHT — FULL SHOT

The Mummy staggers across the cave to the stone mummy case. He fumbles about the base of it for something.

CLOSE SHOT

Kharis pushes against a certain spot in the base of the cave.

CLOSE SHOT — STEVE — IN THE CAVE

Watching. CAMERA PANS to Kharis, as he succeeds in pressing the spring. The mummy case swings about slowly and he staggers through the opening. Steve jumps forward to follow.

MED. CLOSE SHOT — MUMMY CASE

Steve is just too late to get through the opening before the case swings into place. He begins to push frantically at the base of the case.

INT. TUNNEL — NIGHT — MED. SHOT

Kharis slips along the rocky tunnel, grunting animal-like. An eerie, unearthly mist steams upward from the floor.

> *INT. KHARIS CAVE — NIGHT — CLOSE SHOT*
>
> *Steve tries to discover what Kharis had touched to affect the opening. He finally finds the right spot and pushes. The mummy case moves. Steve slips through. The case starts to move back into place.*
>
> *INT. TUNNEL — NIGHT MED. SHOT*
>
> *Steve stands still, listening to Kharis' footsteps.*
>
> *CLOSE MOVING SHOT*
>
> *Kharis' feet splashing through the slime of the tunnel floor.*
>
> *MED. SHOT*
>
> *Steve starts to follow.*
>
> *MED. SHOT — ANOTHER PORTION OF TUNNEL*
>
> *Kharis pauses and turns.*
>
> *MED. LONG SHOT*
>
> *The huge figure of Kharis can dimly be SEEN coming toward Steve. He flattens himself against the wall. Kharis comes closer, stands staring around him, then turns and moves waveringly back the way he had come. Steve follows.*

Now that would have been a truly frightening moment. But when you put those scenes together as writers Jay and Shane have generously done for us, we can see the story was changed for the better. In the film, Steve is being pursued through the tunnel by Kharis. We never actually see Kharis poke around for the secret spring on his mummy case, which causes it to reveal the secret passage. And fortunately, his running abilities were deleted altogether. These sights would have made him appear like nothing more than one of Andoheb's underlings dressed in a mummy suit. This childish prospect was explored 15 years later in *Abbott and Costello Meet the Mummy*. In this scripted version of the climax, Kharis meets his fate in a scene which would have looked like a barroom brawl right out of one of Universal's B Westerns. That approach may have felt natural for Dick Foran and Tom Tyler, who have enough horse operas under their gun belts to open their own matinee, but it may not have made for a very horrific climax. The original script continues:

> *MED. SHOT*
>
> *Steve hurls himself upon the Mummy as he turns to meet his charge. Steve's momentum carries them away from the fluid.*
>
> *CLOSE SHOT — MARTA*
>
> *She watches the fight terrified, and tears at her bonds.*
>
> *MED. SHOT*
>
> *Steve and the Mummy fight desperately — with Kharis trying to reach the vial*

> *of fluid. Time and time again Steve lets loose with rights and lefts to the creature's jaw, which only rock him. Steve can't seem to knock him out.*
>
> CLOSE SHOT
>
> *Marta tries to work loose from the straps that hold her. It is impossible. She gives up and watches the fight.*
>
> FULL SHOT
>
> *Steve and the Mummy crash into Andoheb's transfusion contraption. Steve hurls it at the Mummy. It crashes against him but he starts again for the fluid.*
>
> MARTA: (*screaming*) Steve! He mustn't get it.
>
> *Steve hurls himself at the creature again. They smash into the mummy case of Ananka and it goes over, smashed in pieces. Jewels of all sorts scatter on the floor. The Mummy frees himself and steps back. He looks around him wildly.*
>
> CLOSE SHOT — ROCK *on the floor. The Mummy's hand picks it up.*
>
> CLOSE SHOT — STEVE
>
> *He rises from the wrecked mummy case and charges.*
>
> MED. SHOT
>
> *The Mummy strikes him viciously over the head with a rock. Steve staggers and goes to his knees. Marta SCREAMS. He shakes his head and tries to get up. Blood pours from the wound on his forehead. He can't quite make it. With a little moan, he collapses.*

Kharis eventually reaches the fluid. Things look pretty bleak as the Mummy brings the vial to his mouth. He is about to drink when shots ring out, knocking the fluid from the Mummy's hand onto the floor. It's Babe. Shaking his head, Steve desperately tries to rise from the floor trying to stay conscious.

> BABE'S VOICE: Get him, Steve!
>
> CLOSE SHOT — STEVE
>
> *As the Mummy is about to rise, Steve aims a terrific kick at the monster's jaw.*
>
> CLOSE SHOT
>
> *Kharis travels backward swiftly, crashes into the wall, collapses.*
>
> CLOSE SHOT — MUMMY
>
> *Prone. His eyes flutter, then close. Slowly he shrivels until he is nothing but a skin covered skeleton.*

Is this how all living mummies were destined to meet their fate? A skin-covered skeleton is all that was left of Karloff's Imhotep in *The Mummy* several years earlier. Having Kharis go up in flames, which was his actual fate in the film, is not only a bit more original than having him shrivel up and die, but more conducive to a sequel. Perhaps this is the reason for the red handwritten question mark in the script next to this scene. Many of the ingredients found in this older draft of the script were fortunately dropped. The flashback sequence showing ancient Egypt early in the film cribs more than enough from 1932's *The Mummy*.

In fact, many fans as well as authors mistakenly refer to *The Mummy's Hand* as a sequel to *The Mummy*. Viewing the films back-to-back *can* be confusing to the uninitiated. Back in the '70s, New York's WOR Channel 9 ran the two films together as a double feature several times. This left viewers asking; "Didn't we just see this?" Poor Kharis had the great misfortune of following in Imhotep's footsteps. Even today, this still works against *The Mummy's Hand*. Often times, viewers who are not fully acquainted with the genre and are looking for Hollywood's personification of the shrouded strangler, pick up the more sophisticated Karloff *Mummy* and are disappointed. Fortunately, Universal Home Video has not only saved these treasures for future generations, but they made inexpensive redemption possible.

Those who afford themselves the opportunity to sit back and enjoy *The Mummy's Hand*—and I would strongly recommend doing this late on a Saturday night—are seldom disappointed. Even though George Zucco steals the show as the evil High Priest, lecherously leering at pretty Peggy Moran, Tom Tyler makes a terrific living mummy and is a lot of fun to watch. Universal makeup wizard Jack Pierce created a horror masterpiece the day he gave life to Kharis. Tom Tyler's Mummy application was by far the best of the series. Pierce felt the texture of the Mummy's face should resemble that of a badly wrinkle hippopotamus. Pierce once said, "I covered Mr. Tyler's face, neck and hands with thin slivers of cotton. Then I saturated it with spirit gum. When it dried, it wrinkled like his own skin—only the wrinkles were bigger and deeper." Next came the gray paint and tiny particles of clay. Once Tyler was covered in two-inch strips of gauze, the rest of him was also covered in paint. He was then covered in dust, while his hair was a hideous mixture of glue and clay. How he ever got the stuff out of his hair is anybody's guess! Mummy legend has it that Pierce used acetone, which is quite flammable, and a head-to-toe hot oil treatment. Tyler once commented, "It hurt like the devil."

Speaking of "hurting like the devil," that was quite a spill George Zucco's stunt man took on his way down the temple steps. The temple itself was originally constructed in 1939 for the James Whale adventure *Green Hell*. It was built on the Universal back lot because there was no sound stage large enough. It took 200 sheets of six by eight rock, 1,200 bags of plaster, 90,000 feet of lumber and 100 cubic yards of concrete. When it was completed it stood 125 feet tall and 225 feet across the base.

Despite a cast that featured Douglas Fairbanks Jr., George Sanders, Alan Hale, Vincent Price, Joan Bennett and George Bancroft, *Green Hell* was a box office disappointment. However, Universal was determined to get their money's worth out of this temple investment. In the Spring of 1940, the set was given an Egyptian

This page, top (L–R): George Sanders, George Bancroft, Douglas Fairbanks, Jr., and Vincent Price prepare to climb up to the Inca temple in *Green Hell* (Universal, 1940). It was soon to be transformed into the Temple of Karnak. *This page, bottom:* Universal's famous City Walk attraction under construction in 1990. *Opposite, top:* Inside the Temple of Karnak, George Zucco prepares Peggy Moran to spend eternity with him as the Mummy (Tom Tyler) looks on in *The Mummy's Hand* (Universal, 1940). *Opposite bottom:* Douglas Fairbanks, Jr., and Joan Bennett find romance in an Inca temple, originally built on the studio backlot for James Whale's *Green Hell* (Universal, 1940).

Universal's *Green Hell* temple set served the studio well through the years, from a South American jungle to an ancient Egyptian temple to the sewers underneath the Paris Opera House in *Phantom of the Opera* (Universal, 1943) with Claude Rains and Susanna Foster.

face-lift with the intent of serving the Priests of Karnak and providing a final resting place for the Princess Ananka in *The Mummy's Hand*. When box office receipts for *Hand* began coming in, the expensive set justified its existence.

In the years to come, the rationing brought on by the second World War prohibited the luxury of this kind of spending by Hollywood. As a result, *The Mummy's Hand* would not be the last time moviegoers would see this familiar set. Virtually any time a temple was needed in a Universal film during the early '40s, the old *Green Hell* set was given a new look and pressed into service. It served Maria Montez in *Cobra Woman* and took on the look of the sewers of Paris for Claude Rains in Phantom of the Opera. It even reprised its role as a haunted temple for Abbott and Costello's *Pardon My Sarong*.

The Mummy's Tomb

Eyes that crawl with madness! Hands that creep like cobras!
— Tagline for *The Mummy's Tomb*

Cast: Dick Foran (*Stephen A. Banning*); John Hubbard (*John Banning*); Elyse Knox (*Isobel Evans*); George Zucco (*Andoheb*); Wallace Ford (*Babe Hanson*); Turhan Bey (*Mehemet Bey*); Virginia Brissac (*Mrs. Ella Evans*); Cliff Clark (*Sheriff*); Mary Gordon (*Jane Banning*); Paul E. Burns (*Jim*) [Pedro script name]; Frank Reicher (*Prof. Matthew Norman*); Emmett Vogan (*Coroner*); Lon Chaney (*Kharis, the Mummy*); Eddy C. Waller (*Chemist*); Frank Darien (*Old Man*); John Rogers (*Steward*); Otto Hoffman (*Caretaker*); Fern Emmett (*Dressmaker*); Janet Shaw (*Girl*); Dick Hogan (*Boy*); Bill Ruhl (*Nick*); Guy Usher (*Doctor*); Pat McVey (*Jake Lovell*); Jack Arnold (*Reporter*); Glenn Strange (*Farmer*); Rex Lease (*Al*); Grace Cunard (*Farmer's Wife*); Lew Kelly (*Bartender*); Walter Byron (*Searcher*); Harry Cording (*Vic*); Eddie Parker (*Lon Chaney's stand-in*); Charles Marsh (*Extra*); Mira McKinney (*Extra*). **Crew:** Ben Pivar (*Associate Producer*); Harold Young (*Directed by*); Charles Gould (*Assistant Director*); Griffin Jay, Henry Sucher (*Screenplay*); Neil P. Varnick (*Original story*); George Robinson (*Director of Photography*); Harry Neuman (*Associate*); Jack Otterson (*Art Director*); Ralph M. DeLacy (*Associate*); Milton Carruth (*Film Editor*); Russell A. Gausman (*Set Decorator*); J. Andrew Gilmore (*Associate*); Vera West (*Gowns*); Hans J. Salter (*Musical Director*); Bernard B. Brown (*Sound Director*); William Schwartz (*Sound Technician*); Jack Pierce (*Makeup*).

Steve Banning and the other surviving members from *The Mummy's Hand* expedition into Egypt's forbidden past had a good 30 years to revel in their fame and fortune. But fact or fiction, all good things must come to an end. We're not here to quibble over small details like why it took the High Priests of Karnak 30 years to get their act together. *The Mummy's Tomb* has been torn apart enough times through the years by critics and fans alike that mercilessly magnify the film's shortcomings in an attempt to turn a clever phrase. I think the time has come to give *The Mummy's Tomb* a heartfelt apology. After all, don't we remember the film scaring the tears right out of us as we watched, half amazed and half terrified, during our favorite Saturday night fright-fest? And don't we remember bravely discussing it with our friends, in the safety and light of the next day? Now we're all grown up, more mature, more savvy and more jaded. The fact is, *The Mummy's Tomb* did its job. And how do we repay it as grown-ups? By comparing it to more sophisticated films, as well as schlock masquerading as horror. We simply slap it with the label "kiddie movie" and let it go at that. Is this the way we repay an old friend?

The Mummy's Tomb is surely no *Bride of Frankenstein*, but it never was intended to be. So what if the High Priests of Karnak took 30 years to regroup and pick up the trail of the Banning clan. So what if Babe's last name mysteriously became Hanson instead of Jenson. And so what if Kharis mystically knows exactly where to hone in on his enemies without the use of a crystal ball? You wouldn't dump a childhood friend simply because of a few character flaws, would you? No one is perfect. This rule of thumb applies to movies, too. I can now step down from my soapbox and focus on the business at hand, or Tomb as the case may be.

Stephen A. Banning (Dick Foran), hero from *The Mummy's Hand*, sits comfortably in his New England living room regaling his family with tales of his adventures from 30 years past: "Most of these incidents are so incredible that one would almost have to be there in order to believe them," says Banning. This is indeed the case for his own son John (John Hubbard), who would sooner believe in the tooth fairy than a living Mummy. As Steve continues to captivate his audience with tales from the past, we are treated to some carefully selected flashback sequences from *The Mummy's Hand*. This gets Tomb off to a rousing start, allowing viewers to know immediately what they are in for. Banning's listeners are mesmerized. It's as though his words are forcing him to relive the nightmare over again: "Well, at least I had the satisfaction of having destroyed a terrible monster. And in doing so, rid the world of an awful curse."

Not quite. It took three decades, but back in Egypt, Andoheb (George Zucco) managed to survive that tumble down the temple steps and is not only back on his feet, but sporting a new head of hair. It seems the Priests of Karnak have not only discovered the secret of eternal life but something just as vital, a cure for baldness.

Minus the use of one arm, and bearing one hell of a grudge, Andoheb swears in the new disciple of Karnak, Mehemet Bey (Turhan Bey). In no time, Bey is en route via ocean liner to the United States with some very peculiar cargo, the Mummy. "It is my duty to offer prayers each night, so that the soul of my dear one

2. The Mummy's Tomb

is not left alone to wander lonely and forgotten through the spaces of time," explains Bey to a ship steward (John Rogers).

At his new domain, the Mapleton Cemetery, Bey quickly sets up shop. He informs the obedient Mummy, "Your work begins," and Kharis disappears into the New England night. He keeps close to the shadows and makes his way to the nearby Banning house.

As Steve Banning prepares for bed, he hears the French doors that lead to the terrace open from the outside. Steve recoils in horror at what he sees. He is barely able to bring the word "Kharis" to his mouth. As he backs away, the Mummy advances toward him. With centuries of hate on his face and his one good arm extended, the Mummy strangles the life from the former archaeologist. Banning's scream brings others in the house racing to his aid, but when they arrive, the Mummy is gone, leaving behind nothing but gray marks on Steve's throat. The man who discovered Ananka's tomb is dead.

As the police investigate, repeated reports of a mysterious shadow begin streaming in from the jumpy citizens of Mapleton. When Banning's son John meets his father's former sidekick, Babe (Wallace Ford) at the Mapleton train station, Kharis strikes again. This time the victim is Banning's sister Jane (Mary Gordon). The murder spree continues to baffle police while Babe experiences an awful feeling of *déjà vu*. When he tries to tell John and the local authorities that a 3,000–year-old Mummy is the killer, his warning falls on deaf ears. Soon after, Babe is discovered strangled to death. After Prof. Norman (Frank Reicher) analyzes the gray substance on the necks of each victim and a piece of mummy wrapping found near the Banning home, he concludes that they are "dealing with the presence of the living dead."

Despite the current tragedies, John still plans to wed his fiancée Isobel (Elyse Knox) without delay. However, Bey has other ideas. Like his predecessor Andoheb, Bey succumbs to the weakness of the flesh. He instructs Kharis to kidnap Isobel and bring her to him. Bey promises his reluctant bride eternal life while John and the sheriff rally the troops, or in true Universal fashion, the local villagers. They put two and two together and deduce that Bey is the prime suspect. Suddenly Isobel's mother (Virginia Brissac) arrives in a hysterical state and informs the group that the Mummy has taken her daughter. The mob makes a beeline right for the cemetery.

When Bey hears the men approach, he instructs Kharis to sneak an unconscious Isobel out until he can restore order. But as the confrontation heats up, Bey is fatally shot by the sheriff.

The Mummy, seen carrying Isobel, is tracked down at the Banning house, which is set ablaze by the torch-wielding mob. John not only battles flames to get his fiancée back, but he battles the Mummy as well. While Kharis attempts to throttle the life from the last Banning, the sheriff and deputy fire several shots at the monster from behind. When Kharis turns to pursue his attackers, he allows John and Isobel to escape. The deputy thrusts a torch into the Mummy's eyes. He and the sheriff narrowly escape, leaving the Mummy to perish in the flames.

The Mummy's Tomb fiery finale is clearly the most elaborate climax of the four Mummy films. The film also treats us to some of the best scenes from *The Mummy's Hand* via flashbacks. However, *Tomb* does not reach the bar set by *The Mummy's Hand*. Removing the Mummy from his native Egypt and turning him loose on someone else's turf immediately places him at a disadvantage. Although Kharis appears to find his way around the sleepy New England town without much difficulty, he is in his adversaries' ballpark.

The brilliant Foran-Moran-Ford chemistry from *Hand* is noticeably absent in *Tomb*. John Hubbard pales as a leading man when compared to Dick Foran. And there is not much the attractive Elyse Knox can do with the role of Isobel Evans except to sit or lie around looking cute. Peggy Moran's Marta Solvani had much more spunk. Paired with Foran, their sparring provided *Hand* with a bit of sexual tension. In *Tomb*, Hubbard and Knox portray characters that are already engaged to be married. There are no relevant exchanges between the two, just a lot of picnicking and handholding. Blah!

George Zucco is back as Andoheb despite being shot several times and taking that nasty spill down the temple steps in *Hand*. Only the mighty Gods of Egypt know how he survived. His role in *Tomb* is reduced to little more than a cameo. Fortunately, Turhan Bey is able to pick up the slack and is quite convincing as the sinister High Priest, Mehemet Bey. Bey does the most with the role of Andoheb's successor. From the moment we are introduced to him, he appears as dedicated to Amon-Ra as ever a priest there was. He never gives the impression that a pretty face can turn his head. But too much work and not enough play can make Bey a dull boy.

As for Chaney's Mummy, Kharis had either been binging while waiting 30 years to seek revenge on the Bannings, or those tana leaves are loaded with carbohydrates. The husky Mummy moves from shadow to shadow snuffing the life from Mapleton's seniors. Is this because of a curse, or because Kharis is now too heavy to pursue anyone under the age of 65?

Despite the padding of the first 15 minutes of *Tomb* with scenes from *Hand*, the first half of *The Mummy's Tomb* does offer adequate suspense. As the body count rises, the only clue police have, besides the grayish marks found on the throats of each victim, is a mysterious shadow being reported by some of Mapleton's most prominent citizens. The shadow first passes across a couple parked at a lover's lane, and then it passes by a bedroom window, waking the woman inside. A fearful sensation of "lock your doors and stay inside" is created until the town learns what they are up against, then the suspense is diminished. The hunter becomes the hunted as the sleepy town shows they're made of some pretty stern stuff after all. The monster racks up an impressive number of victims before the town turns the tables on him. *Tomb* also provides us with food for thought. What if the Banning family migrated to a heavily populated city like Manhattan? Curse or no curse, it would have been considerably more difficult for a 3,000-year-old mummy to get around unnoticed in the city that doesn't sleep. Luckily, *The Mummy's Tomb* didn't take place among urban sprawl, although you can bet that in 1942, many small-town patrons left their local movie theaters feeling spooked. In addition to the price of admission, the film surely cost younger viewers some sleep as well. I know I certainly paid the price. But for the memories it left me with, it was well worth the cost.

It's easy to criticize *The Mummy's Tomb* when comparing it to *The Mummy's Hand* mostly because of the lack of character development. In a way, *Tomb* cheats. It relies on our previous acquaintance with the characters from *Hand* that are now getting bumped off in *Tomb*. The flashback sequences from *Hand* are fun to see, especially since it was the only Mummy film not reissued. Audiences of the '50s were denied the opportunity to see *Hand* when all the other Universal horror films were making their re-release rounds, courtesy of Film Classics and Realart Pictures. Maybe we would feel a greater sense of loss for our old friends from *Hand* if the flashback clips put a bit more emphasis on how likable they all were and a bit less emphasis on the Mummy's mayhem.

Criticism notwithstanding, *The Mummy's Tomb* is a fun 60 minutes and is a very welcome addition to anyone's late-night movie line-up. Sixty years ago, no one could have comprehended the technology that we would have today which allows such in-depth comparisons of these films. Granted, there is never an excuse for such a continuity error like Babe Jenson's name becoming Babe Hanson. To give the film the benefit of the doubt, let's just assume Babe might have changed his name to throw any succeeding priest of Karnak off the track, and let it go at that. Besides, when vampire hunter Van Helsing's name was mysteriously changed to Von Helsing for *Dracula*'s sequel, *Dracula's Daughter*, few eyebrows were raised.

Another reason why *The Mummy's Tomb* is often criticized is its brief running time, 20 percent of which is padded with scenes from *The Mummy's Hand*. In fact, not one of the studio's four Mummy films during the '40s reached the length of even the shortest Frankenstein film.

As with *The Mummy's Hand*, incredibly tight shooting schedules usually resulted in scenes being deleted if there were no time for retakes. While this is also true in *The Mummy's Tomb*, the most noticeable differences between script and final film were the shortening of already existing scenes. Steve's retelling of his adventures in Egypt some 30 years past dissolves to the temple where Andoheb begins explaining to his new disciple Bey, "Thirty years ago an infidel sought to destroy me." However, about three pages of dialogue between Andoheb and Bey, missing from the film, survive in the script:

> CLOSE SHOT — STEVE
>
> STEVE: Well, at least I can find some solace in the knowledge that I destroyed two horrible monsters spawned in the very depths of antiquity. And in this manner, I rid the world of an awful curse. The curse...
>
> QUICK WIPE TO: INT. ALTAR ROOM AT KARNAK — CLOSE SHOT — ANDOHEB
>
> ANDOHEB: (*his voice weird and unearthly*) ...of Amon-ra, King of all the

gods. who shall defile the temples of the ancient gods of Egypt, a cruel and violent death shall be his fate, even though he travels to the farthest corner of the earth. Never shall he find rest…unto eternity!

Andoheb, whom we thought killed in the preceding sequence, kneels over the pool of Kar, praying. He is dressed in the ancient robes of the High Priests of Karnak, and is now an old man.

MED. SHOT

On the door into the altar room. MEHEMET BEY, a much younger Egyptian, enters and stands looking about him. His face contains something of that fanatical zeal that burns also in Andoheb's countenance.

FULL PANNING SHOT — REVERSE ANGLE

The room looks much as before, except that now it is even more ancient and crumbling. CAMERA PASSES from torches set in the walls, ACROSS the base of an idol of Isis. The torches cast a weird, flickering light on Andoheb, who sits on a stone throne behind a low altar. His left arm is useless and is held in a broken position. Incense pots burn at either end of the altar. CAMERA MOVES IN toward Andoheb.

MED. SHOT

As Mehemet Bey reaches the altar.

MEHEMET BEY: I have answered your summons, O Master.

Andoheb leans a little toward him, his eyes very bright and piercing.

ANDOHEB: Even as numerous others before you have answered a like summons, my son.

CLOSE SHOT — MEHEMET BEY

ANDOHEB'S VOICE: And even as I responded many years ago … for the single purpose of fulfilling the destiny of the High Priests of Karnak. You are prepared?

MEHEMT BEY: I am prepared, father.

CLOSE SHOT — ANDOHEB *with a smile of satisfaction and triumph.*

ANDOHEB: Civilizations have risen! Civilizations have crumbled! But here in the ruined tombs and temples, the ancient gods still rule despite the efforts of modern man to substitute his modern god!

MED. SHOT

Mehemet Bey stands with bowed head.

ANDOHEB: For many years you have been trained carefully … painstakingly … for this moment.

MEHEMET BEY: Yes, father.

ANDOHEB: Beneath the idol of Isis, you will find a copper box. Bring it here.

Mehemet bends under the statue and brings out a copper box, as CAMERA PANS with him. He places it before the altar.

2. The Mummy's Tomb

ANDOHEB: Open it.

CLOSE SHOT — BOX

Mehemet's hands lift the lid. Inside are a number of dried leaves.

MEHEMET'S VOICE: Tana leaves!

CLOSE SHOT — THE TWO MEN

ANDOHEB: (*intently*) You know the purpose of tana leaves?

MEHEMET BEY: They grew from a bush that disappeared from the face of Egypt many years ago, O Master. According to modern belief they were used for embalming.

ANDOHEB: Go on.

MEHEMET BEY: The Book of the Dead, known only to the Priests of Karnak, states a different purpose. Used correctly, they can preserve life indefinitely.

Andoheb nods.

ANDOHEB: Take three of them.

CLOSE SHOT — BOX

Mehemet Bey's hand ENTERS SCENE and picks up three leaves.

INT. TOMB — MED. SHOT

A torch in a bracket of the stone wall spreads a flickering light through the weird place. Here and there water trickles down and the walls are covered with hieroglyphics and drawings of the demon gods of Egypt. Against one wall stands a mummy case, covered with dust and spider webs. Andoheb and Mehemet Bey are before it.

ANDOHEB: Here in the very womb of the mountains waits the reason for our existence. A crypt that can never be looted by archaeologists because there is no record of its existence. A crypt that is cursed and damned forever.

(C.S.)

A huge rat comes from an accumulation of dust and dirt and moves about.

ANDOHEB'S VOICE: Centuries ago, Kharis was buried here and thus he was maintained by the priests of Karnak...

(C.S.)

A large, hairy spider, its little eyes gleaming, comes from a web, straight for CAMERA.

ANDOHEB'S VOICE: ...to guard the tomb of the princess Ananka. Such is his destiny and neither time nor place can change it.

MED. CLOSE SHOT

ANDOHEB: Thirty years ago, an infidel sought to destroy me and to destroy Kharis. Both attempts failed! The bullet he fired into me only crushed my arm.

Lest we forget that tumble he took down the temple steps.

This is where the film resumes after Banning concludes his tale of terror from the safety of his living room.

This first edit was taken almost word-for-word from *The Mummy's Hand* screenplay, only most of the dialogue never made it to the final release print of *Hand* either. *Tomb* writer Griffin Jay, who also penned the screenplay for *Hand*, apparently realized that the scene did not survive *Hand*'s final cut and attempted to crib it for use in the sequel. But it would not be until the next Kharis film, *The Mummy's Ghost*, where the scene would finally make it to the big screen.

In *Tomb*, Andoheb succumbs again, albeit this time a bit more peacefully. In the film, the scene now ends, but the script provides an additional surprise that should not have been cut:

> MEHEMET BEY: In my hands is the power of life and death. May I use it to the best of my ability!
>
> *The remote HOWL of a jackal comes OVER SCENE.*
>
> EXT. MOUNTAINS — NIGHT (M.C.S.)
>
> *A jackal points his nose at the sky and HOWLS mournfully.*
>
> INT. TOMB— CLOSE SHOT — MUMMY
>
> *The monster's one eye flickers open and stares with the horror of centuries straight INTO CAMERA. It looks out of a socket that is nothing but a burned, blackened hole.*

Kharis doesn't appear to be completely dormant. His one good eye making contact with the camera would have been a chilling touch.

The film dissolves to the ocean liner moving through the fog. During the voyage across the Atlantic, Bey administers the tana fluid to Kharis. Again, the script indicates the monster making eye contact with the camera. After Bey pours the elixir into the Mummy's mouth in the film, Kharis stirs a bit, but does not open his eye.

In the States, Bey wastes no time in sending the Mummy out on his murderous mission. The script indicates several shots of Bey looking on as the Mummy climbs a trellis at the Banning home on his way to kill Stephen Banning. Having Bey on hand for the first Mummy murder would have helped justify how Kharis was able to find the Banning house so easily. Instead, Bey sends the Mummy out on his own without so much as a clue as to Banning's location. This is just another one of those details fans tend to overlook.

When the Mummy returns from killing the first defiler, Bey tucks him back into his coffin, so to speak. "Three remain, only three. And then we can return to the land that gave us birth." The scene fades to black and continues in a chemical lab, but not according to the script. Another quick look at a Mapleton newspaper flashing headlines to the strains of the music of Hans J. Salter:

Mehemet Bey (Turhan Bey) tucks the Mummy (Lon Chaney) in for the night, in between killings in *The Mummy's Tomb* (Universal, 1942).

> *FADE IN: INSERT — NEWSPAPER bearing the name: "MAPLETON DAILY NEWS." On the front page is a picture of the upper front porch of the Banning house. Just climbing over the railing is a figure that is entirely blacked out. No features at all are observable. Over the top of the picture are the words: "WHO IS THIS MAN?" Beneath the picture are the further questions: "WHERE DID HE COME FROM? WHERE DID HE GO?"*
>
> *CAMERA IRISES DOWN to a portion of the accompanying article, which reads: "…authorities are as much in the dark today as to who committed the murder of Stephen Banning as they were the night the crime took place. The gray marks found upon the throat of the deceased, upon the upper porch railing and upon the rose trellis, remain the only clue. Efforts are being made to analyze these marks in order to trace the former actions and perhaps whereabouts of the fiend…"*

The film continues in the lab with the coroner (Emmett Vogan), a chemist (Eddy Waller), Sheriff Elwood (Cliff Clark) and John Banning (John Hubbard). It isn't very likely that anyone will read the scene above and feel the film suffered because of this cut, especially since it breaks away three other times to reveal news headlines. Any more newsbreaks and viewers might think that they couldn't be more familiar with this tabloid if they had a subscription.

Most cuts do help the film move along at a reasonable clip. The next edit probably saved the film altogether. John and Isobel's picnic was originally two full pages longer than it actually ended up being in the film. Now, Elyse Knox is a lovely sight to take in visually, but unless you're the one lying next to her on a picnic blanket, cracking open the bottle of vino, this could get tiresome:

> *INT. ISOBEL'S ROADSTER — DAY — TWO SHOT (PROCESS)*
>
> *John is leaning back in the seat, a bit tired, but enjoying the air and scenery. Isobel is driving.*
>
> JOHN: Where are we going?
>
> *Isobel glances out of the corner of her eye at him.*
>
> ISOBEL: Remember the brook that ran close to the cemetery grounds — the place where we used to play when we were kids?
>
> JOHN: (his eyes lighting up somewhat) Yeah…
>
> ISOBEL: Well, I hear tell it's still there…
>
> *Some of John's weariness appears to vanish. His expression would seem to suggest that the idea is an enjoyable one.*
>
> ISOBEL: (watching John out of the corner of her eye) John — would you reach in back and get that basket…
>
> *John, looking at her questioningly a moment, reaches back and brings out a picnic basket. He starts to open it as Isobel stops him with her hand.*
>
> ISOBEL: Unh-unh — no peeking. Wait till we get there.
>
> *EXT. WOODS NEAR BROOK — DAY — MED. CLOSE SHOT (PROCESS)*
>
> *John and Isobel are seated on the ground, the picnic basket before them. They seem to be enjoying it immensely.*
>
> JOHN: (taking a bite of sandwich) I'm trying to remember the first time I ever proposed to you.
>
> ISOBEL: I can tell you — when you had the desk behind me at school.
>
> JOHN: I thought I was too busy pulling your hair — and pouring ink down the back of your dress.
>
> ISOBEL: You managed to propose, though.
>
> *DISSOLVE TO: EXT. WOODS — DAY — LONG SHOT*
>
> *Far in the distance a figure can be seen approaching. By his curious action, moving from tree to tree, we know that the figure is trying to avoid being seen.*
>
> *DISSOLVE TO: EXT. WOODS NEAR BROOK — DAY — MED. CLOSE SHOT (PROCESS)*
>
> *The picnic is now finished. John has moved close to Isobel. They both lean against a tree.*
>
> *EXT. BUSHES — DAY — CLOSE SHOT*

2. The Mummy's Tomb

> *A RUSTLING in the b.g. is HEARD as the bushes are parted and INTO VIEW comes Mehemet Bey. He stares o.s.*
>
> *MED. SHOT — FROM MEHEMET BEY'S ANGLE — FAVORING ISOBEL*
>
> **JOHN:** Don't you think I propose better now than when I was a youngster?
>
> **ISOBEL:** Oh, yes — you've improved a whole lot...

I've heard of dipping a girl's ponytail into the ink, but dumping the bottle down someone's dress? Banning had a peculiar way of displaying his affection for poor Isobel.

And how many times has John actually proposed to her?

This dialogue would have put audiences to sleep back in 1942. Today it would provoke sarcastic laughter.

The one thing that it does succeed in doing is explain why Bey always happens to be in the right place at the right time, leering at Isobel. The final cut of the film in no way indicates where John and Isobel are picnicking, but in the above missing dialogue, Isobel tells John they're going to "the brook that ran close to the cemetery grounds." This makes the likelihood of Bey catching a glimpse of their picnic a calculated risk, not to mention that they are probably only yards away from the dormant Kharis. Wouldn't it have been interesting if John and Isobel elected to picnic under the moonlight? This meal may have been John Banning's last, as Kharis would not have needed to wander very far to knock off the groom-to-be.

However, there is no rest for the Mummy. Kharis must continue to secretly make his way through Mapleton after sunset, keeping close to the shadows. Perhaps working off some of those tana leaves may be in his best interest anyway. His next encounter takes place on High Street, with a very close call for one of Mapleton's own, Nick Lanston (Bill Ruhl). Here is another scene we never get to see:

> *EXT. EDGE OF TOWN — NIGHT — MED. CLOSE SHOT*
>
> *The Mummy comes directly at CAMERA, his one good eye blinking mercilessly. CAMERA PANS as he shuffles down a dimly-lighted street.*
>
> *EXT. STREET — NIGHT — MED. SHOT*
>
> *The Mummy makes his way along, going as rapidly as he can. He pauses suddenly beside a fence and looks o.s.*
>
> *MED. FULL SHOT — FROM HIS ANGLE*
>
> *A car with headlights is coming toward him slowly.*
>
> *MED. SHOT*
>
> *Kharis looks about him and then dodges into the shadows between two houses.*
>
> *EXT. ALLEYWAY — NIGHT — MED. CLOSE SHOT*
>
> *His feet stumble into the litter of old cans. They roll away rattling.*

> CLOSE SHOT
>
> *A huge black cat jumps from an ash-can to the ground and stands there, back arched, spitting. OVER SCENE comes FAINTLY the HOWL of a dog.*
>
> MED. SHOT
>
> *Kharis makes his way rapidly down the alley. The angle of the shot makes his figure monstrous.*
>
> EXT. STREET — NIGHT — MED. SHOT
>
> *NICK LANSTON, a typical New England father — a man in his late forties — carrying a little girl in his arms, walks slowly along. The child is sleepy and nestles against his shoulder. CAMERA MOVES with them.*
>
> NICK: (softly) Did you have a good time?
>
> CHILD: Uh-huh.
>
> NICK: I'm glad you did, but you shouldn't be out this late. How are you ever going to grow up and be a big girl if you don't get your beauty sleep?
>
> CHILD: I don't want to grow up and be a big girl. I just want to stay like this and have you carry me — always 'n' always.
>
> NICK: I...
>
> *He stops abruptly and CAMERA PANS QUICKLY to the side of a building, as the outline of the grotesque shadow of the Mummy appears.*
>
> CLOSE SHOT
>
> *Nick goes rigid with terror. His arms close tightly about the slight figure of the little girl in his arms. He turns and runs in the opposite direction.*
>
> MED. CLOSE SHOT — AT SIDE OF BUILDING *as the monster comes INTO VIEW. He starts out of the alley into the street.*
>
> DISSOLVE TO: EXT. STREET — NIGHT — CLOSE SHOT
>
> *The Mummy shuffles INTO SCENE, glances about, and then goes on, his feet making no sound as he moves. CAMERA PANS with him.*
>
> WIPE TO: EXT. ANOTHER STREET — NIGHT — MED. SHOT
>
> *The Mummy stares at something o.s. CAMERA PANS ABOUT to disclose several men coming toward CAMERA. CAMERA PANS BACK. The monster darts down an alley between buildings.*

Until reading the script, I never quite understood what that man said to clear the bar so quickly when he later bursts in screaming. But apparently it was, "The killer! He's out again! Just frightened Nick Lanston on High Street — the sheriff and he are down there now." Perhaps he should have spoken more clearly, or perhaps the father and daughter scene should not have been deleted. It's doubtful it was ever filmed because when Nick bursts into the sheriff's office and excitedly tells him that he saw the "shadow" along High Street, the following dialogue from the script

2. The Mummy's Tomb 47

matches the dialogue from the film exactly, except for one line, which is highlighted:

> INT. SHERIFF'S OFFICE — NIGHT — CLOSE SHOT — AT DESK
>
> *The sheriff is talking on the phone. From his conversation we know it is to someone of authority.*
>
> SHERIFF: I know — I know ... I've heard that laughing-stock routine before. Now what do you want me to do? (*pauses and listens a while*) Sure — the whole town is afraid of their own shadows now. I'm following up on it. Goodbye.
>
> LONGER ANGLE
>
> *The sheriff no sooner hangs up the phone than in bursts Nick Lanston. As the sheriff turns in his swivel chair, Nick comes to face him.*
>
> NICK: Sheriff, it's out again ... I saw that shadow ... I saw it with my own eyes!
>
> SHERIFF: You saw a shadow? Well what else did you see?
>
> NICK: I didn't wait for anything more...
>
> SHERIFF: That's fine — that's a great help!
>
> CLOSER SHOT
>
> NICK: **Well, I had my little girl with me**. You didn't think for a minute I was taking any chances...
>
> SHERIFF: Where'd you see it?
>
> NICK: I was walking along High Street...

The bold line of dialogue is the only difference between the script and the final release print of the film. Perhaps a later draft, if there is one, excludes this line.

With all the prowling done by the Mummy, it's only natural that he leaves evidence behind. When John Banning finds potential proof of the Mummy's existence in the shape of a strip of bandage hanging on a tree limb, he asks Isobel to drive him to see Prof. Norman at the university. He quickly darts into the house to first phone the professor, leaving Isobel outside. What we never get to see is Bey, who in the script, just happens to be in the neighborhood, again! At least Bey has the consideration to restrict his gawking over Isobel to the daylight hours or Mapleton would be buzzing about two shadows around town:

> MED. CLOSE PANNING SHOT
>
> *Mehemet Bey walks down the street near the Banning house. He stops for a moment, staring intently at something o.s. There is more than casual interest in his eyes.*
>
> MED. SHOT — FROM MEHEMET BEY'S ANGLE

> *Isobel stands with her back to Mehemet Bey; her summer dress fits her figure beautifully. She is unaware of Mehemet Bey's scrutiny.*
>
> CLOSE PANNING SHOT— MEHEMET BEY *as he starts to move slowly down the street. A sort of inward conflict is manifest upon his face, as though he were terrifically drawn to the girl and yet struggling within himself against it. He collects himself and starts OUT OF SCENE with a faster pace.*

Yes, Bey is everywhere. Where will he turn up next? Under Isobel's bed perhaps? In the film, there is a scene that takes place in Isobel's bedroom as the bride-to-be is trying on her wedding dress. The pre-wedding banter between Isobel and her mother runs a bit longer in the script, and time is running out for Bey:

> INT. ISOBEL'S BEDROOM— NIGHT— MED. SHOT
>
> *Isobel goes to the window and leans against it, looking out at the full moon above. In spite of all the horror that has been going on in the town, for the moment she is happy. Tomorrow she will be married. Her mother comes INTO SCENE quietly.*
>
> ISOBEL: Mother, were you excited the night before you were married?
>
> MOTHER: (*smiling, her mind going back*) Well, I did knock over a big glass of ginger ale…
>
> ISOBEL: How was Pop?
>
> MOTHER: (*smiling a little*) Somebody told him not to worry about a thing. Just to find out where the ceremony was going to be held and at what time. Then, to be there!
>
> ISOBEL: That's like Pop. You've been happy, haven't you mother?
>
> MOTHER: (*suddenly bustling*) We'll talk about that later. I have a hundred things to do before tomorrow. It's time you were in bed. Come on, now. Move!
>
> *Isobel smiles and starts away from the window.*

No Bey this time. He's back at the cemetery instructing Kharis to kidnap Isobel. The script resumes:

> EXT. ISOBEL'S BEDROOM WINDOW— NIGHT— MED. CLOSE SHOT
>
> *The monster comes INTO SCENE, looking about him, and stops at the open window. He looks inside.*
>
> INT. ISOBEL'S BEDROOM— NIGHT— MED. SHOT— FROM HIS ANGLE
>
> *Isobel can be seen in bed, asleep. She moves restlessly.*
>
> CLOSE SHOT— MUMMY'S FACE *coming straight for CAMERA and FILLING SCREEN.*

2. The Mummy's Tomb

INT. ISOBEL'S BEDROOM — NIGHT — CLOSE SHOT

Isobel, in bed, stirs again restlessly. The shadow of the Mummy falls across her.

CLOSE SHOT — MUMMY *staring* INTO CAMERA, *his one eye blinking evilly.*

CLOSE SHOT — ISOBEL

The shadow of the monster still across her. Her eyes snap open and go wide with terror.

INT. ISOBEL'S HOME — NIGHT — MED. SHOT

This is the corner section of a room. Isobel's mother is busily occupied, ironing on an old-fashioned ironing board in preparation for tomorrow. A SCREAM *from the rear of the house* COMES OVER. *The iron she has in her hands falls to the floor.*

MOTHER: (*her lips barely framing the word*) Isobel…

She turns and exits the scene.

INT. ISOBEL'S BEDROOM — NIGHT — CLOSE SHOT — ON THE DOOR

Her mother opens it and freezes in terror.

MED. SHOT — REVERSE ANGLE

The Mummy, with Isobel under his arm, faces her. He turns and goes for the window, taking it out with him.

MED. CLOSE SHOT

Isobel's mother SCREAMS *at the top of her lungs.*

CLOSE SHOT — ISOBEL'S MOTHER SCREAMING.

EXT. SIDE OF ISOBEL'S HOUSE — NIGHT — MED. SHOT

The Mummy hesitates and then makes off towards the rear of the house. The mother's SCREAM *again rings out.*

CLOSE SHOT — A WINDOW IN AN ADJOINING HOUSE *going up suddenly. A woman sticks out her head.*

INT. ISOBEL'S BEDROOM — NIGHT — MED. SHOT

Hysterically, her mother goes toward the broken window. She starts to scramble and climb through.

EXT. SIDE OF ISOBEL'S HOUSE — NIGHT — MED. SHOT

The mother stumbles INTO SCENE, *crying and carrying on. She is very near hysteria.*

LONGER ANGLE

The mother screams hysterically:

MOTHER: Isobel … Isobel…!

She comes rushing toward CAMERA, *with the scream of "Isobel!" still on her lips.*

> *EXT. EDGE OF WOODS — NIGHT — MED. SHOT*
>
> *The Mummy, going as swiftly as possible, emerges from the edge of town and goes toward the trees.*

In the film, Isobel's mother bursts into the room just as the Mummy is carrying Isobel through the window. She screams and moves quickly toward the camera. Nothing after that made it to the final release print. But more importantly, Bey has made his move, and so have the townspeople.

Quite a few scenes toward the end of the film have been snipped in order to keep the action moving at a lively pace. As the troops are congregating at the Banning house, Isobel's mother arrives, hysterical. She runs into John's arms, barely able to speak. "Isobel … the monster … took her away…"

A handwritten note to the right of the dialogue on the script suggests John be "more dramatic" for the remainder of the scene. Ironically, it is not even included in the film:

> JOHN: Men, there's no time to lose. We've got to find that monster and find him right away!
>
> *MED. CLOSE SHOT*
>
> *The sheriff then faces the crowd…*
>
> SHERIFF: I want one third of you men to follow Henry Turner, here. You'll approach the cemetery from the south. Another third will follow John. The remaining third will follow me. Now, let's get going!
>
> *CLOSE SHOT — GROUP — FAVORING JOHN AND ISOBEL'S MOTHER*
>
> *He turns to one of the men.*
>
> JOHN: See her home for me, will you Al?
>
> AL: Sure John, sure.
>
> *MED. FULL SHOT*
>
> *The crowd organizes in groups. A ROAR comes from them as they move.*

Didn't we see this in a Frankenstein movie once?

When the villagers descend on Bey's cemetery cottage, he sends the Mummy out until he can restore order. Bey and John finally face off. Bey denies any knowledge of Isobel, and John's patience expires. In the film, one of the searchers makes his way up to them:

> SEARCHER: The Mummy! Isobel! (*points*) Through the woods!
>
> *(in a very quick scene also removed)*
>
> *John's face tightens.*
>
> *CLOSE SHOT — MEHEMET BEY reacting to the impact of the above words. His lips form a thin, cruel line. He realizes everything is over — for him.*

2. The Mummy's Tomb

> **MEHEMET BEY:** Banning!
>
> *MED. SHOT*
>
> *John turns slowly.*
>
> **JOHN:** (his voice like ice) Well?
>
> **MEHEMET BEY:** (*grimly*) For those who defile the temples of ancient Egypt, a violent death shall be their fate… (*his hand leaps from his pocket; it contains an automatic*) …and yours is the death of…
>
> *A gun ROARS.*
>
> *As he staggers beneath the impact of a heavy bullet. His own automatic swivels in his fingers…*

After the crowd disperses in pursuit of Isobel and the Mummy, Bey is left to be judged by his ancient Egyptian gods. What follows is a continuation of the scene taken from the script, which was not in the final film:

> *EXT. CARETAKER'S HOUSE — NIGHT — MED. SHOT*
>
> *Not a person is now visible.*
>
> *EXT. MAUSOLEUM — NIGHT — MED. CLOSE SHOT — AT THE DOOR*
>
> *Mehemet Bey, unable to walk upright, drags himself through the opening.*
>
> *INT. MAUSOLEUM — NIGHT — CLOSE SHOT — WINDOW through which pours the moonlight. CAMERA PULLS BACK and PANS DOWNWARD to TAKE IN Mehemet Bey standing erect, his face turned toward the sky.*
>
> *CLOSE SHOT — MEHEMET BEY*
>
> *His face contorted by pain and exertion. A terrific sadness is in his manner.*
>
> **MEHEMET BEY:** Oh, mighty gods of Egypt, forgive me. Above all other mortal men I have put myself — and even above you! I have failed!
>
> *CLOSE SHOT — WINDOW with the moonlight streaming in.*
>
> **MEHEMET BEY'S VOICE:** (*weakly*) I have proven unworthy of the mantle of High Priest of Karnak. Earthly desires and earthly thinking has consumed me…
>
> *CLOSE SHOT — MEHEMET BEY*
>
> **MEHEMET BEY:** …miserably … utterly! But may — there be compassion … when… (*he sinks down upon his knees, one arm upon the altar*) …I stand before you… (*he sinks still lower*) …in … judgment….
>
> *He pitches forward, one hand striking the base of the metal tripod as he does so.*
>
> *CLOSE SHOT*
>
> *The tripod goes over and the metal pot hits the floor with a crash.*

> *CLOSE SHOT*
>
> *The dark liquid spreads over the floor. It reaches the embers from the fire that had heated it. A minor explosion takes place and flame darts across the stones. It moves toward Mehemet Bey's inert hand and wrist at one edge of the frame.*
>
> *CLOSE SHOT — THE FLAME burning brightly.*

This edit certainly denies Turhan Bey a spectacular death scene. And now Isobel will marry her childhood sweetheart of numerous proposals, the more conservative, and certainly less interesting, John Banning. But before the wedding commences, there's still the little matter of the Mummy.

Kharis, with Isobel in hand, makes his way to the Banning house with the villagers hot on his heels. Once inside, there is no way out. John and the sheriff race in to free Isobel from the Mummy's clutches while the mob fling their torches at the house and set it ablaze.

Inevitably, John rescues his betrothed and Kharis perishes in the inferno, at least temporarily.

The primary difference between the script and the film are the close shots of the Mummy in the flames. Watching poor Kharis struggle during the film's fiery finale is almost sad, but the script provides a pathos that almost makes one reach for the tissues. He is like some poor animal, trapped in a blazing holocaust, desperately trying to free himself. He attempts to scream from the pain, but cannot, as the fire consigns him to his inevitable doom. He finally collapses as the flames completely engulf him.

Instead of the rush-rush ending of more news headlines and Isobel's single, looped line, "I'm glad we managed to sneak out while the folks are celebrating," the script concludes with John and Isobel actually on their way to the train station via taxi cab:

> *INT. TAXI — CLOSE SHOT (PROCESS)*
>
> JOHN: Say — I wonder if they allow officers to live outside the barracks...?
>
> ISOBEL: Well, maybe you should've thought of that before you decided to take me along.
>
> JOHN: Oh well — at least you'll be able to live somewhere near there.
>
> ISOBEL: I'm so glad we managed to sneak out. I just hated the thought of having to say goodbye to everybody in town.
>
> JOHN: (grinning) Will they be surprised when they find us gone.
>
> *DISSOLVE TO: EXT. TRAIN STATION— NIGHT — FULL SHOT*
>
> *The street by the station is deserted.*
>
> *CLOSER SHOT*
>
> *As the cab pulls in to a stop, John and Isobel get out. John quickly reaches in for the traveling bags, hands the driver the fare. As he and Isobel start toward*

> the station entrance, all hell pops loose. The townspeople start pouring out of the station, tossing old shoes, confetti, tin cans. They have to run the gauntlet amid ad libs:
>
> AD LIBS: Tried to get away with it huh?... You weren't fooling us for a minute...
>
> SHERIFF: I ought to have you arrested for that.
>
> CLOSE GROUP SHOT as Isobel and John make their way through the crowd. Isobel's mother runs up, stops long enough to kiss John and Isobel. As John and Isobel start toward the station, the CAMERA MOVES IN on Isobel's mother as she calls after them:
>
> MOTHER: Be good to her, John...
>
> FADE OUT.

Wartime audiences deserved a happy ending and usually got one. The evil force, whether it is a monster or Nazis, if they're not one of the same, is always extinguished by the closing credits. Just imagine, in a more modern horror film, it wouldn't have been the townspeople waiting for John and Isobel at the train station, it would have been an over-cooked Kharis who would have escaped the flames and certainly gotten in the last word in a surprise ending.

However, by marrying into the Banning family, Isobel places her name on the Egyptian High Priest hit list. It's a good thing the mission of the High Priest in the follow-up, *The Mummy's Ghost*, was to reunite Kharis and Ananka, and not continue the Banning onslaught.

Elyse Knox shared some of her mummy memories with me regarding the making of *The Mummy's Tomb*. They bear something of a resemblance to the memories Peggy Moran wrote for this book's introduction, pertaining to her work on *The Mummy's Hand*.

Ms. Knox recalls, "*The Mummy's Tomb* was filmed on the back lot of Universal Studios— about 58 years ago. Most of it was shot at night, which made it all seem a little spooky!"

Ms. Knox also gave me a bit of insight on her experience of being on the set with Lon Chaney. "Lon Chaney was very pleased I didn't weigh more," she said, "because in my unconscious state, the Mummy was called upon to carry me a great deal! If I remember correctly, he only had the use of one arm."

In a *Filmfax* article, Turhan Bey also recalls Chaney's discomfort in the Mummy suit:

> The Mummy, Kharis, was played by Lon Chaney, who really suffered in that costume. We shot the film during summer, and he had to spend all his time in the wrapped-up costume. Of course, he had a zipper in the back, so he could withdraw to his dressing room, slip out of the bandages and take a break. Lon did not complain, however. It was kind of funny talking to him. Everything came out muffled, of course, but you could make out what he said. It is a strange experience holding a conversation with a mummy between the shots.

Lon spent most of his time in the dressing room where he sneaks a smoke with a cigarette holder or a drink with a straw. When an actor is in heavy makeup, they do try to make him comfortable whenever they can. I enjoy doing horror films. I particularly liked *The Mummy's Tomb.*

Following are a few further noteworthy facts from the script that were changed before the final release print:

- Dick Foran's character, Steve Banning, has a line in the script during his checker game with John: "You kind of cramped for space ain't you son?" The Steve we knew from *The Mummy's Hand* never would have said "ain't." In fact, he once corrected his buddy Babe when he said "ain't." As it turned out, Steve does say, "You kind of cramped for space, aren't you, son?" in the film. Perhaps Foran, who formerly attended Princeton, felt that "aren't" flowed a bit easier and took it upon him to make the correction during the take.
- The Bannings' caretaker, Jim, portrayed by Paul E. Burns, was formerly named Pedro.
- Babe walks into the bar and orders a beer, but the script calls for him to order a whisky and soda. Whisky must have been too strong for the censors in the Breen office.

3

The Mummy's Ghost

> Nameless ... fleshless ... deathless...
> —Trailer for *The Mummy's Ghost*

Cast: Lon Chaney *(Kharis, the Mummy)*; John Carradine *(Yousef Bey)* [*Ahmed Bey* script name]; Ramsay Ames *(Amina Monsouri)* [*Amina El Harun* script name]; Robert Lowery *(Tom Hervey)*; George Zucco *(High Priest)*; Barton MacLane *(Inspector Walgreen)*; Frank Reicher *(Professor Norman)*; Claire Whitney *(Mrs. Ellen Norman)*; Harry Shannon *(Sheriff Elwood)*; Emmett Vogan *(The Coroner)*; Lester Sharpe *(Dr. Ayad)* [*Dr. Nagel* script name]; Oscar O'Shea *(Watchman)*; Jack C. Smith, Jack Rockwell *(Deputies)*; Stephen Barclay *(Harrison)*; Carl Vernell *(Student)*; Dorothy Vaughan *(Mrs. Blake)*; Mira McKinney *(Mrs. Martha Evans)*; Bess Flowers, Caroline Cooke *(Mapleton Women)*; Eddy Waller *(Ben Evans)*; Anthony Warde *(Detective)*; Ivan Triesault *(Scripps Museum Guide)*; Martha MacVicar *(Girl Student)*; Peanuts and King *(Dogs)*; David Bruce *(Voice of Radio Actor)*; Pietro Sosso *(Priest)*. **Crew:** Joseph Gershenson *(Executive Producer)*; Ben Pivar *(Associate Producer)*; Reginald Le Borg *(Directed by)*; Melville Shyer *(Assistant Director)*; Griffin Jay, Henry Sucher, Brenda Weisberg *(Screenplay)*; Griffin Jay, Henry Sucher *(Original Story)*; William Sickner *(Director of Photography)*; John B. Goodman, Abraham Grossman *(Art Direction)*; Saul Goodkind *(Film Editor)*; Russell A. Gausman, L.R. Smith *(Set Decorations)*; Vera West *(Gowns)*; Hans J. Salter *(Music Director)*; Bernard B. Brown *(Sound Director)*; Jess Moulin *(Technician)*; Jack Pierce *(Makeup Artist)*.

Of the four Mummy films produced by Universal during the wartime era, *The Mummy's Hand* clearly stands out as the best of the bunch. But among fans of the genre, *The Mummy's Ghost* gives *Hand* a good run for its money with the popular vote. Reasons being, Ramsay Ames is absolutely gorgeous. Second, the Mummy has much more screen time in *Ghost*, than in *Hand*. Third, Ramsay Ames is gorgeous. Fourth, the Mummy shows greater emotion here than in the other entries. Fifth, Ramsay Ames is gorgeous.

One cannot really dispute any of the above reasons. Ramsay Ames is stunning as the Princess Ananka, and Lon Chaney as the Mummy appears just ten minutes into the film, allowing fans to relish the action right away. Chaney visibly gives the role quite a bit more here than he did in *The Mummy's Tomb*, especially during the murder scenes. As Kharis bursts in on poor Prof. Norman, you can see the rage on the Mummy's face just before he moves in for the kill. Or perhaps its just Chaney displaying his discomfort in the Mummy makeup. And just as the Princess Ananka slips through Kharis' moldy fingers one night in the Scripps Museum, the Mummy flies into a rage and has to be calmed by his mentor. Unfortunately, the night watchman shows up when Kharis is displaying his worst temper outburst. He is in no mood for infidels. Needless to say, the watchman is quickly dispatched. Then, of course there is the obligatory double-crossing High Priest who literally falls victim to the enraged Kharis.

An interesting aspect of *The Mummy's Ghost* screenplay is that there are very few scenes that failed to make it into the final film. There are no missing Mummy murders or shadows in dark alleyways. However, many final scenes from the film have been shortened or trimmed before released to theaters. In order to keep this book coherent, these scenes have been included in their entirety.

Yousef Bey (John Carradine) answers the sacred summons of the High Priest (George Zucco) of Arkam (formerly Karnak). When Bey arrives at the temple, he is sworn into the cult and given his mission. He is to travel to America, not to do away with surviving members of the Ananka expedition as attempted by the previous acolyte, but to return the mummies of Ananka and Kharis (Lon Chaney) to their rightful resting places in Egypt.

Miles away in Mapleton, Massachusetts, Prof. Norman (Frank Reicher) lectures to his students about the ill-fated Ananka expedition and the marauding Mummy who terrorized their town not long ago. Later that night, Norman is tinkering with tana leaves in his home. As he translates Egyptian hieroglyphics, he slowly places nine leaves into a burner. Vapor begins to rise into the air. Suddenly Kharis emerges from the nearby woods. He passes by the window of a sleeping co-ed, Amina Monsouri (Ramsay Ames). As his shadow passes across her, she slowly rises from her bed and begins to sleepwalk.

Now the Mummy approaches Prof. Norman's house. He pauses for a moment, then advances toward a pair of open French doors. As the monster looks in, Prof. Norman suddenly senses someone else in the room with him. He turns toward the doors to see the horrifying figure of Kharis. The enraged Mummy stalks toward the terrified professor, who gets up from his chair and attempts to escape.

3. *The Mummy's Ghost*

But Kharis' outstretched arm blocks his exit. Norman, paralyzed with fear, slowly backs away from the advancing Mummy. He eventually backs himself into a corner and Kharis strangles the life from the horror-stricken man. Kharis quickly downs the fluid and exits. As he does so, the sleepwalking Amina, now close to Prof. Norman's house, comes out of her trance-like state, sees the Mummy and does what any young girl in a 1940s horror film would do—faints.

The next morning, the whole campus is buzzing over Prof. Norman's murder. The coroner (Emmett Vogan) deduces that Norman was strangled and the killer left traces of mold on the victim's throat. The sheriff's apprehensive conclusion, "The Mummy."

The police are now questioning Amina, who was found unconscious outside the late professor's house. Her boyfriend Tom Hervey (Robert Lowery) bursts in, insisting she is innocent. As the police dismiss the couple, Tom notices a strange white streak in Amina's hair, but he makes no verbal remark.

Soon, the local newspaper headline reads, "Mummy believed to be back in New England." The town is warned to stay indoors at night, except for the able-bodied who will patrol the streets after dark.

In the woods on the outskirts of town, it's feeding time once again. Bey is brewing the tana leaves to summon Kharis, but not before the Mummy takes care of one of the villagers (Eddy Waller) coming home from street patrol.

Later, at the Scripps Museum, Bey and several touring spectators gaze down at the mummy of Ananka as she lies in her sarcophagus. As the others move on, Bey stays behind. He hides in the museum until it closes. Kharis arrives and Bey has some good news for him. "The hour of fulfillment is at hand," he proclaims. "Behold her, Ananka, the princess of your forbidden love."

Yet the best-laid plans of mice and men and mummies.... Kharis leans over to touch his bride, literally for the first time in centuries, and she all but disintegrates, leaving nothing but the bandages she was wrapped in. Bey informs the enraged Mummy that Ananka's soul "has entered another form." Kharis vents his frustration on the other displays in the museum. He smashes a glass case, knocks over another mummy coffin, you name it. All the ruckus sends the night watchman (Oscar O'Shea), gun in hand, charging into the room. But he only sees Bey. As he instructs Bey to step away from Ananka's mummy case, the watchman fails to see Kharis sneaking up behind him, in a very bad mood. Thanks to Kharis, there is now an opening for a night watchman at the Scripps Museum.

Meanwhile, back in town, Amina awakens suddenly, insisting she felt someone touching her.

The next day at the museum, Inspector Walgreen (Barton MacLane) and Dr. Ayad (Lester Sharpe) examine the wrappings in Ananka's coffin and are baffled. They deduce that with no wrappings cut, there is no way Ananka's body could have been removed. And yet, it is gone. Since the murdered guard has the same mold on his throat as the victims in Mapleton, the Inspector decides to pay a visit to the small town.

After conversing with the local authorities, Walgreen and the police devise a trap for the Mummy. They repeat the experiment Prof. Norman was conducting the night of his death, with the hopes of trapping the Mummy in a camouflaged pit just outside Norman's house. With the tana leaves brewing and Prof. Norman's widow secure in her room, they wait. But Kharis is a no-show. Instead, he has kidnapped Amina, whose streaked white hair is now more noticeable than the Mummy mold on the throats of Kharis' victims. The Mummy is headed with Amina to Bey, who is waiting atop of an old elevated mining shack at the edge of town.

By the time Kharis arrives, Amina's hair is now completely white. The Mummy places his bride on a table as Bey prepares to return her to a mummified state. Kharis anxiously stands guard just outside the shack, while Bey is inside, doing serious battle with his conscience. Finally, he dares the anger of Amon-Ra, not to mention the hot-tempered Kharis just a few feet away. He decides to follow in the footsteps of previous men of the cloth by allowing the blood to rush from his head to somewhere else. He not only succumbs to the temptation of Ananka, but also has the unmitigated stupidity to announce aloud, "I'm going to make you immortal. And I too shall drink and be immortal. We will not return to Egypt!"

You would think that by now, Kharis would be wise to these Priests. Kharis overhears the proclamation and comes back into the shack to find Bey attempting to administer the life-preserving tana fluid to the girl. Outraged, Kharis approaches his double-crossing mentor and knocks the cup from his hand. With nowhere to run, Bey attempts to reassure Kharis that they *will* return to Egypt, but Bey's number is up. Kharis sends him crashing to the other side of the shack. Amina's beau Tom has now shown up and can see the goings-on from below. With one mighty blow, Kharis sends Bey hurtling down to his death. For the third time in three outings, Kharis has outlived the film's High Priest.

As Tom charges up to attack the advancing Mummy, he too loses his battle with Kharis. Fortunately, he is only knocked unconscious. Kharis returns to the shack, picks up the girl and takes off into the woods.

Now the Sheriff and townspeople have caught up with Tom. After finding the mine shack empty, they deduce that Kharis must have taken Amina into the woods.

Poor Kharis. Now with no mentor (I can't see him buying a boat ticket for two back to Egypt) and the mob hot on his heels, he heads for the swamp. As he slowly moves through the brush, Amina begins aging rapidly. Her skin dries up and shrivels practically before our eyes. (For Ramsay Ames fans, this has to be the saddest scene in the film.) Suddenly, the bog becomes thick and deep. With no place to turn, Kharis and his bride, who is now nearly as mummified as he is, sink lower and lower into the mire. Tom covers his face in horror as he watches the swamp swallow them completely. The townspeople can do nothing but watch helplessly.

As mentioned in the previous chapter on *The Mummy's Tomb*, having the Mummy in America should have been much more of a novel idea than a staple. But since he is here to stay, *The Mummy's Ghost* toyed with a few different ideas. It was the first of the Kharis series to take on the subject of reincarnation. Not since Karloff's 1932 *The Mummy* did Universal incorporate this theme into one of their Mummy films. However, *The Mummy* had a much happier ending. In the last reel, the heroine was saved from the clutches of the dead in the nick of time. She presumably survived to marry the film's hero, David Manners, whereas in *The Mummy's Ghost*, Amina ceased to exist as the mummy of Ananka prevailed.

Having the monster killed off by the closing credits does not, by any means, imply that you're guaranteed a happy ending. The monster may have been destroyed by the hero, but what about the heroine? This is a trend followed by several Universal horror films:

In *Son of Dracula* (1943), Kay Caldwell (Louise Allbritton) plans to obtain eternal life from Count Alucard (Lon Chaney) so she can pass it on to her childhood sweetheart Frank Stanley (Robert Paige) and attain eternal bliss. But her plan backfires. After polishing off the Count, who is really Dracula, Frank seeks out his fiancée Kay. She is lying dormant in a coffin awaiting the sunset. He removes the ring from his finger, places it on hers and proceeds to set the coffin ablaze with her in it.

In *House of Frankenstein* (1944), young Ilonka (Elena Verdugo) is love-struck for Larry Talbot (Lon Chaney), and becomes the Wolf Man's last victim of the film. But not before she manages to fire the single shot that does him in.

In *House of Dracula* (1945), Talbot (Chaney) is cured of his lycanthropy and walks off with the leading lady (Martha O'Driscoll). But despite this good fortune, *House of Dracula* presents arguably the most sorrowful ending of a Universal horror film.

To start, Dr. Edelmann (Onslow Stevens) attempts to give Dracula (John Carradine) a transfusion, but the double-crossing Count deliberately backs some of his blood into the kindly doctor. This gives him Jekyll and Hyde–type tendencies with a dash of vampirism added for good measure. In the end, Dr. Edelmann viciously attacks and kills his sweet hunchbacked assistant (Jane Adams), then tosses her lifeless body aside like a rag doll. After curing Talbot and attempting to rid the world of all its evil beings, including Dracula and the Frankenstein Monster (Glenn Strange), Dr. Edelmann is shot down and killed by the former lycanthrope.

The Mummy's Ghost received its share of bad reviews, as most sequels do. But the fans that lined up in droves outside theaters in the summer of 1944 couldn't care less. Despite more inconsistencies, moviegoers came out in hordes to see their favorite Egyptian put the squeeze on his latest round of victims.

Priests of Karnak were mysteriously renamed Priests of Arkam in the film (it remained Karnak in the script), the hill of the Seven Jackals became the hills of Arkam, and there is no attempt whatsoever to explain how Kharis survived the inferno of the Banning house, or why he looks less singed after being consumed by flames at the end of *Tomb*. Perhaps this is where the film title comes into play. Maybe *The Mummy's Ghost* was intended to imply that this is the spirit of Kharis. After all, with just a sniff of freshly brewed tana fluid, he reappears. Or perhaps *The Mummy's Ghost* refers to the spirit of Ananka.

Whatever the title was meant to imply, the Egyptian cat goddess Bast was out of the bag in *The Mummy's Ghost*. Only minutes into the film, we learn that tana leaves are now as familiar to students of Egyptology as they are to us. And immediately following the first Mummy killing, Kharis is the one and only suspect. Unless one has seen the previous series entries, the automatic conclusion that Kharis is their man seems a bit hokey. After all, who would look at a murder victim, find mold on the throat and automatically deduce "The Mummy," as though he were some legendary creature who finally paid the town a visit?

Perhaps if the Mapleton citizenry were a little sharper, the Mummy would not have gathered the momentum to knock off four victims in a 60-minute film. They appear a bit too occupied with planning for weddings and digging ditches.

The Mummy's Ghost utilized the least stock footage of all the Mummy films. There's the often seen shot of the full moon, and what about the High Priest? Is that really John Carradine, or is it George Zucco walking up the temple steps via *Mummy's Hand* stock footage at the opening of *Ghost*? It may have been Zucco from afar, but it was new footage of Carradine entering the altar room seconds later in the film:

> *INT. ALTAR ROOM AT KARNAK — NIGHT — MED. FULL PAN SHOT*
> *CAMERA PASSES SLOWLY from burning torches set in the walls of the ancient and crumbling room, ACROSS paintings of the gods of Egypt, which under their coating of dust are almost obscure in the flickering light, ACROSS disintegrating stone statues of forgotten deities, and STOPS at the base of a huge idol of Set. Ceremonial lamps burn at either side of this idol and incense smoke whirls upward in the lethargic atmosphere. An old man, a temple priest in ancient temple costume, is replenishing the incense containers. Another man, also in temple robes, is seated on a stone throne beneath the idol. A third man, the one who was seen climbing the stairway, comes INTO SCENE. CAMERA MOVES IN toward these three men.*
>
> *MED. SHOT*
>
> *We see now that the occupant of the throne is much older than the man standing before him. His face is lined and wrinkled but his body is strong and vigorous, his eyes sharp and penetrating. The man before him reverently faces the HIGH PRIEST of Karnak. The High Priest waves his hand and the priest attending the incense burners withdraws.*
>
> HIGH PRIEST: (*to the newcomer*) Before our god, Amon-Ra, you are Ahmed Bey, son of Abd el Malik, bazaar keeper of Alexandria?
>
> AHMED BEY: (changed to YOUSEF BEY) I am, oh father. I have answered your summons.
>
> HIGH PRIEST: Even as others before you have answered. Even as I answered many years ago ... to fulfill the destiny of the Priests of Karnak.
>
> AHMED BEY: Yes, master.
>
> HIGH PRIEST: You have been schooled in the concepts of the modern world ... You have been admitted to the mysteries of our own ancient Egypt.

3. The Mummy's Ghost   61

> Thus your faith has been strengthened by knowledge, that you might better serve our gods in the proper time. That time is now at hand.
>
> *CAMERA STARTS TO MOVE into a CLOSE SHOT of the High Priest, whose eyes begin to burn with inner zeal.*
>
> CLOSE SHOT — HIGH PRIEST
>
> HIGH PRIEST: The modern world scoffs at the powers of our ancient gods … our ceremonies … our beliefs! We are untouched by such derision.
>
> CLOSE SHOT — AHMED BEY
>
> *Listening.*
>
> HIGH PRIEST'S VOICE: For here … in these ruined temples and tombs, truth lies buried and hidden from the infidels. Here, the ancient gods still rule supreme.
>
> MED. CLOSE SHOT
>
> *The High Priest looks steadily at Ahmed Bey.*
>
> HIGH PRIEST: You are prepared to undertake a mission?
>
> AHMED BEY: I am.
>
> HIGH PRIEST: And to live your life according to the pattern decreed by the Priests of Karnak?
>
> AHMED BEY: I am.
>
> *The High Priest's expression shows that he is satisfied.*
>
> HIGH PRIEST: Here then… (*pausing impressively*) Three thousand years ago lived the Princess Ananka and a young man, Kharis. They dared love each other. But Ananka was a Princess initiate of Karnak, and such a love was forbidden. The princess died, her soul cursed forever.
>
> CLOSE SHOT — AHMED BEY *listening to the High Priest's story.*
>
> HIGH PRIEST'S VOICE: Kharis was buried with her. But … Kharis was not dead! He never died. He was kept alive through the ages to guard Ananka's tomb, to destroy anyone who might attempt its violation.
>
> CLOSE SHOT — HIGH PRIEST *the fanatical gleam in his eyes intensifying.*
>
> HIGH PRIEST: Kharis became a thing without feeling… His only mission in life … and in death … was to kill! He obeyed only the Priests of Karnak! (*he pauses*) Then, thirty years ago…

From "Kharis was buried with her" to "Then, thirty years ago…" George Zucco's dialogue in the script was cut noticeably, as it was in *The Mummy's Tomb*. Could it be the old gods had it in for this wonderfully wicked thespian for his sacrilegious acts two films ago? Non-believing infidels would say the cuts were made for the sake of pacing.

Interestingly, a detail that is seldom if ever noticed is contained in the credits for *The Mummy's Ghost*. Zucco is billed as the High Priest. In *The Mummy's Tomb*, he *was* Andoheb. So in reality, Andoheb truly and finally died in *The Mummy's Tomb*. It was based purely on assumption by fans and critics alike that Andoheb returned in all his quivering, trembling glory for *The Mummy's Ghost*.

Meanwhile, Ramsay Ames, billed in the credits simply as Amina, became Ananka by the time she and her beau were swallowed up by the murky Mapleton marsh. She opened the film as a spooked college student who got the chills at the very mention of anything to do with Egypt. And 60 minutes later she *literally* became part of her country's history by metamorphosizing into Ananka:

> HERVEY: (*puzzled*) What is it Amina? Why do you always get so jittery if I mention anything about Egypt?
>
> AMINA: (*abruptly*) Please, Tom! Do we have to talk about it?
>
> CAMERA ANGLE WIDENS *as she goes toward a small mirror beside a window.*
>
> HERVEY: Why not? You're Egyptian. That makes it important and interesting to me. But when I speak of it, you freeze up!
>
> CLOSE UP — INTO MIRROR
>
> *Amina's face can be seen staring straight before her.*
>
> AMINA: I know. I can't help it! Something happens to me when I think of Egypt. I see tombs ... dark, dreadful tombs! Long underground tunnels ... black and with dripping water. Rot ... decay ... death!
>
> *Hervey steps up behind her and his face, too, can be SEEN in the mirror.*
>
> HERVEY: But darling ... Egypt isn't like that! It's as modern ... as up-to-date as any other country.

Okay, consider the subject changed. Back in Egypt, the High Priest in the temple is putting the final touches on his speech to the cult's new acolyte, the complete version is written below which we were denied via editing:

> HIGH PRIEST'S VOICE: The world believes they have destroyed Kharis. But through the sacred message brought to us by the most holy spirit of Amon-Ra ... we know that he still lives!
>
> CAMERA PULLS BACK *into a MED. SHOT. The High Priest, who holds some tana leaves, and Ahmed Bey are disclosed standing among the hills, the moonlight bright about them. Ahmed Bey is aghast at what he has just heard.*
>
> AHMED BEY: Kharis ... still ... lives!?
>
> CLOSE SHOT — HIGH PRIEST
>
> HIGH PRIEST: Lives only for the purpose for which he was created. To

3. The Mummy's Ghost 63

> guard Ananka's tomb until the end of time! Your mission is to bring him back to Egypt, and with him, Ananka, his beloved princess!
>
> *MED. CLOSE SHOT as the High Priest raises his head toward the heavens in prayer.*
>
> **HIGH PRIEST:** (*praying*) Oh mighty gods of Egypt, the fate of those who defy the will of the ancient gods shall be a cruel and violent death. For it is said...
>
> *DISSOLVE TO: INT. AMINA'S ROOM — NIGHT — MED. SHOT*
>
> *White curtains at the window billow inward. Amina tosses restlessly in her sleep, the moonlight very bright about her. The High Priest's VOICE COMES OVER in a weird, far-away tone.*
>
> **HIGH PRIEST'S VOICE:** (*continuing prayer*)...that the descendants of the Priests of Karnak shall never rest — even unto eternity — and our prayers shall be heard even to the far corners of the earth ... and they shall be called to our aid ... to help us in our sacred mission...
>
> *Amina shows she is under a great stain. She mutters something in her sleep and her restlessness increases.*
>
> *DISSOLVE TO: MED. CLOSE SHOT*
>
> **HIGH PRIEST:** (*praying*) ...and may you find in this man, a priest worthy in every respect to carry on the sacred trust now delivered into his hands. May he never succumb to any temptation that might lead him from his path!

Mummy addicts can recall the High Priest's line dubbed in at the end of the film as we see the shot of the motionless swamp. "The fate of those who defy the will of the ancient gods, shall be a cruel and violent death!" While Kharis himself may have lost the ability to frighten, that line still has the potential to raise a few hairs. Having the voiceover come in at the end of the film works as a subtle reminder to fans of the series not to mess with Egypt's ancient gods.

Another line cut from the High Priest's dialogue was also a retread. Mummy aficionados recall, "...and may you find in this man (young follower), a priest worthy in every respect to carry on the sacred trust now delivered into his hands." These are almost Andoheb's last words after swearing in Mehemet Bey in *The Mummy's Tomb*. This High Priest (Zucco) is also the first not to expire upon delivering the responsibilities of the ancient sect to the new disciple. But it is only the youngster who travels abroad.

Mapleton has barely recovered from the nightmare inflicted upon it by Kharis. Now, Ahmed Bey is among the citizenry. He unobtrusively mixes right in with the locals. In fact, he casually stands by, smirking, as he eavesdrops on two women who pass right by him on the street:

> 1st Woman: All the money in the world wouldn't get me out tonight.
>
> 2nd Woman: I remember the last time this happened. It was pretty horrible.

This bit of dialogue was missing from the typewritten version of the script. It was written in by hand, leaving the reader to assume it was either a last-minute idea or simply left out accidentally when the script was being typed. In any case, it was a neat idea. The camera pans along with the two women, then stops on Bey, who eavesdrops with a devious grin on his face.

Little bits of dialogue and quick intercuts are all it takes sometimes to create a memorable scene. Then, there are those that are, or would be, forgettable.

Mrs. Evans (Mira McKinney) is asleep in her room. Her husband Ben (Eddy Waller) is due back soon from his late night Mummy vigil from the courthouse roof. Suddenly, King, the family dog begins barking frantically:

> *EXT. BARN— NIGHT— MED. SHOT*
>
> *An extremely large dog, vicious-looking and powerful, stands looking across the field, BARKING loudly. The dog bounds forward, then swerves back, hair bristling, but still barking and growling.*
>
> *INT. EVANS' BEDROOM— NIGHT— MED. SHOT— AT BED*
>
> *The room is illuminated by moonlight. A shotgun stands near the wall. Mrs. Evans stirs restlessly. The BARKING of the dog is HEARD distinctly. Mrs. Evans half wakes and mutters to herself:*
>
> Mrs. Evans: Now what's got into old King, I'd like to know.
>
> *She turns over and goes to sleep again.*
>
> *EXT. BARN— NIGHT— MED. CLOSE SHOT— ON DOG who is in a frenzy of rage and fear, leaping toward the CAMERA and backing away, not quite daring to attack what he sees.*
>
> *REVERSE SHOT— FROM BEHIND DOG*
>
> *Kharis is coming on, swaying and searching the air as before. The terrified dog keeps leaping toward and away from the monster. Without stopping, Kharis swerves slightly, sniffing the air. The scent and the harrying of the dog turn him toward the interior of the barn, the door of which is open.*
>
> *INT. EVANS' BEDROOM— NIGHT— MED. CLOSE FOLLOW SHOT*
>
> *The BARKING of the dog is wilder than before. Mrs. Evans sits up abruptly. She reaches for the alarm clock.*
>
> Mrs. Evans: Land sakes! It's way past midnight!
>
> *She gets out of bed, draws an old bathrobe about her and crosses to the window.*
>
> Mrs. Evans: *(leaning out calling)* King! King!
>
> *EXT. BARN— NIGHT— MED. SHOT as King appears in doorway of barn, BARKING violently.*

3. The Mummy's Ghost 65

> INT. BEDROOM — NIGHT — CLOSE SHOT — MRS. EVANS
>
> MRS. EVANS: (*calling out*) What's the matter, boy?
>
> *The crunching of steps on gravel is heard.*
>
> MRS. EVANS: That you, Ben?
>
> EVANS' VOICE: Yep, it's me!
>
> MRS. EVANS: And about time, too!
>
> EXT. YARD — NIGHT — MED. PAN SHOT *as Ben Evans approaches the house through the shrubbery.*
>
> MRS. EVANS VOICE: (*continuing*) Old King's been carrying on like crazy —
>
> EVANS: (*a little edgy*) I hear 'im! Go back to bed Martha!
>
> *He lifts his rifle and starts for the barn.*
>
> INT. BARN — NIGHT — MED. SHOT — ON KHARIS
>
> *The barn is filled with shadows, which make shapeless masses of all its contents. Kharis, in the center, turns slowly, sniffing the air, lumbering and confused. In this setting he seems more gigantic and monstrous than ever.*
>
> EXT. BARN — NIGHT — FULL SHOT *as Ben crosses to the barn. The dog is leaping at him, whining. The contrast between the towering monster we just saw in the barn and the figure of Evans, made smaller in the full shot of the barnyard, is very sharp. Evans tries to quiet the dog.*
>
> EVANS: All right, boy — all right. Take it easy, now.
>
> *Evans starts into the barn.*
>
> INT. EVANS' BEDROOM — NIGHT — MED. CLOSE PAN SHOT
>
> *Mrs. Evans is still at the window.*
>
> MRS. EVANS: Night after night, after night!
>
> (*crossed out, replaced with "Prowlers."*)
>
> *Suddenly her muttered complaints are interrupted by several shots. These are followed by the wild BARKING of King. Mrs. Evans face is frozen with terror. Then she cries out:*
>
> MRS. EVANS: Ben! Ben!
>
> *She rushes toward the door o.s.*

The only scene in the Evans bedroom to survive was when Mrs. Evans quickly puts her robe on after hearing the gunshots. It's also unusual that it never dawns on Mrs. Evans that her husband may be going one-on-one with the Mummy in her own barn. Upon hearing the shots fired, she races down, finds her husband dead, sees an enormous hole in the barn wall and still believes she was burglarized. What a non-believing infidel! The script continues:

> EXT. BARN — NIGHT — FULL SHOT *as the dog races, howling, toward the*

house and back again, and again toward the house. The cries have ceased. From within the barn is suddenly HEARD a shattering, tearing SOUND of great volume. Mrs. Evans comes running INTO SCENE. The dog rushes toward her. She stops for a moment looking around.

Mrs. Evans: *(calling, fearfully)* Ben! Ben!

The dog races toward the barn, and she follows. As she disappears into the barn, the dog after her, the CAMERA HOLDS on the empty barnyard. Only the whining of the dog, o.s. is HEARD. Then there is a terrible SHRIEK from within the barn.

INT. BARN — NIGHT — MED. SHOT

Mrs. Evans is kneeling beside the body of Ben Evans, which is BELOW FRAME. She is moaning in a dazed, stunned manner. The dog is on his haunches beside her, howling. The group is clearly illuminated by a broad path of moonlight, which we did not see before in the barn. Mrs. Evans lifts her head and gazes dazedly before her.

MED. LONG SHOT — WALL — MRS. EVANS' ANGLE

A great jagged hole has been made in the wall as though a tank had gone through it. It is through this that the moonlight pours. The MOANING of the woman, and the HOWLING of the dog COME OVER.

EXT. HILLS — NIGHT — CLOSE SHOT

Ahmed Bey stands in a tense attitude. The fire from the tripod beside him casts a flickering light across his face.

Ahmed Bey: Kharis! Kharis! Turn your steps into the hills! Here is new life for you; life everlasting.

EXT. SIDE OF ROAD — NIGHT — FULL SHOT

Kharis smashes from the woods and crosses the road. He disappears in the hills, which can be seen in the b.g.

DISSOLVE TO: INT. BARN — NIGHT — MED. GROUP SHOT

Sheriff Elwood and the coroner are bending over Ben Evans' body BELOW FRAME. Three or four deputies stand by. Mrs. Evans sits on a box, sobbing quietly. The dog is at her feet. She talks in a monotone, almost whispering.

Mrs. Evans: If he'd been home where he belonged, this wouldn't've happened. Wouldn't nobody come to steal except they knowed he was sittin' on the courthouse roof half the nights, watchin' for a mummy.

The coroner straightens up, rubbing the telltale gray mold between his fingers. The sheriff looks up, touches the mold; they exchange a glance and nod gravely. One of the deputies wanders out.

Sheriff: It was no thief killed Ben, Mrs. Evans.

She looks up questioningly. He looks toward the jagged hole in the wall and others follow his glance.

MED. LONG SHOT— WALL— GROUPS ANGLE

SHERIFF'S VOICE: And nothing human tore through that wall.

A deputy's VOICE is HEARD calling o.s.

DEPUTY'S VOICE: Sheriff! Come out here a minute!

EXT. FIELD NEAR BARN— NIGHT— MED. SHOT

The deputy is bending over the ground. He looks up as the sheriff comes running IN to him.

DEPUTY: (pointing his flashlight at ground) Look at this!

CLOSE SHOT

Huge, formless footprints can be seen pointing toward the hills.

MED. SHOT

DEPUTY: If the Mummy didn't make those prints, I'll eat 'em!

The sheriff turns. CAMERA ANGLE WIDENS to include the others who have come up.

SHERIFF: He's making for the hills. One of you men call my office to send out more men.

Deputy nods and runs FROM SCENE.

SHERIFF: (*continuing*) The rest of you spread out and comb this country inch by inch! If you spot the Mummy don't try to tackle him. Just keep him in sight until we get more help!

The men nod and start out in different directions. The Sheriff and coroner run straight for the dark hills.

EXT. HILLS— NIGHT— MED. SHOT

Ahmed Bey stands listening. The SOUND of Kharis' approach can be HEARD. Ahmed Bey's face lights up.

AHMED BEY: The gods have heard my prayer…

Kharis bursts INTO SCENE and seizes the tana fluid. As he drinks, Ahmed Bey lifts his face reverently.

AHMED BEY: (*praying*) Mighty Amon-Ra … I thank thee for guiding Kharis to me and for delivering us from the hands of those who would destroy us.

Kharis has finished the tana fluid. Ahmed Bey takes the vessel from him and the tripod, and starts away. Kharis follows him off, and we…

DISSOLVE TO: EXT. HILLS— NIGHT— MED. SHOT

The sheriff and coroner run INTO SCENE and pause for a moment, looking about. Suddenly the coroner grasps the sheriff's arm and points o.s.

CORONER: Look!

CAMERA PANS QUICKLY and we see the spot in which Ahmed Bey had

> *been standing. A pile of warm ashes can be seen where the tripod stood. The sheriff and coroner run toward it.*
>
> MED. SHOT
>
> *The sheriff and coroner run INTO SCENE and up to the ashes. The sheriff touches them carefully.*
>
> SHERIFF: (*grimly*) Still warm!
>
> *He looks around as running footsteps can be HEARD.*
>
> MED. FULL SHOT
>
> *His other men come INTO SCENE from different directions.*
>
> DEPUTY: There are no more footprints, sheriff. Nothing but rocks.
>
> SHERIFF: (*looking grimly at ashes*) Then we've reached a dead end again.
>
> EXT. ROCKY HILL — NIGHT — MED. TWO SHOT — AHMED BEY AND KHARIS.
>
> AHMED BEY: Now, mighty gods, grant me the wisdom and the skill to complete our mission and return the Princess Ananka to the tombs of Karnak. And only thy will be done. In this world and in the next! (softly) Come, Kharis…
>
> *CAMERA PANS as they make their way between the rocks and are lost to view.*
>
> DISSOVE TO: EXT. BUSY STREET — DAY — FULL SHOT
>
> *A large, imposing building can be seen in the b.g.*
>
> CLOSE SHOT — METAL PLAQUE *with the words:* SCRIPPS MUSEUM

During the scene in the barn, we do not hear the "shattering, tearing sound of great volume," as indicated in the script (which, of course is Kharis crashing through the wall of the barn). If it *is* there, the music score may have drowned it out. But after looking *and* listening to the scene several times, there was no sound of Kharis ripping his way through the barn wall.

Mrs. Evans also does not stop to look around after exiting the house. She runs quickly into the barn, narrowly missing her own encounter with Kharis. Surprisingly, her "shriek from within the barn" was mysteriously crossed out from the script.

The two excerpts of Bey summoning Kharis were edited together to create one scene in the film's final cut. Also, the sequences of the police searching in the hills for Kharis were noticeably trimmed down.

In fact, all references to the Mummy "heading for the hills" as it were had been eliminated altogether, probably to avoid the time-consuming use of another set.

The entire scene of the sheriff and the coroner discovering the warm ashes in the hills was also slashed. That specific page was marked with a big X. Also excluded was the busy street scene with the imposing Scripps Museum building in the background. The shot of the plaque indicating "Scripps Museum" remains.

3. The Mummy's Ghost

Inside the museum, a guide is just concluding the story of Ananka to a group of spectators. Among them is Bey. As the guide exits the room, the spectators follow, but Bey stays behind. He hides among the shadows of the Egyptian room until everyone has left and the museum is closed:

> INT. EGYPTIAN ROOM — NIGHT — FULL SHOT
>
> *The room is now deserted and filled with shadows. Moonlight streams through the windows. A door opens and a thin ray of light falls across the floor.*
>
> MED. SHOT
>
> *An old watchman ENTERS and switches on a room light. He looks around.*
>
> FULL SHOT — FROM HIS ANGLE
>
> *Ananka's case can be seen in the center of the room but not a thing moves. Everything is in order.*
>
> MED. SHOT
>
> *Talking to himself, the watchman inserts his key into the signal box beside the door and turns it. Then he snaps out the light, vanishes through the door, closing it after him. CAMERA PANS and MOVES SLOWLY ACROSS the room until it STOPS in a CLOSE SHOT of a recess behind two mummy cases. Ahmed Bey can be seen standing in the shadows. He moves forward silently.*
>
> MED. SHOT — ANOTHER ANGLE
>
> *Ahmed Bey comes INTO SCENE and stops beside Ananka's case, which is bathed in moonlight from a high window. His face is tense and his eyes bright with purpose.*
>
> AHMED BEY: (*murmuring, like a ritual*) From the far off land of her birth have I come to return the body of this Priestess initiate to her resting place in the hills of Karnak.
>
> MED. SHOT — ANOTHER ANGLE
>
> *Ahmed Bey takes two ceremonial lamps, which adorn the Egyptian room, moves them into place, one at either end of Ananka's case, and lights them. The flickering light makes the scene more eerie than ever.*
>
> CLOSE SHOT — AHMED BEY
>
> AHMED BEY: (*softly*) Amon-Ra … Isis … Osiris … help me!
>
> EXT. MUSEUM — NIGHT — FULL SHOT
>
> *Deep within the shadow cast by the building, the Mummy shuffles rapidly toward the front door.*
>
> CLOSE SHOT
>
> *The monster glances around, his eye blinking evilly.*
>
> MED. SHOT — AT FRONT DOOR

> *The Mummy comes INTO SCENE and up to the door. He glances about once more and then puts his massive shoulder to it.*
>
> *INT. STOREROOM — NIGHT — FULL SHOT*
>
> *This room is a storeroom for the museum. It is cluttered with all sorts of odds and ends, including a good-sized semi-nude statue of a woman with an outstretched hand. The old watchman comes INTO SCENE, hangs his hat on the outstretched hand and flips on a small, portable radio. Loud dance music blares out.*
>
> *EXT. FRONT OF MUSEUM — NIGHT — CLOSE SHOT*
>
> *The Mummy breaks through the front door.*
>
> *INT. STOREROOM — NIGHT — MED. SHOT*
>
> *The watchman tunes the radio to another station. A man's VOICE issues from the instrument, weird and unearthly.*
>
> **VOICE:** This, is the hour … of murder…!

Among the most noticeable differences between the script and the film at the museum is the absence of the "in joke." As the watchman listens, the voice continues, "Did you ever meet a killer, my friend? You will, tonight. A killer's at large tonight, my friends. He enters the darkened study of Doctor X, the Mad Doctor of Market Street." The script made no mention of either of the two Lionel Atwill titles.

While closely observing the watchman when he enters the storeroom, we see him turn the radio on but there is no sound. This is where the loud dance music was supposed to blare out for a few seconds and then cut-away to Kharis smashing through the entrance of the museum. He would not have been heard over the music. Only moments later the watchman changes the channel to the much quieter mystery program. Kharis was last seen pounding on the delivery entrance door to no avail. We never do see him actually enter the museum, only the Egyptian room where Bey awaits him. Bey informs Kharis that their search is over. "Behold her! Ananka the Princess of your forbidden love!" In the film, upon Kharis' touch, she crumbles to dust, leaving only the bandages that bound her:

> *MED. SHOT*
>
> *Ahmed Bey's face registers fury and frustration as he looks up from the case.*
>
> **AHMED BEY:** Too late! Too late! Her soul has entered another form!
>
> *With a snarl of rage, Kharis goes wild and begins to smash everything within his reach.*
>
> *INT. STOREROOM — NIGHT — MED. SHOT*
>
> *The watchman looks up sharply and switches off the radio. The SMASHING SOUND from the Egyptian room COMES OVER. He gets to his feet and hurries toward the door.*

3. *The Mummy's Ghost*   71

The watchman (Oscar O'Shea), dead on the floor, lost his battle with the Mummy (Lon Chaney) and Yousef Bey (John Carradine) in *The Mummy's Ghost* (Universal, 1944).

Bey manages to calm the outraged Mummy by the time the watchman reaches the Egyptian room. As the guard comes in, he only sees Bey standing by Ananka's case. The two exchange words while Bey is held at gunpoint. The guard, thinking he has the upper hand, is unaware that Kharis has appeared behind him and is ready to strike. The script continues:

> *Ahmed Bey only smiles disdainfully. At this moment, the watchman turns at a sound from one side.*
>
> CLOSE SHOT
>
> *Kharis shambles toward CAMERA, one hand coming up.*
>
> MED. SHOT
>
> *The watchman, his face a mask of horror, gives ground before him. He snaps a glance at Ahmed Bey, who has not moved, and then sends shot after shot from his automatic, ripping through Kharis' body. The monster continues to advance. Realizing that bullets won't stop the creature, the watchman throws his gun into his face. Then he jumps for the alarm box near the door.*
>
> MED. SHOT — ANOTHER ANGLE

> *Kharis follows rapidly and reaches him just as he turns the key in the box. The alarm starts RINGING. The man fights back with all his strength. The two smash into paraphernalia and equipment. The watchman stumbles.*
>
> CLOSE SHOT
>
> *Watching the struggle o.s. without expression. There is a man's partly throttled scream, a gasping sound and then all is quiet.*
>
> MED. SHOT
>
> *Kharis raises up from the body of the watchman, which is BELOW FRAMELINE. CAMERA PANS as he looks toward Ahmed Bey. The RINGING of the alarm can be heard. Ahmed Bey starts for the door.*
>
> AHMED BEY: Come, Kharis!

Here in the script, the watchman does quite a bit more to defend himself than any of Kharis' other victims, even to the point of hurling his gun into the monster's face. However, Mummy experts know that in the film, Kharis had the feisty guard by the throat before he had the opportunity to heave his weapon. Why this detail never made it to celluloid is most probably due to Chaney.

Universal horror historians are familiar with the old breakaway glass story. The glass doors in the museum were not changed to breakaway glass in time for the day's shooting. So director Reginald Le Borg instructed Chaney not to crash into the glass during the strangulation scene with the watchman. Well, despite the change in instruction, Chaney was on the guard and through the glass so fast that the poor watchman, who had to be caught off guard, no pun intended, never had the chance to toss his gun. And while the watchman's hand *does* reach the alarm box on the wall, it is not clear whether he actually activates it or not. We have to assume there was no alarm sounded because we never *do* hear it and because the watchman's body isn't discovered until the next day.

It's baffling enough to police how a museum guard is found strangled with mold on his throat, miles away from Mapleton, but what really takes the biscuit is that despite the uncut bandages in her coffin, Ananka's body is missing. This brings the police *and* us right back to Mapleton, and to Amina. Has she now become Ananka completely?

Immediately following the murder in the museum, we see Amina in her bedroom being consoled by her landlady, Mrs. Blake (Dorothy Vaughan). The landlady came to Amina's room after hearing the girl wake up screaming just as Kharis placed his hand on the mummy of Ananka back at the museum. A lengthier scene followed this brief scene with Tom Hervey, missing from the release print. In the script, Amina truly feels she's one taco short of a combination plate:

> EXT. LIBRARY—DAY—MED. SHOT
>
> *Hervey comes INTO SCENE and runs up the steps. Harrison and other students, just coming out of the building, call to him as they pass:*

STUDENTS: Hya, Tommy!

Hervey, a troubled look on his face, continues on as though he hasn't heard. He disappears through the door into the library. Harrison and the other students look at each other with amused surprise, and then continue on down the steps.

HARRISON: (*singing to the tune of "Too Much Texas"*) He's got a touch of Egypt on his brai-ain

He winks at the other students.

INT. LIBRARY OFFICE — DAY — MED. SHOT

Amina turns from the window as Hervey ENTERS. There are dark circles under her eyes and she looks nervous and distraught.

HERVEY: (*anxiously*) Amina! What in the world happened? I stopped at the house ... Mrs. Blake told me...

AMINA: (*trying to control herself*) I don't know, Tommy. My mind is breaking into little bits. I don't think I can stand it much longer!

HERVEY: (*with determination*) You're not going to! Not if I have anything to say about it!

AMINA: What can we do, Tommy?

HERVEY: We'll do something! I'm certainly not just going to sit around and watch you go to pieces!

Hervey paces away and back, grimly thoughtful, CAMERA PANNING with him. He stops before Amina.

HERVEY: Will you let me handle this my way?

AMINA: Anything you say, Tommy!

HERVEY: (*smiling*) That's my girl! (*patting her cheek*) First of all, get someone to relieve you here and go home. Find a nice spot in the sun and relax. I'll be over later, and I'll have news for you.... Okay?

AMINA: (*huskily*) Okay!

He gives her shoulder an affectionate little shake and goes out.

WIPE TO: INT. SHERIFF'S OFFICE — DAY — MED. SHOT — TAKING IN DOOR

A deputy opens the door.

DEPUTY: Tom Hervey wants to see you, Sheriff.

SHERIFF: Let him come in.

Hervey enters, CAMERA PANNING as he approaches the sheriff's desk.

SHERIFF: Morning Hervey. What's on your mind, this time?

HERVEY: Sheriff, is it still necessary for Miss Harun to remain in town?

SHERIFF: Why?

HERVEY: She needs a change! This thing has affected her terribly! She's on the verge of a nervous breakdown! I want to take her to New York.

MED. SHOT — ANOTHER ANGLE

SHERIFF: Why should if affect her more than anyone else in this town? She's not the only one who was shocked by the murders.

HERVEY: (*heatedly*) She's the only one who was found unconscious near the scene of one of them!

SHERIFF: (*dryly*) Yes, I was thinking of that!

HERVEY: (*realizing he has blundered*) All I meant was her shock was greater ... I've got to take her away!

SHERIFF: I'm afraid I can't agree to that. I'm not saying that Miss Harun is actually implicated in any way. But this is a serious business, and there's a doggone lot we don't know about yet... Just to make things a little more involved, a man was murdered in the Scripps Museum last night —

HERVEY: And I suppose Amina's mixed up in that, too!

SHERIFF: I didn't say that at all. But until this business is cleared up — everything remains as it is.

HERVEY: You mean you refuse to let her go!

SHERIFF: I'm sorry!

HERVEY: (*angrily*) Okay, sheriff! Thank for the interview.

He turns abruptly and the CAMERA ANGLE WIDENS as he strides from the office. The sheriff looks after him. The door BANGS shut and is reopened immediately as a deputy admits the coroner, Walgreen, and Dr. Nagel.

FULL GROUP SHOT as the sheriff comes forward to his callers.

SHERIFF: Well, gentlemen, have you dug up anything new?

All ad-lib greetings. The sheriff indicates chairs and all sit, as the CAMERA ANGLE WIDENS.

CORONER: We've been out to the Evans place, Sheriff, but the Sergeant wants you along at Norman's...

WALGREEN: (*nodding*) I saw the photograph of the footprints, and I saw the side of the barn torn out. Your coroner corroborated our findings about the mold on the victim's throat... But I still can't get it through my head that a live mummy committed the murders...

SHERIFF: We've got a few old tombstones here in Mapleton, Sergeant, to prove that the Mummy did exist. And we've got two new ones to show that he still exists!

Walgreen stares at him for a few seconds.

WALGREEN: And if he isn't trapped mighty quick, there's no telling how many more tombstones he'll be setting up.

3. The Mummy's Ghost   75

> SHERIFF: That's right!
>
> WALGREEN: Have you made any progress at all?
>
> SHERIFF: (*shaking his head*) We've had men combing the country ever since Norman was killed, but...
>
> *He shrugs helplessly.*
>
> WALGREEN: (*rising*) Can we have a look at the Norman place now?
>
> SHERIFF: Sure!
>
> *All rise and start for the door, as we DISSOLVE TO INT. PROFESSOR NORMAN'S LABORATORY — DAY — FULL SHOT*

Mummy's Ghost experts will recognize only about a third of the abovementioned scenes. The rest have been omitted from the film. It's always fascinating to learn little tidbits and details about a film after a half of a century, no matter how inconsequential they may be.

Poor Amina is stressed almost to the breaking point (if this were not a mummy movie about reincarnation, one wonders if she might be a prime candidate for Prozac). Hervey gives her his dog Peanuts to keep watch over her while Inspector Walgreen can't get over the fact that a living mummy is responsible for the reign of terror and the sheriff has the tombstones to prove it. This is interesting to read from a historical viewpoint. But from a production standpoint for a film with a running time of 60 minutes, that scene would have been too long to go without an appearance from the Mummy, so cuts were inevitable.

When Mrs. Blake is awakened by the sound of the barking Peanuts, she gets up from bed to look out the window just in time to catch a glimpse of Kharis walking off with Amina. Mrs. Blake quickly calls Tom Hervey. Their complete phone conversation is the length of an entire page of script. In screen time, this would be close to a minute. Again, far too much time without any action. Here's what was cut:

> INT. HERVEY'S BEDROOM — NIGHT — CLOSE SHOT — AT BED
>
> *Hervey is asleep. The telephone at his bedside RINGS. He stirs in his sleep. It RINGS again, and he wakes with a start and seizes the phone.*
>
> HERVEY: Yes?
>
> MRS. BLAKE'S VOICE: (*hysterically*) Tom! — Amina! — It's got her!
>
> HERVEY: What are you talking about?
>
> MRS. BLAKE: The Mummy! He took Amina!
>
> *Hervey's face seems to break with shock and grief for a moment. He cannot speak.*
>
> INT. MRS. BLAKE'S ROOM — NIGHT — CLOSE SHOT — AT PHONE
>
> *Mrs. Blake is near collapse.*
>
> MRS. BLAKE: Tom — Tom — do you hear me?

> HERVEY'S VOICE: I — yes — wait — I —
>
> MRS. BLAKE: What shall I do?
>
> INT. HERVEY'S ROOM — NIGHT — MED. CLOSE SHOT AT PHONE
>
> *Hervey pulls himself together. His face is tragically grim.*
>
> HERVEY: Get help.... Hurry!
>
> MRS. BLAKE'S VOICE: Yes, yes, Tom ... I'll...
>
> *Hervey doesn't wait to hear more, but hangs up, leaps out of bed and grabs his clothes.*

Had the scene been done as written, it would have allowed us to hear both ends of the conversation and witness how unglued Mrs. Blake had become. Instead all we get in the film is Tom quickly blurting out; "Yes, what about Amina? (pause) Wait a minute, I... (pause, again) Get help. Hurry!" But it's all we need. The hysterical woman quickly made her point and Tom is off like a top to protect his beau and confront his 3,000-year-old competition. But not only has Kharis, who has all the speed of Cecil Turtle, gained quite a lead on our hero, poor Hervey has no idea where to start looking.

Kharis has made his way to the old abandoned mining shack with Amina in his arms, where Bey awaits them. This scene in the script is also considerably longer than the final release print. There's more talk with Amina, or by now Ananka, but more importantly, Bey does a far greater amount of battling with his conscience before finally breaking down. The script reads:

> INT. MINE SHACK — NIGHT — FULL SHOT
>
> *The shutters on the window are still open and moonlight floods the large table. The rest of the room is in shadows. Ahmed Bey faces the door when Kharis ENTERS.*
>
> *Holding Amina before him, like an offering, the creature advances slowly into the room.*
>
> CLOSE SHOT — AHMED BEY *staring at him with fanatical frenzy.*
>
> CLOSE SHOT
>
> *Kharis places Amina down on the moon-flooded table and steps back into the shadows. Amina's right arm swings limply at her side.*
>
> CLOSEUP — HER WRIST
>
> *The birthmark shows plainly in the light.*
>
> MED. SHOT
>
> AHMED BEY: (*softly and reverently, lifting her hand*) The light — and the sign! Ananka!
>
> CLOSE SHOT — KHARIS IN SHADOWS *staring at Amina o.s.*
>
> MED. CLOSE SHOT

Ahmed Bey stands looking down at her.

AHMED BEY: She's beautiful, Kharis … as she was centuries ago. (to Kharis) And she has returned to you! The will of Amon-Ra has been done!

CLOSE SHOT — AHMED BEY as he continues, something like sadness and a great longing in his eyes, as his glance returns to Amina.

AHMED BEY: Now I can understand how you dared to defy the gods themselves, for her sake…

He shakes the mood from him and raises his head. He begins to pray, softly, as CAMERA WIDENS to include Kharis.

AHMED BEY: Oh, mighty Amon-Ra … we thank thee for thy guiding hand in this night… Help us now to return safely to the hills of Karnak and to the tombs of our sacred dead. Help us to be eternally worthy in thy sight.

He bows his head, reverently, then moves toward coffins. CAMERA PANS to Amina and starts to MOVE IN to a CLOSE SHOT of her.

AHMED BEY: Kharis, we turn our eyes toward home —

MED. PAN SHOT — AT COFFIN

Ahmed Bey takes a cord from a coffin. He returns to the still unconscious Amina and binds her to the table. His actions are gentle. Kharis is NOT IN THE SHOT. Suddenly, Amina's eyes open, and she stares, terrified, at Ahmed Bey.

AMINA: (*her voice thick with fear*) Who are you? Why am I here?

CLOSE SHOT — AHMED BEY looking at her o.s. with admiration in his eyes.

AHMED BEY: (*softly*) I am a Priest of Karnak … and you are here because the gods have willed it so…

MED. SHOT

AMINA: (*struggling against her bonds*) Let me go!

AHMED BEY: Do you not know who you are?

AMINA: I am Amina El Harun. I…

AHMED BEY: You are the Princess Ananka, third daughter of Amenophis — one time Pharaoh of all Egypt.

AMINA: You're mad!

AHMED BEY: Centuries ago you died a cursed death … because you dared return the love of Kharis.

AMINA: (*horrified*) No!

MED. CLOSE SHOT

Ahmed Bey turns her right hand and turns the wrist so that the birthmark is visible.

AHMED BEY: The birthmark of Ananka ... the symbol of the Priests of Karnak! You cannot escape your destiny.

AMINA: It's not true!

CLOSE SHOT — AHMED BEY smiling at her, o.s.

AHMED BEY: It is true.... That is why the footsteps of Kharis were led to you this night ... because the hour had come!

CLOSE SHOT — AMINA

AHMED BEY'S VOICE: ...because you are Ananka, reborn! Because you first knew life three thousand years ago!

AMINA: (*frantically*) You're lying! I am young!... Young! Tomorrow I shall marry...

MED. CLOSE SHOT

Ahmed Bey's face begins to harden.

AHMED BEY: (*interrupting*) You may never marry. No bridegroom but the tombs of Karnak wait to receive you.

CLOSE SHOT — AMINA looking at him now with mortal terror in her eyes.

AHMED BEY'S VOICE: For those who defy the will of the ancient gods, a cruel and violent death shall be their fate. Never shall they find rest unto eternity.

As he speaks, a huge shadow falls across Amina, blotting out the moonlight. Slowly and fearfully her head turns as she senses some new danger from the shadow. She looks o.s. Her eyes dilate with terror. She sees:

MED. LONG SHOT — AMINA'S ANGLE

Kharis has moved from the shadows into the path of the moonlight. His great, swaying hulk seems enormous. Slowly he advances.

CHANGED ANGLE — TAKING IN AMINA

Her head is raised as far as she can lift it. Her eyes are filled with horror. Her lips struggle to articulate but she seems voiceless. Then as the monster comes a step closer, the moonlight pouring over him, Amina gives a dreadful shriek and faints again.

EXT. FIELD BEHIND AMINA'S HOUSE — NIGHT — MED SHOT

The sheriff, Walgreen and the coroner look at Kharis' footprints in some mud of the field by means of a flashlight. The sheriff looks up.

FULL SHOT — FROM HIS ANGLE

Men search in various directions for more footprints.

MED. SHOT

The sheriff turns slightly as a deputy runs IN to them.

DEPUTY: Prints are fading out, sheriff, but they point toward the woods...

3. The Mummy's Ghost

The sheriff nods. They all look up.

SHERIFF: That makes sense. Mrs. Blake said the Mummy headed that way... (*to one of the deputies*) Pass out the torches.

The deputy turns to a pile of torches. The men gather to receive and light them.

INT. MINE SHACK — NIGHT — MED. CLOSE SHOT

Amina is still unconscious. A startling change has taken place in her! Her hair has now turned almost completely white, but in the moonlight it is like spun silver and lends a new and unearthly beauty to her face. Ahmed Bey stands a little to one side carefully preparing a small hypo. We HEAR the VOICE of his mind talking to him. The VOICE is his own, soft, insistent and with an eerie quality.

VOICE: You have done your work well, Ahmed Bey. The gods will look with favor upon you. Why do you not rejoice?

Ahmed Bey's hands tremble and pause in their task. He looks over at Amina.

VOICE: Perhaps because it grieves you to consign this lovely girl to death again. Why should she not live, Ahmed Bey? Why should you not live?

CLOSE SHOT — AHMED BEY *as he struggles inwardly against this temptation that is beginning to take hold of him.*

AHMED BEY: I live! I live to fulfill my destiny as a Priest of Karnak!

VOICE: But what of your destiny as a man? You are thousands of miles from the tombs of Karnak. She is thousands of years from her sin. Kharis dared to love her.... Are you less brave than he?

CLOSE SHOT — AMINA

VOICE: (*coming over*) The world of love has beauty that is nowhere else.... It could be your world — yours and hers...

CLOSE SHOT — AHMED BEY

VOICE: Happiness, Ahmed Bey, is for those who dare to command it!

Ahmed Bey's eyes, bright and reflecting the inner struggle, stare straight at CAMERA. Beads of perspiration begin to stand out on his forehead.

Off in the distance, Hervey moves rapidly through the brush. From another direction, Walgreen, the sheriff and the coroner advance, aided by many townspeople. It is only a matter of time before they discover what they are searching for:

INT. MINE SHACK — NIGHT — CLOSE SHOT

Ahmed Bey stands in the center of the room, his hands clasped before him.

AHMED BEY: Oh, mighty Isis, protect me in this my hour of temptation. Give me the strength to fulfill my vows as Priest of Karnak!

> *His head sinks upon his breast. The VOICE in his brain can be HEARD again.*
>
> VOICE: (*softly, insistently*) The tana leaves, Ahmed Bey!
>
> *Ahmed Bey raises his head.*
>
> VOICE: (*continuing*) Tana leaves…! They would keep her young and beautiful forever. And you, too, Ahmed Bey! Tana leaves … offering you eternal youth, eternal beauty, eternal love.
>
> *Almost in a daze, Ahmed Bey crosses to one side of the room, CAMERA PANNING. He stoops over a box on the floor.*
>
> CLOSE SHOT — BOX
>
> *Ahmed Bey's hand ENTERS SCENE and picks up a quantity of the long tana leaves.*
>
> VOICE: Take them, Ahmed Bey. You and Ananka together, forever. Forever!
>
> *Ahmed Bey straightens up and walks back to the ceremonial lamp.*

Hervey continues moving breathlessly while the other searchers continue to pour through the countryside as if they were closing in.

> INT. MINE SHACK — NIGHT — CLOSE SHOT
>
> *Ahmed Bey pours tana fluid into a small bowl. His movements betray his repressed excitement. CAMERA PANS as he goes to Amina's side. The girl is still unconscious. Ahmed Bey puts the bowl down on the table and starts to unfasten the bonds across her shoulders. His eyes have an insane look.*
>
> AHMED BEY: (*to Amina — although she can't hear him*) There is nothing more for you to fear. Not death, nor decay, nor damnation. Here in this cup is my gift of life to you.
>
> CLOSE SHOT — AMINA *stirring slightly.*
>
> AHMED BEY'S VOICE: I am going to make you immortal. And I, too, shall drink and be immortal.
>
> *A door rasps faintly upon dry hinges.*
>
> CLOSE SHOT
>
> *The Mummy can be seen standing in the shadows just inside a door on the far side of the room.*
>
> AHMED BEY'S VOICE: We will not return to Egypt. Our world shall be wide, and our time shall be without end. Has any man before offered a gift of eternal life to his bride?
>
> *The Mummy begins to whine and he shakes his great head from side to side.*
>
> MED. SHOT
>
> *Ahmed Bey now has the bonds loose from across Amina's chest. He raises her up partially and picks up the bowl containing tana fluid once more.*
>
> CLOSE SHOT — THE MUMMY

3. *The Mummy's Ghost*

His motions are now more frenzied. He sways from side to side.

CLOSE SHOT

Ahmed Bey is about to pour some of the liquid between Amina's lips. The girl's face looks lined and drawn ... a little like parchment.

FULL SHOT

With a snarl, Kharis hurls himself toward Ahmed Bey, knocking the bowl from his hands. Ahmed Bay staggers back.

CLOSE SHOT — KHARIS staring at Ahmed Bey, animal sounds issue from his throat. His body sways back and forth.

MED. SHOT

Ahmed Bey turns slowly and stares at Kharis. The monster faces him, swaying.

CLOSE SHOT — KHARIS as he advances slowly, straight into CAMERA.

CLOSE SHOT — AHMED BEY

Retreating slowly. Horror of Kharis is growing upon him.

Ahmed Bey: Kharis! Stop!

CLOSE SHOT — KHARIS

Still advancing — slowly... Faintly from a distance can be HEARD the BARKING of Peanuts.

MED. CLOSE SHOT

Ahmed Bey stumbles over a box and nearly falls. He recovers himself and then faces the monster with every bit of will power he commands.

Ahmed Bey: You will obey me, Kharis! I am your master! I am a Priest of Karnak! Go back!

He retreats until his back is pressed against the wall. Still Kharis advances.

EXT. THE TRESTLE — NIGHT — MED. PAN SHOT

Peanuts, BARKING, races to the foot of the trestle.

INT. MINE SHACK — NIGHT — MED. CLOSE TWO SHOT

Kharis' hands rise and move to Ahmed Bey's throat.

Ahmed Bey: (reading his death in that single glittering eye) I'll take her back, Kharis! Together we'll go to Karnak! The three of us! I swear it! I...

His words are shut off by Kharis' mighty hand clasps his neck. Ahmed Bey rises to remove the hand with both of his, but the monster forces him o.s.

CLOSE SHOT — AMINA still unconscious and unaware of the horrible thing going on there in that room with her.

MED. SHOT

Kharis has back to CAMERA. Slowly he straightens up and looks toward the

> *open window through which the moonlight streams. He reaches down, picks up Ahmed Bey from the floor and raises him above his head.*
> CLOSE SHOT — AHMED BEY'S FACE
> *His lips barely move.*
> **AHMED BEY:** Gods of Egypt ... Isis ... forgive me. May my soul...
> MED. SHOT
> *Kharis hurls Ahmed Bey toward the window.*
> EXT. SHACK AND TRESTLE — NIGHT — MED. SHOT
> *Peanuts is barking furiously as Hervey runs INTO SCENE. He looks up, and his face shows his horror as he sees:*
> *FULL SHOT as Ahmed Bey's body hurtles down through the air, bangs against the trestle and disappears on its way to the ground.*

Monster and master actually have a nice moment together until Bey shows his treacherous true colors. He has flattering words for Kharis that reflect the Mummy's good taste in women.

Once again, one has to feel sorry for the poor Mummy. Upon learning he has again been double-crossed by the Priest that has sworn to look after him, he begins to make grunting, animal-like sounds of desperation. As in *The Mummy's Tomb*, he has been abandoned by his mentor and left to fend for himself in a strange land, automatically eliminating the chance of getting safe passage back to Egypt.

One also has to ponder the potential mistrust that could have been fermenting in Kharis' head. After all, this is the third entry into the series and all the poor creature has ever known was double-crossing masters. First George Zucco had the Mummy kidnap Peggy Moran in *The Mummy's Hand*, then Turhan Bey sends him after Elyse Knox in *Tomb*. Did Kharis think Carradine would be any less horny? He started out amiably enough with two coffins awaiting occupancy by Kharis and Ananka, but Ramsay Ames just proved too much a temptation, causing him to go the way of his predecessors.

In fact, the script suggests a sensation of *déjà vu* several times. Both Bey and Amina impersonate the cast of *The Mummy's Tomb* while Amina lies strapped to the table, she informs the High Priest that tomorrow she is going to be married. Bey's response; no way. "You may never marry."

Apparently Miss Ames was also going to mimic Zita Johann from *The Mummy*, as she screams at Karloff's 3,700–year-old Imhotep; "I am young... Young!" In all likelihood, writers Griffin Jay, Henry Sucher and Brenda Weisberg spent some time in the screening room with the previous Mummy films before they began putting this assignment on paper.

But the greatest impersonation would have come from John Carradine's Ahmed Bey, who, according to the script, was supposed to go flying out of that elevated shack like Superman, at the hands of Kharis. While Bey *does* become the first High Priest to perish at the hands of the Mummy, his death was supposed to be more impressive. In the film, Kharis deals the priest a severe blow, which sends him hurtling to his untimely demise. If Kharis had lifted Bey over his head and tossed him out the window, the scene would have been far more impressive. Universal horror fans can no doubt recall the far more memorable J. Carrol Naish death scene at the hands of Glenn Strange's Frankenstein Monster in House of *Frankenstein*. The monster picks up the murderous hunchback (Naish), heaving him out the laboratory window to his death.

Regardless of how the Mummy does away with his mentor, he and Ananka are now on their own. He takes his beloved in his arms and heads for the swamp only minutes ahead of the pursuing townspeople. In the script, there's a bit more dialogue:

> **SHERIFF:** (*to Walgreen*) He's heading for the marshes... (*turns to one of the deputies*) Joe — take some of the boys and cut him off at the left bank. (*Turns to another deputy*) Al ... you follow through in the other direction.
>
> *FULL SHOT as the men separate into groups. The sheriff, Walgreen, Hervey and the coroner lead one group in the direction of the Mummy, and the other groups flank them on both sides.*

Inevitably, they surround the Mummy and his love, which by now doesn't look a day over 3,000, and drive them into the murky water. Together they sink lower and lower into the swamp, almost as though it was waiting for them. Kharis attempts to keep his princess' head elevated, but it is no use. Before she sinks completely, Hervey, Walgreen, the sheriff and the coroner witness the girl's hideous transformation into Ananka from the edge of the swamp. They cannot believe their eyes. In the script, Walgreen verbalizes what he sees:

> **WALGREEN:** (*muttering, as they go*) I saw it! ...I saw it with my own eyes!...

Kharis and his Princess may not have made it back to Egypt, but at least they are together. It is a world that did not exist when they last walked the earth together, 3,000 years ago, and it certainly was not the most glorious burial. There were no Kings or royalty present, no singers or mourners, only the local authorities, a jilted lover, and fans to remember them for almost 60 years!

4
The Mummy's Return

About the same time Kharis carried his Princess Ananka into Universal's back lot swamp, but long before the birth of Brendan Fraser, screenwriter Leon Abrams sat before his typewriter and saw to it that the world's longest love affair would not be halted by a simple wrong turn into the mire.

"The Mummy's Return" should not be confused with the action-adventure *The Mummy Returns* (2001). "The Mummy's Return" was a 23-page treatment banged out by Abrams. It was an idea that eventually evolved into what we know today as *The Mummy's Curse*. The reason "The Mummy's Return" receives its own chapter in this book is because the treatment bears no resemblance whatsoever to *Curse*, the final entry in the classic series. However, there are several episodes within the story that remind us of other films in Universal's gallery of terror. In the quest to unearth anything new from the Mummy movies, some may find "The Mummy's Return" to be the most fascinating chapter in this book.

The treatment begins with a field of daisies being bathed in the moonlight. It is a typical spring evening. The sound of twittering birds nesting can be heard in the distance. An old man tends to his livestock. He brings in a couple of calves. The mood is very peaceful, calm and pastoral.

The quiet is suddenly broken by the sound of something dragging along the ground. The sound is heavy and ominous. It gradually gets louder. Then a shadow passes across the old man. He is oblivious to it. Then, without warning, he is quickly struck down. A large, monstrous figure crosses in front of the camera.

The scene then dissolves to a woman outside hanging her wash on the line. Once again, the heavy dragging sound gradually becomes audible. This time we can see a large bandaged foot dragging along the ground. The woman sees what is approaching and begins to scream. She too becomes a victim. Again, this huge hulk of a figure obstructs the view of the camera.

Another one or two murders occur in the same fashion. The victims do not know what is happening or what is upon them until it is too late.

All of these are quick dissolves. After the last murder, we get a quick glimpse of what is doing the killing. It is Kharis, the Mummy. As he disappears, the scene dissolves to a meeting of the Society of Psychic Research. A famous criminologist is addressing a group who have come from all corners of the planet (Sweden, Spain, Russia, China, India, etc.) His voice is somewhat theatrical in his delivery. He is telling the story of Kharis and his maniacal killing spree: "It is the most mysterious case history in all the annals of crime."

The meeting is taking place at the Egyptian exhibit of Stanley College. The room is decorated with hieroglyphics on the walls, mummy cases and glass cases filled with other ancient Egyptian artifacts. The speaker continues, "The story is of intense interest to a society endowed to study occult phenomena, for the Mummy was not of our world, but was brought back from beyond the pale from which few visitors ever return."

Astounded by what they hear, the audience begins to whisper to each another. The murmur is loud enough to be heard throughout the room.

The speaker continues, "With the final disappearance of Kharis in a dismal swamp, the science of metaphysics has suffered its greatest loss." As the speaker concludes, the scene changes to a group of Italian migrant workers who are excavating and dredging the swamp. They accidentally dig up the Mummy. They are curious about this find, but no one really knows what it is. The foreman thinks it is a dummy. The rest of the workers simply have a good laugh and even joke around with it.

It is now lunchtime and all the men take a break. A farmer has arrived in a pick-up truck. He has come to bring the men fresh milk and eggs. He notices the Mummy.

"I can use that," he says. He receives no argument from the migrant workers. They help the farmer lift the corpse and place him face down in the truck.

The scene then dissolves to the hideous figure of Kharis propped up in a very awkward manor, in a field. Someone, we presume the farmer, has draped him in an old overcoat and a beat-up old hat. There are many crows that fearlessly fly around him as if they are taunting him, daring him to take action. One bird brazenly lands on his head. The scene fades out.

When it fades in, we see three men in a trailer who are passing by the field. They are on their way to the local fair and carnival. The driver is a young, good-looking man by the name of Jim Oakley. Doc is the proprietor of the show. He sees the scarecrow in the field and stops to examine it. Doc is in his sixties and quite dapper. He is smooth-shaven with slight patches of gray around his temples. Gus is his shill or decoy. He is a cross between Dopey of the Seven Dwarfs and Wimpy, the hamburger guzzler from Popeye. He is asleep in the back of the trailer.

As Doc takes a close look at the scarecrow, he is taken aback with surprise.

4. "The Mummy's Return" 87

He calls to Jim, "Look, it's a mummy." Jim's response is that it is a phony, but a good quality phony. Doc continues, "A grand prop. We can use it in the act." Jim and Doc take the Mummy down and put him in the back of the trailer next to the sleeping Gus. Without so much as opening his eyes, Gus, now objecting to the crowded space, gives the Mummy a shove. "Move over." The scene fades out.

After the fade-in, we now return to the college. The Psychic Research meeting is still in progress. The chairman says that the horrific Mummy murders made sensational reading in the newspapers. He continues. "Abdullah Bey, a fellow member of our Society, has just arrived from the University of Cairo. He will tell us the little known story of the Mummy, when he knew life as you and I know it, before the spirit of Kharis came back to this earth again enslaved in a strange half-world of horror."

Then, the Bey rises. (The original writer used the term "the Bey" throughout the treatment.) He is clothed in European attire. He is also very eastern–Old World in appearance. He is poised, clean-shaven and wearing an Egyptian fez.

As the Bey begins to speak, his dialect is somewhat Middle Eastern. "It is the tragedy of an Egyptian slave who lived and loved on the banks of the Nile three thousand years ago." As the Bey continues to speak, the scene dissolves to the land of the Pharaohs, the Sphinx, the Pyramids of Choeps and the endless sand that is the Sahara Desert. Each of these shots is intended to be a series of quick dissolves using stock footage.

The Bey begins to tell the love story between Kharis, a slave and the young High Priestess of Arkam, Princess Ananka. There is a bed of very high-pitched Middle Eastern music underneath the Bey's soft voice. He explains, "To appease the outraged God Amon-Ra, the young lovers were mummified alive and buried in a tomb of the temple of Karnak."

A series of dissolves, again using stock footage, show what happened in ancient Egypt 3,000 years ago. For the first time, we see the beautiful Ananka in her ancient Egyptian surroundings. The Bey's voice continues to tell the story.

"The Mummy of Kharis was brought to life by a sacred drug brewed from tana leaves." He informs his listeners that this secret formula was known only by the High Priests of ancient Egypt, and that this plant has now become extinct and the formula is lost forever. The scene fades out.

It is nighttime and the annual fair has begun. It is an elaborate carnival with all of the usual attractions, and then some. There is a Ferris wheel along with several other rides. The sideshows feature all kinds of freaks, a snake charmer, a hula dancer, a bearded lady, etc. Again, the treatment called for the use of stock footage.

At the medicine show, the Mummy is propped up on a stand for all to see. Next to the Mummy is Jim Oakley, doing a barker routine. He does his pitch, asking the patrons to come closer and gather 'round. Doc is standing beside him holding a bamboo cane. He is wearing a turban and dressed very elegantly in burnoose. He has brown stain on his face. As Jim continues his routine, Doc strikes the Mummy with his cane. Now Jim includes the Mummy in his spiel. "[T]his is a symbol of the ancient civilization that built the pyramids and gave us the mystic science of astrology." As Jim continues to speak, Doc strikes the Mummy again with his bamboo cane.

The many different sounds of the carnival can be heard in the background. Various different melodies are meshed together as the cries of vendors can be heard selling peanuts, hot dogs, etc.

Gus, the shill, has called Doc behind a large canvas wall. He informs Doc that the dairy farmer from whom the Mummy was taken has recognized the Mummy on display and wants him back. Doc makes the farmer an offer of five dollars. The farmer hesitates, then Doc offers a couple of free passes for the show and the farmer agrees. He asks for a bill of sale, gets it and then leaves the tent.

As the farmer walks away, Doc signals a shifty-looking man from the crowd. The man has a cigarette dangling from his mouth and is wearing a hat which is pulled down so far that his eyes are barely visible. The man is known as Flutter. The reason for this nickname is because other people's possessions somehow always manage to turn up in his hands. Doc calls the farmer to Flutter's attention. Doc says he just gave the farmer five dollars for the Mummy. Flutter acknowledges him and exits the scene, which dissolves to an out-of-commission Greyhound bus near the fairground.

The music from the carnival can be heard in the background. The passengers are milling around outside the stalled bus. The driver informs them that it will be a couple of hours until they can get back on the road.

One of the passengers is a smartly dressed young woman named Maggie Wynn. She is a special writer for the United News Bureau. She was on her way to cover the meeting of the Psychic Research Society at Stanley College when the bus broke down. Maggie finds a pay phone to telephone one of her peers to explain that she will be late and to catch the first speaker on her behalf. With nowhere else to go, Maggie walks to the carnival to look around a bit. The propped-up Mummy at Doc's medicine show seems to captivate her interest, so she stops. The fact that Jim Oakley is good-looking doesn't hurt either. Jim is doing his routine before the crowd. He picks up a small bottle and urges, "Step closer, folks—step closer." He goes on with the usual schtick one would hear at a carnival medicine show, "It makes old men young and young men wise—"

As a man steps closer, he removes his hat to reveal he has no hair. He asks Jim, "Will it grow hair?" The crowd begins to laugh as the man is pushed back from where he came. Jim continues his routine. "[I]n this little bottle is the elixir that gave Cleopatra what it takes to ensnare Mark Anthony—"Gus, the shill, quickly approaches Jim and buys five bottles.

Jim spots Maggie in the crowd. Immediately attracted to her, he includes her in his routine. But suddenly there is a disturbance in the crowd. A man yells out, "My wallet!" It is the same farmer that sold the Mummy to Doc for five dollars. Jim's routine ends. The farmer is whisked away. Maggie just stands there and grins at the whole episode. She knows exactly what is going on. She's seen these scams before.

As the crowd begins to disperse, Maggie happens to look down and notices

4. "The Mummy's Return"

her pocket book is open and her purse is gone. Maggie is a no-nonsense woman. She walks directly over to Jim, the barker, and makes quite a scene. Jim calmly responds to her insisting that he knows nothing about it. "I don't believe you," she says. Jim abruptly turns and walks away from her. He enters his trailer behind a canvas sheet. There he is surprised to find Flutter handing the farmer's wallet to Doc. Jim starts to get tough.

"Give me the girl's purse," says Jim. Doc argues. Flutter gives the purse to Jim, who leaves the trailer. He returns the purse to Maggie, who is still angry. She takes her purse but does not thank Jim.

"I could forgive anything but being a cheap crook," she says. She turns around quickly and heads back towards the bus. Jim just stands quietly and watches her walk away. He appears stunned by her cutting words. The scene fades out.

At the fade-in, we return back to the Society of Psychic Research at the college. Maggie has just arrived. She is breathless and a bit disheveled. She is just in time to fill her place as one of the speakers. She is barely in the door when Abdullah Bey greets her. As the two exchange pleasantries, a mysterious look between them is very obvious. From their discussion, we know that Maggie has met and interviewed him a few days earlier upon his arrival in New York.

The chairman continues to speak. He announces that the mummy of Princess Ananka, which was stolen from the Scripps Museum, has been recovered. The audience is stunned. The chairman informs the audience, "It is now on exhibit here at this college." The excited listeners begin to murmur among themselves.

The chairman announces that the next guest, Maggie, will tell them how the mummy of the Princess was recovered. Maggie takes center stage. She begins to tell the story. As she does, her voice continues through a dissolve. We now see a gang of construction men dynamiting a riverbed. The look is as though industrial progress is being made in leaps and bounds. There is a pair of loud explosions, which send the water blasting skyward.

Down the river, a couple sits in a rowboat. Suddenly they see a body floating in the water, face down. But the fast-moving current turns the body over, and it is now plain to see that it is the body of a woman.

The scene changes to a gangster seated in Sing Sing prison death house. Maggie is also present. He is telling her about the theft of Princess Ananka from the museum.

The voice of the condemned man can be heard over a dissolve. We can see the mummy of Ananka being taken from the museum and put in the back of a car. After the Mummy is inside, the car makes a quick getaway. As the car moves along the highway, another car pulls up next to it and attempts to hijack it. Stock footage is used to show the cars speeding along next to each other. A gunfight breaks out.

And as the fight continues, the car with the Mummy inside is sideswiped. It loses control and crashes through a bridge guardrail and ends up at the bottom of a river.

Back to the couple inside the boat; they recover the body that is floating. They discover it is not a drowning victim, but a female mummy. The mummy would later be proven to be the body of Ananka, stolen from the museum. Maggie is just finishing her story back at the college, and the members are very excited to hear what she had to say on the subject.

Later, the meeting of the Society comes to an end. The members begin to disperse and Maggie and the Bey exchange a few more words. But this time, their conversation is a little more mysterious.

"Did you bring it with you?" asks Maggie. The Bey nods. He replies, "I will wait for you at my hotel."

Later, the Bey is inside his hotel suite. He is wearing the robe of his native land. Part of his baggage in the room includes a water pipe. The Bey takes a medallion, which was concealed under his robe, from around his neck. It is the medallion of the High Priest. He clasps it between his hands and lifts his head to the heavens, offering a prayer to the ancient gods of Egypt.

"May it please the great spirit of Amon-Ra to help me to return the body of the Princess Ananka to its rightful resting place in the tombs of Karnak."

The Bey is startled by an unexpected knock on the door. He tucks the medallion back, removes his robe and puts on a jacket. He now shows his more modern-day manner as he greets Maggie at the door. Maggie appears to have her work hat on, like she is out for the big scoop. She has learned that Kharis was brought back to life by a secret formula brewed from the now extinct tana leaves. She not only knows that this was a secret known only to the High Priests of Egypt, but that Abdullah Bey is a member of the sect.

Maggie has persuaded the Bey to attempt the same life-giving experiment on the mummy of the Princess Ananka. "If this experiment is successful, it will be the biggest news scoop in the history of journalism," says Maggie.

Her plan is to be certain there is no guard at the museum on the night her and the Bey arrive. He now walks her back to the door. Maggie cannot conceal her excitement. "Tonight," says Maggie, "only you and I will know." As she leaves, the Bey closes the door behind her. He whispers softly to himself, "Only I will know." The scene fades out.

When we fade in, it is night and the clouds pass across the moon very ominously. Maggie has managed to maneuver the guards out of position so that she and the Bey can be alone in the room of the Princess. They brew the leaves and the Bey siphons the fluid into a hypo. Maggie waits breathlessly, but nothing happens. Is seems that the experiment failed. As the Bey expresses genuine disappointment, they both leave the museum.

The annual fair is playing in the college town where the Society was having its meeting. It is also where the mummy of Ananka in on exhibition. Maggie and the Bey visit the carnival. She has told him about the fake mummy on display at the medicine show. He is extremely curious to see it. But Maggie shows some hesitation about bumping into Jim Oakley again. When the Bey persists, she agrees, but when they arrive at the exhibition, she does not stand next to him.

Gus sees Maggie in the crowd. He attempts to correct the injustice that has been done earlier — the possible romance between Maggie and Jim that went wrong

4. "The Mummy's Return"

because of Gus' own dishonesty. Gus approaches Maggie and tells her that Jim had nothing to do with the robbery. He also informs Maggie that Jim has quit the show as a result of that incident.

Inside the trailer of Doc's medicine show, Doc is trying to persuade Jim Oakley to come back to the show and resume his old job. He promises Jim that from now on it's the straight and narrow. No more stealing. Jim finally agrees and he leaves the trailer. As soon as Jim is gone, Doc tells Flutter to continue to operate as usual.

Outside, Maggie and Jim meet again. She apologizes for walking away so abruptly and then introduces him to the Bey. The Bey says he would like to have a closer look at the Mummy. Jim obliges. As Jim reveals the hideous figure of the Mummy, the Bey is shocked. He makes a careful examination of the Mummy. "This is the best fake I have ever seen," he says. As the Bey continues to look at the Mummy, Jim and Maggie go for a walk.

A truck shot follows Jim and Maggie as they make their way around the fairgrounds. The two exchange wisecracks and insults. But this hostility gradually evolves into romance. The two confess an instant attraction to each other. Love at first sight. This transforms into a love scene between them.

Jim later says that he is really a press agent between jobs and that being a barker is not his true profession.

The truck shot now has taken in the colorful background of the carnival.

All of the carnival workers are having their dinner. The Bey and the Mummy are alone. The Bey knew upon first glance that this was the Mummy of Kharis. He looks toward the heavens. Clouds pass over the full moon. The Bey whispers, "It is the cycle of the full moon." He takes out his medallion and prays to the ancient gods of Egypt. He thanks them for guiding him to Kharis in this strange and foreign land. He takes out the hypo full of tana fluid and gives it to the Mummy.

Later we see the sideshow open up for the evening. Jim and Maggie separate as Jim goes to do his routine. This time, the departure is a friendly one. Maggie rejoins the Bey.

Once again, the fair is in full swing. The lights and sounds of the carnival can be seen and heard all throughout. Crowds of patrons are everywhere. Jim is out in front doing his schtick while Doc, dressed in a turban and robe, stands behind him. "[S]tep closer, folks, step closer—"

Maggie and the Bey are part of the crowd. Doc, in his turban and robe, strikes the Mummy with his bamboo cane just as he did before. But this time, he does not notice that the tendons in the Mummy's face begin to twitch slightly.

"[I]t makes old men young and young men wise—"

The Mummy's eyelids begin to flutter and muscles start to twitch. As the rotating lights of the carnival shine on the Mummy, we can see his only good eye is now open. It beams with an unearthly glow.

"[I]n this little bottle is the elixir that gave Cleopatra what it takes to ensnare Mark Anthony—"

Doc again strikes the Mummy in the face with his cane. Now the Mummy's mouth opens. As Doc attempts to strike the Mummy one more time, the cane manages to wedge right inside the Mummy's mouth. Believing this is all part of the act, the crowd begins to laugh hysterically. Doc, completely caught by surprise, pulls the cane from the Mummy's mouth and strikes him again.

The Mummy has now come to life, but he is behind Doc and out of his view. Only the crowd can see the Mummy start to move. Thinking it is still part of the act, they continue to laugh. Then Doc, reacting to the crowd's laughter, sees the Mummy moving. He calls this to Jim's attention, but Jim's back is to him. Jim believes the crowd is laughing at the act. He is busy with Maggie. He makes another funny wisecrack, but Maggie doesn't laugh. Everyone is laughing except Maggie. She sees what is going on with the Mummy. She does not know that the Bey has given the Mummy the tana fluid, yet she knows instinctively something is wrong. The look on her face suggests that she suspects what might have happened. Immediately, she starts scanning the crowd for the Bey, but he is nowhere to be found.

Suddenly, almost all at once, the crowd stops laughing. The joviality turns to bewilderment. Then the bewilderment turns to genuine horror as they witness the Mummy strangle Doc to death before their eyes. The monster drops the mangled body to the floor. The faces on the speechless crowd now change from horror to terror as the Mummy slowly advances toward them!

The crowd is now in a mad frenzy to escape the fair. They knock each other down in a frantic effort to escape the advancing Mummy.

But two carnival patrons are unlucky enough to be too close to the stage and not beyond the reach of the Mummy's murderous hand. The monster claims two more victims.

A minute or so later, Jim actually saves Maggie from the Mummy's murderous grip.

As the last of the patrons run for their lives, the Mummy destroys the medicine show stand and a couple of other carnival sideshow attractions and then disappears into the darkness. The scene fades out.

Next comes a series of stock shots of police cars racing down the highway with sirens blaring. The sheriff has organized a large posse of men. Most of them are carrying torches. A series of quick dissolves show the police cars racing down the road, the men with torches on the move and several short-wave calls coming over police radios. A radio announcer makes an official broadcast warning all listeners about the danger of the Mummy. The short-wave radio calls are intercut with scenes of the Mummy moving through the darkness and leaving a trail of death behind him.

This scene cuts to Jim and Maggie driving in a car. They stop at a gas station. While at the station, they hear over the radio of the Mummy's return. The announcer mentions the places where the bodies of murder victims have been found that night. Maggie checks the names of the places against a road map to see if she can guess where he might strike next.

"He's heading for the museum," cries Maggie. "Come on!"

"I won't let you go," says Jim.

4. "The Mummy's Return" 93

"Why not?"

"The danger!"

"Danger, my grandmother! What a story!"

The leaves on the trees start to blow about as the wind begins to kick up. Clouds pass over the full moon temporarily obstructing it from view. Maggie and Jim brave the gusts of wind and make their way toward the museum.

Two motorcycle cops are speeding down the road when the word comes over their short-wave radio that the Mummy is close by. No sooner do they hear this announcement than both policemen see the Mummy. They draw their revolvers and empty them into the advancing monster. But the Mummy continues forward as the bullets do not even slow him down.

Before the officers can escape, the Mummy grabs one of them and strangles him. The other retreats, then turns around and drives his motorcycle at full speed directly into the Mummy. Like bullets from a gun, this too has absolutely no effect on the Mummy. It's like hitting a brick wall! The motorcycle is completely wrecked. The Mummy takes it and throws it, along with the policeman, off to the side of the road, like they were nothing. Both policemen are now dead.

Inside the museum, the Bey is standing before the mummy of Ananka. He takes out his medallion and again begins to pray, "I humbly thank the great god Amon-Ra for blessing my sacred mission with the help of the Mummy Kharis."

After his prayer, he takes a hypo containing tana fluid and inserts the needle into one of Ananka's mummified arteries.

Nearby, an elderly couple is in a very old-fashioned buggy being pulled by a horse. They are just returning from church and are dressed in their Sunday best. The woman is holding a Bible and a small bunch of flowers. Then another announcement comes over the radio warning about the Mummy.

The wind continues to pick up. The sky begins to darken. The Mummy emerges from a wooded area on the side of the road.

The old man sees the Mummy, quickly stands up and cracks the whip. The horse takes off, the driver loses control and the buggy crashes. The couple perishes in the crash.

Back at the museum, the Bey is with the mummy of Ananka when Jim and Maggie arrive. They quietly enter the Egyptian exhibition room and observe the Bey's experiment with the tana leaves and the mummy of Ananka. Jim has no idea what is really going on, so Maggie informs him. They continue to watch carefully. Seeing the Bey attempt to revive the mummy of Ananka confirms what Maggie has suspected. It was the Bey who was responsible for returning life to Kharis.

The sky continues to get darker. The air is hot and uncomfortable. The barometer is falling quickly. The Bey interprets this sudden change in weather as a sign, a voice from the ancient Gods of Egypt. It is actually a fast-approaching cyclone.

Maggie informs Jim that it was the Bey who revived Kharis, and he is trying to do the same with Ananka. Jim is outraged that it is the Bey who is responsible for the reign of terror. He is not the slightest bit interested in the news value of the story. He walks away from Maggie and reveals himself to the Bey. He demands an explanation. The two have a heated exchange of words. Then the Bey attempts to strike Jim with a heavy object. They begin to fight.

The two men and Maggie have been so occupied with what is going on in the museum that all three fail to hear the dragging leg or see the shadow as Kharis approaches. By the time any of them notice Kharis' presence, the monster is upon them and there is no way out of the room. Kharis has blocked the exit.

The two men now stop fighting. The Bey quickly stands up and speaks to the approaching Mummy with authority. "I am an ancient Priest of Egypt. You will obey me."

He instructs Kharis to kill Maggie and Jim. The Mummy starts to move menacingly toward Maggie. Jim attempts to keep the Mummy from reaching her. He tries to attack the monster but is sent flying into a wall. The Mummy is now closing in on Maggie. As the Mummy is about to strike, he hesitates for some unknown reason. He stands before her, looking confused.

Again, with a great deal of authority in his voice, the Bey commands Kharis to kill Maggie, then Jim. But Kharis behaves as though he cannot hear the Bey's commands. He turns and with his one good eye seems to look right through the Bey at the body of his Princess Ananka. Maggie and the two men are bewildered. Their eyes follow the Mummy's gaze.

Maggie, Jim and the Bey are mesmerized at what they see. The Mummy of Ananka, long dried and shriveled, has now transformed back into the ancient beauty that existed more than 3,000 years ago. Apparently the Bey's earlier experiment with the tana leaves did not fail after all.

Ananka's eyes are no longer sunken. Her face is no longer hollow. And her body is no longer a dried, lifeless shell. She is once again the beautiful woman that she was centuries ago. Those present, including Kharis, are breathless, completely stunned by the thing of vibrant beauty before them.

"God of Amon-Ra!" exclaims the Bey. He approaches the Princess and he sinks to his knees. He is completely humbled. Princess Ananka has returned to life.

Ananka's eyelids begin to flutter ever so slightly. Then her eyes open. She stares into space as if she can see nothing, almost as though she were in a trance. The Princess begins to look around slowly until her eyes fall upon Kharis. She stares at him intently, showing no fear. The Mummy starts to move toward Ananka. The Bey quickly maneuvers between Ananka and Kharis and cries out "Stop! Stop, Kharis!"

Kharis grabs the Bey and positions him so that the monster can raise his foot and breaks the Bey's neck. Then he kicks the broken corpse aside and continues toward the Princess.

Ananka still gazes at Kharis. She does not display any reaction or emotion at all to the murder that has just taken place before her. In fact, she moves right into Kharis' arms. The monster's mighty arms embrace her. He draws her youthful body still closer to be embraced by his hideous one.

Kharis and Ananka are reunited!

Maggie and Jim are completely enthralled by what they see. The two stand there in complete disbelief.

4. "The Mummy's Return"

The scenes of Jim and Maggie and Kharis and Ananka are intercut with scenes of the on-coming cyclone. A huge black funnel cloud can be seen approaching.

Kharis slowly raises his head and looks at Maggie and Jim. He loosens his grip on Ananka but the Princess still clings to him. It appears he is almost about to release her. "He's coming for us again!" cries Maggie.

We will never know for sure because at this moment, the twister strikes the museum.

There is montage of quick cuts and flashes, using stock and process shots.

Kharis begins to stagger. Even his colossal strength is no match for nature's tremendous fury. The walls, covered in Egyptian hieroglyphics, begin to tremble as though an earthquake of great magnitude has struck. Then the walls collapse and fall upon the ancient Egyptian. He manages to rise up again through the debris.

But within seconds, a deafening roar descends upon the museum. The twister's vacuum sucks everything up. Virtually everything is carried off. Maggie and Jim hold on for their lives as the world around them is being destroyed in a great apocalyptic blast of wind.

It is now early dawn and the sun is coming up. The cyclone has passed. The destruction it has left in its path is indescribable.

We see a close shot of Jim and Maggie. They look around in disbelief at the damage caused by nature's wrath. What was once a museum is now nothing more than a pile of rubble. Maggie walks over to the car to see if it is still there. She turns on the radio to hear if there is any news.

Maggie returns to Jim and stands close to him. She tells him that the Mummy and Ananka have disappeared completely. Suddenly they are both startled by the sound of a squawking noise that seems to be coming from one of the mummy cases behind them. Still on edge, they quickly turn around to face it.

From around the corner of the mummy case comes a tiny chick, followed by a small parade of newly hatched chicks. A proud-looking hen is bringing up the rear.

The twister carried the nest and the eggs within it into the mummy case. Miraculously, all survived.

The mysteries of life from the planets rotating in the uttermost confines of space to nature's smallest miracles continue endlessly.

FADE OUT

The End

Lack of continuity notwithstanding, the treatment of "The Mummy's Return" certainly makes for interesting reading. And before we hang writer Abrams out to dry for these inconsistencies, let us remember that this is an early draft of the original story, destined for numerous changes before a first draft of the screenplay would be banged out.

Most of these inconsistencies revolve around the Mummy himself. Then again, it all depends on who is telling the story. We already know right out of the chute (*The Mummy's Hand*) that Kharis was buried alive for attempting to use the life-preserving tana leaves to revive his love, Princess Ananka, 3,000 years ago. Then two films later (*The Mummy's Ghost*), the love that Kharis and Ananka shared was forbidden.

Now "The Mummy's Return" literally has made a slave of the Mummy. And due to the ancient hanky panky, Kharis and Ananka were *both* buried alive. The correct use of the tana fluid is also a miss. Since when does a mummy have to "shoot up" to achieve its life-preserving effects? The key word here is life-preserving. The original use for the tana fluid is that it must be administered once each night during the cycle of the full moon. The fluid from three tana leaves can preserve life. Nine can restore motivation. But if one is dead, tana leaves will not bring you back. That trick is reserved for Frankenstein films. Apparently, Abrams had not yet had the opportunity to scan the previous Mummy films.

The story is also very talky. Its 23 pages begin with several Mummy killings to establish the mood. Then it proceeds to make the poor monster look as undignified as humanly possible. First he in unceremoniously dumped into the back of a construction worker's pickup truck. From then on it only gets worse. The once mighty monster finds himself as a scarecrow in the middle of a field for the sole purpose of keeping unwanted birds away. A farmer has dressed him in an old coat and a battered hat, which is not even frightening enough to dissuade the crows from landing right on top of his head.

His last stop before resurrection is to act as a prop in a carnival sideshow. Here, after being sold for a scant five dollars, he is mercilessly struck in the face several times by a moron with a cane. His 1955 meeting with Abbott and Costello would prove to be more dignified then this. But at least our Mummy *does* have the last laugh.

Although the Mummy is present through most of the 23 pages of treatment, he is not revived until page 16. But once he is, things really start to buzz. In fact, the death toll in this would-be Mummy melodrama actually reaches double figures, a claim that no other Universal Mummy movie can make.

While the number of homicides in "The Mummy's Return" separate it from the other Mummy films, several sequences strike similarities to other films in the genre. At the meeting of the Society of Psychic Research, the chairman speaks to the other members about the Mummy's brutal killing rampage, just as Prof. Norman did before his class in *The Mummy's Ghost*.

The idea of Kharis on display, as undignified as it may be, worked in Universal's all-star monster fest *House of Frankenstein*, that same year. Dracula (John Carradine) found himself on display as part of Lampini's Chamber of Horrors, revived by a vengeful Dr. Niemann, portrayed by Boris Karloff. In fact, coincidentally, *House of Frankenstein* was paired with *The Mummy's Curse*, formerly "The Mummy's Return," on a double-bill in December 1944.

When the Mummy is revived in "The Mummy's Return," he makes his way toward the terrified carnival patrons, much the way the Frankenstein Monster (Bela Lu-

4. "The Mummy's Return"

gosi) made a personal appearance at the festival of New Wine in *Frankenstein Meets the Wolf Man* the previous year.

The elderly couple coming home from church in their buggy meets an untimely demise as the Mummy emerges from the nearby woods; this bears a similarity to a sequence from Universal's *Man Made Monster*. In that film, Lon Chaney, Jr., portrays Dynamo Dan, part of a carnival sideshow act. He displays immunity to small doses of electricity until mad scientist (Lionel Atwill) really turns on the juice, enabling him to withstand even greater doses, including the big one, the electric chair. After escaping from prison looking like the world's biggest nightlight, Dynamo Dan emerges from the woods and frightens the occupants of a hayride. The horses pulling the wagon also get spooked. The driver is killed, the hay is set ablaze and the wagon crashes off the road.

The film that "The Mummy's Return" bears the closest resemblance to is Hammer's 1959 *The Mummy*. The scene in which Abdullah Bey is murdered by Kharis is so similar to the same sequence in the 1959 film that one has to wonder if the film's writer, Jimmy Sangster, cribbed the idea from "The Mummy's Return" treatment. When Abdullah Bey orders Kharis to kill Maggie and Jim, he is met with quite a bit of resistance from the Mummy. Kharis not only defies his master, but also proceeds to snap his spine. In the Hammer film, Mehemet Bey (George Pastell) instructs the Mummy (Christopher Lee) to kill an Ananka look alike (Yvonne Furneaux). But it's not so easy to kill someone who so closely resembles the one you love, regardless of how many centuries have passed. So Kharis does the next best thing and breaks Mehemet Bey's back.

Whatever the particular mission, the Mummy never appears to be enjoying himself, which is very understandable, especially from the vantage point of Lon Chaney, Jr. Maybe the heavy makeup would have been more tolerable if the Universal brass took the hot California summers into consideration. Filming schedules for the Mummy films always seemed to coincide with summer.

Chaney would don the Mummy makeup for three films; "The Mummy's Return" or *Curse* would be the last. How would the other characters from *Return* have been cast? Would we have seen the same actors who appeared in *The Mummy's Curse* fill the roles for "Return"? If so, that would mean that Virginia Christine's role would have been severely cut for her portrayal of the Princess Ananka, having come to life just prior to the arrival of a giant twister, then disappearing.

Peter Coe, who portrayed the role of the High Priest Ilzor Zandaab in *Curse* would have been Abdullah Bey in "Return."

Dennis Moore, who portrayed *Curse*'s hero James Halsey, would have fit the bill of Jim Oakley, while the heroine, Kay Harding, might have been Maggie, the reporter.

It is anyone's guess as to whom the roles of Doc, Gus, Flutter and the farmer would have gone to. The seedy talents of Martin Kosleck would have been wasted on any of these remaining characters. While the jolly Kurt Katch, the grouchy Addison Richards and empathetic Holmes Herbert would have been sorely miscast as well.

Regardless, the metamorphosis of "The Mummy's Return" into *The Mummy's Curse* was the natural order of evolution.

5

The Mummy's Curse

Resurrected in horror! Rising out of death! Egypt's ancient lovers live again in evil to fulfill ... The Mummy's Curse.

Cast: Lon Chaney *(Kharis, the Mummy)*; Peter Coe *(Dr. Ilzor Zandaab)* [*Ismail* script name]; Virginia Christine *(Princess Ananka)*; Kay Harding *(Betty Walsh)*; Dennis Moore *(Dr. James Halsey)*; Martin Kosleck *(Ragheb* [*Abbas* script name]; Kurt Katch *(Cajun Joe)* [*Big Joe* script name]; Addison Richards *(Pat Walsh)*; Holmes Herbert *(Dr. Cooper)*; Charles Stevens *(Achilles)*; William Farnum *(Michael, the Sacristan)*; Napoleon Simpson *(Goobie)*; Herbert Heywood *(Hill)*; Ann Codee *(Tante Berthe)*; Nina Bara *(Cajun Girl)*; Eddie Abdo *(Pierre)*; Tony Santoro *(Ulysses)*; Al Ferguson *(Extra)*; Heenan Elliott *(Extra)*; Budd Buster *(Extra)*. **Crew:** Ben Pivar *(Executive Producer)*; Oliver Drake *(Associate Producer)*; Leslie Goodwins *(Directed by)*; Mack Wright *(Assistant Director)*; Bernard Schubert *(Screenplay)*; Leon Abrams, Dwight V. Babcock *(Original Story and Adaptation)*; Virgil Miller *(Director of Photography)*; William Dodds *(Second Camera)*; John P. Fulton *(Special Photography)*; John B. Goodman, Martin Obzina *(Art Direction)*; Fred R. Feitshans, Jr. *(Film Editor)*; Russell A. Gausman, Victor A. Gangelin *(Set Decorations)*; Paul Sawtell *(Music Director)*; Song: "Hey You"; Oliver Drake *(Music)*; Frank Orth *(Lyrics)*; Bernard B. Brown *(Director of Sound)*; Robert Pritchard *(Sound Technician)*; Edwin L. Wetzell *(Rerecording & Effects Mixer)*; Paul Neal *(Music Mixer)*; Ted Richmond *(Continuity Writer)*; Ernie Smith, Eddie Case *(Props)*; Jack P. Pierce *(Makeup)*; Vera West *(Gowns)*; Eddie Parker, Bob Pepper *(Lon Chaney Doubles)*; Carey Loftin, Teddy Mangean *(Stunts)*.

After three Mummy films in four years, and after providing Kharis with every excuse under the full moon to strangle the life from the uninitiated, Universal executives decided that the series needed a shot in the arm or, in this case, an extra dose of tana fluid. Leon Abrams' treatment "The Mummy's Return" underwent a complete overhaul. The locale was changed from New England to the swamps of the Louisiana bayou and, most importantly, the Mummy was once again on his own turf for the first time in three films. It wasn't the sacred hills of Egypt, but the swamp worked for him just fine. And despite further continuity inconsistencies (this time deliberate), the plan worked.

The legend of Kharis succeeds in keeping most of the populace away from the swamp. To quote one of the locals, "Too many people, they go in the swamp, they *nevaire* come out." He is, as most nervous villagers are in these films, right.

By now everyone in the area knows about the Mummy and how he carried a girl into the swamp 25 years ago. And the more superstitious folks would rather stand on the unemployment line than work anywhere near the murky marsh. But there is a government project going on, so neither rain nor snow nor killer Mummy would prevent the draining of this swamp.

The Mummy's Curse begins in Tante Berthe's Café, a watering hole where the local citizenry gather regularly for a few belts. Owner, Tante Berthe (Ann Codee) also doubles as the house entertainment. She has just wrapped up a little number to the applause of the patrons. Moving over to the bar, she is greeted by Cajun Joe (Kurt Katch), who boasts that the government swamp-draining project will soon bring wealth his way. However, the mood begins to change when Achilles (Charles Stevens), one of the workers, insists that the work is finished now. It seems only Cajun Joe and a few others are willing to continue the job because they fear that the Mummy haunts the swamp. Achilles is soon joined by others who share his belief.

Meanwhile, project coordinator Pat Walsh (Addison Richards), tries to convince the superstitious crew that the swamp is being drained for their benefit. However, when Achilles comes out with the news that Antoine, another one of the workers, is the latest to disappear in the swamp, the level of fear increases. Just as Walsh insists everyone get back to work, two representatives from the Scripps Museum, Dr. James Halsey (Dennis Moore) and Ilzor Zandaab (Peter Coe), arrive. They have special permission to excavate the swamps for the bodies of Kharis and Ananka and return them to the museum.

Frustrated with the work situation and skeptical of the story about the mummies, Walsh's only fear is that this swamp-clearing job will never get done. But his niece Betty (Kay Harding) defends the new arrivals (where would we be without a love interest?). Suddenly, another worker, Goobie (Napoleon Simpson), bursts into the office with the news that Antoine's body has been found with a knife in his back. The few remaining workers threaten to quit.

They all congregate at the scene where the body was found. Then Halsey discovers a hole in the ground that looks like the imprint of a large body. If this isn't enough to convince Walsh that he has a bigger problem than just superstitious workers, a Mummy wrapping has also been found near the site.

5. *The Mummy's Curse*

Later that night, Ilzor goes into the swamp where he meets Ragheb (Martin Kosleck), who is waiting for him. The two make their way through a swamp path to a long flight of steps. The steps lead up a hill to an abandoned monastery. Inside is a sarcophagus where Kharis (Lon Chaney) lies in a dormant state. It turns out that Ilzor is none other than the latest High Priest of Arkam, sent to the swamp to recover the bodies of Kharis and Ananka and return them not to the Scripps Museum, but to their tombs in Egypt. Ragheb is his acolyte.

Ragheb takes his sacred vow, swearing to the mighty god Amon-Ra. Now that he is officially sworn in, Ilzor explains the full purpose of their mission.

Over 3,000 years ago, the Princess Ananka died. Her lover, Kharis, refused to believe he lost his true love forever. So one night, he tried to revive her using the forbidden tana leaves, but he was discovered. For this sacrilege, Kharis was condemned to be buried alive. First, his tongue was torn from his mouth and then he was buried in an unmarked grave in the middle of nowhere. Then to ensure that the location of the grave would remain a secret, the priests killed the slaves who buried him. Later, the priests removed Kharis and placed him in a cave inside the mountain where Ananka was laid, together with an ample supply of tana leaves. There he would be kept alive through the centuries by the secret cult of High Priests, to guard Ananka's tomb forever.

Ilzor further explains that Kharis is in America to attempt to bring Ananka back to Egypt after the Banning expedition defiled her tomb years ago.

With the tana leaves brewed, Ilzor pours the fluid into the Mummy's mouth. He sits up in his coffin, again ready for action. Just to get warmed up, Kharis kills Michael (William Farnum), the self-ordained caretaker who walks in on them at the wrong time.

The next day, as a bulldozer plows over the mud, the earth begins to move very slightly. Suddenly, withered and wrinkled fingers make their way through the slime, then a hand, followed by an arm. Within a minute, the entire body of a woman (Virginia Christine) has emerged, looking as though she is wearing a head-to-toe mud-pack. It is Ananka. Barely able to walk, she makes her way to a small pond and cleans herself. When she reappears, she is perfectly groomed, but still quite dazed.

When Cajun Joe makes his way through the swamp about to call it a day, he and Ananka cross paths. As Joe attempts to learn her identity, Ananka, in a trance-like state, utters the name of Kharis. This piques the interest of Ragheb, who is also passing by. Ragheb overhears Joe tell Ananka he is taking her to Tante Berthe.

Ragheb returns to the monastery that night and tells Ilzor he's seen Ananka. Ilzor tells Kharis, and Kharis makes a nocturnal beeline, albeit a slow beeline, to Tante Berthe's. As Tante Berthe attempts to care for Ananka, Kharis comes barging in. Ananka sees him, recoils in horror and makes a quick escape. Tante Berthe is not as fortunate. While attempting to get between Kharis and his ancient beau, she is promptly strangled to death.

Kharis follows Ananka and the chase through the swamp is on. Despite the speed at which Ananka is running, Kharis is never far behind.

Finally, collapsing from exhaustion, Ananka is rescued by Halsey and Betty,

Ever get the feeling there's someone looking over your shoulder? Betty (Kay Harding) narrowly escapes the Mummy's (Lon Chaney) clutches in the final chapter of the Kharis saga, *The Mummy's Curse* (Universal, 1944).

who are driving down a road adjacent to the swamp. They are unaware that they have barely escaped Kharis. The Mummy returns to the monastery empty-handed.

In the morning, Ananka wakes up in Dr. Cooper's (Holmes Herbert) tent, near the construction area, not knowing who she is. The good-natured Halsey gives her some minor lab work to keep her occupied. In doing so, he discovers that she knows quite a bit about ancient Egypt. She gives Halsey more information on the strip of Mummy bandage than he would ever want to know. Yet she cannot even begin to explain how she knows any of it. Then when Ilzor shows up, she appears mesmerized by him. Ilzor denies knowing the woman, but he knows it's Ananka. When Ilzor walks away, Ananka again reverts back into a trance-like state, calling the name of Kharis.

That night, Ilzor sends the Mummy out for another attempt at retrieving his long-lost love. Ananka does not give herself up without a fight. At the sight of Kharis, she once again takes off, this time to Dr. Cooper's tent. (It's enough to give poor Kharis a complex.) She isn't there long before Kharis makes his way through the good doctor's tent flap. The doctor gallantly tries to protect Ananka, but the Mummy sends him the way of Tante Berthe. Ananka once again flees.

5. The Mummy's Curse

Meanwhile, back in Walsh's office, he is blaming all recent tragedies on Halsey and Ilzor. He threatens to have the plug pulled on their excavation project, but when they learn that the woman is missing, that takes precedence. Halsey, Cajun Joe and a few of the other workers volunteer to penetrate the swamp to search for her. Mistake number one, they all separate. Cajun Joe sees Ananka from his rowboat and calls to her. She is still in a trance-like state and does not respond. He beaches the boat, gets out and continues to call. Suddenly, Kharis emerges from the trees in pursuit of Ananka. When he sees Cajun Joe, he changes direction and heads toward him, ready to attack. Cajun Joe takes aim at the advancing Mummy with his rifle. He fires at him, but the Mummy keeps coming. As Cajun Joe quickly turns to escape back to his boat, Kharis grabs him.

Ananka wanders back to the campsite, still somewhat dazed. She enters Betty's tent and stays with her for the night. Nearby, Ragheb secretly watches. Soon Kharis makes his way to the campsite and breaks into Betty's tent, bringing it down on top of them. In the confusion, Kharis abducts Ananka.

Ragheb observes the incident from a distance. After the Mummy is gone, he makes his presence known. Betty accompanies Ragheb when he promises to take her to Halsey. Instead, he leads her back to the monastery.

When Halsey arrives at the campsite, he finds Goobie investigating the collapsed tent. Fearing Kharis has swiped Betty, Halsey tells the frightened Goobie that it looks like the Mummy is the cause. While Halsey follows the tracks, Goobie wakes Walsh and a few of the other men.

Kharis returns to the monastery with Ananka and is met by Ilzor. The Mummy places the ancient princess in a sarcophagus. Ragheb and Betty arrive. Ragheb is trying to put the moves on Betty when Ilzor unexpectedly interrupts him. The Priest accuses his underling of betraying his sacred trust; unless Betty is sacrificed, the secret of the tana leaves cannot be sustained. After a strong verbal exchange, Ragheb produces a knife and stabs his master in the back.

Meanwhile, the Mummy's footprints have led Halsey up the steps and into the old monastery. Inside, he sees Betty and Ragheb. Ragheb tries to pull the same knife on Halsey, but this time, he's in for a fight. Halsey temporarily knocks the treacherous acolyte unconscious, then examines Ilzor's body. Ragheb shakes off his daze, grabs his knife and again attacks Halsey. Kharis comes out of the adjacent chamber where he placed Ananka. Just as the treacherous Ragheb is about to finish off Halsey with a terrific blow to the head, he is interrupted by the unlikeliest of heroes, Kharis. After finding Ilzor dead on the floor, the enraged Mummy goes after the sleazy Ragheb. The terrified killer retreats from the advancing Mummy into a nearby chamber and locks the door.

In his rage to reach the double-crosser, Kharis smashes through the door and rips steel bars from the mortar, literally bringing down the entire wing around them and burying them both. When Walsh and the troops arrive, all they find is Ananka, who has metamorphosed back to a mummified state. When Halsey tells Walsh that this is the woman that was brought to the camp, he scoffs. Walsh is just happy that Halsey will be clearing out of the swamp, leaving the project coordinator free to complete his job. Halsey walks off, hand-in hand with Betty, and Kharis is left to be dug out and carted back to the Scripps museum with Ananka.

It is important to remind the reader that the names of several characters differ between the script and the film. For consistency, this chapter will refer to the characters using their script names. Specifically, the film characters Ilzor, Ragheb and Cajun Joe will be referred to as Ismail, Abbas and Big Joe, respectively.

The main theme in *The Mummy's Curse*, as in *The Mummy's Ghost*, is reincarnation. In *Ghost*, we gradually witness the transformation of Amina into Ananka through the use of her hair as a metaphor; it gradually becomes lighter as the film proceeds. When we are introduced to Virginia Christine's character in *The Mummy's Curse*, she already *is* Ananka.

In addition to the reincarnation theme is the idea of Kharis haunting the swamp. This was the factor that gives *The Mummy's Curse*, and the series, the boost it needed. The shots of the swamp, previously seen under the main titles of *The Wolf Man* and *The Ghost of Frankenstein*, are also seen underneath the main titles of *The Mummy's Curse*. When the credits fade out, instead of opening the film with Ann Codee belting out a tune at Tante Berthe's Café, a much more atmospheric introduction was suggested in the script:

> *As the CREDIT TITLES FADE OUT, to the UNDERSCORING of mood music like Debussy's "Clair de Lune," we FADE IN*
>
> EXT. JUNGLE SWAMP AND FOREST — DAY — (LS)
>
> *It is dark, forbidding and impenetrable. Over it is SUPERIMPOSED THE TITLE: "Deep in the Bayou country is a swampland of entangling vines and jungle growth..."*
>
> STOCK SHOTS (TO INTERCUT)
>
> *of crocodiles slipping into the water — coveys of birds flushed from marshland, or any other animal life indigenous of the Bayou country*
>
> DISSOLVE
>
> EXT. JUNGLE SWAMP AND FOREST — DAY — AN OLD GNARLED LIVEOAK OR KINDERED TREE — (CS)
>
> *struggling to keep alive against entangling vines wrapped about its trunk. From a branch, Spanish moss hangs — long and thick — like a beaded oriental curtain shutting out the light. With the MUSICAL UNDERSCORING CONTINUING, OVER THE SCENE IS SUPERIMPOSED THE TITLE:*
>
> *"For countless generations it has remained a dwelling place of dreaded fears and superstition..."*
>
> DISSOLVE
>
> EXT. LOW SWAMPLAND — DAY — (CS)
>
> *surrounded by shrubbery and glutted with wild reeds and stumps of rotted trees. With the MUSICAL UNDERSCORING CONTINUING, OVER*

5. The Mummy's Curse

> *SCENE IS SUPERIMPOSED THE TITLE: "…stubbornly resisting man's effort toward enlightenment and progress…"*
>
> *CLOSE SHOT — SHRUBBERY NEAR WATER'S EDGE*
>
> dark and forbidding like the preceding scene. Suddenly, from o.s., we HEAR a cacophony of noises,— man-made noises of motors chugging, steam engines in operation, and the shouts and cries of men at work. INTO THE CAMERA comes crashing a bulldozer, which ruthlessly tears tangled brush apart, and floods the SCENE with sunlight, as we DISSOLVE TO CLOSE SHOTS — A SERIES OF QUICK SCENES
>
> *GANG OF LABORERS,* digging a water shed to catch the water drained off the swamp. Suddenly, another worker edges INTO SCENE, whispering to one. They start whispering among themselves and stop work.
>
> *STATIONARY ENGINE PUMP,* pumping water over Spillway. As the CAMERA HOLDS ON IT, the water diminishes, finally comes to an abrupt stop.
>
> *HEAVY STEAM ROLLER,* pounding down a road — evidently being cut through the swampland.
>
> *A native ENTERS SCENE,* whispers to operator of the steamroller. The operator stops the roller, takes his coat and lunch pail, hops out, leaving the machine right in the middle of the road.
>
> *TRUCKS,* being loaded with gravel and earth from a derrick.
>
> *DERRICK SHOVEL,* loading the earth. It remains stationary in mid air.
>
> *DISSOLVE TO EXT. CONSTRUCTION CAMP — DAY — CLOSE SHOT — ON WOODEN SHINGLE SIGN bearing the lettering: OFFICE SOUTHERN ENGINEERING COMPANY P. Walsh, Supt.*
>
> *OVER THE INSERT we HEAR WALSH'S vehement and forceful VOICE.*
>
> **WALSH'S VOICE O.S.:** It's up to you to get those men back to work.

This opening scene from the script is far more atmospheric than the merriment we see in the film, courtesy of Tante Berthe's vocals. The above deleted scene segues into Walsh lecturing the superstitious workers, a scene that remains in the film, but doesn't appear for another few minutes.

In the script it is Tante Berthe's one-minute ditty "Hey You" that doesn't appear until page 14. By then, we've already met nearly everyone except Kharis and Ananka. Even sparks from the love interest between Halsey and Walsh's niece Betty become ignited faster. The weak love interest in the film could have been made a little more enticing if certain cuts had not been made. Comparing the script with the final edited version of the film, scenes featuring Halsey and Betty were shortened or eliminated from the film completely.

In the film, when the two first meet in Walsh's office, Betty practically undresses Halsey with her eyes. Without a single word of dialogue, we know what to expect. But it is as though the film's editors have it in for the potential young lovers by making cuts in their very first scene together. When Halsey arrives in Walsh's office and tells him why he and his assistant Ismail are there, Walsh immediately balks in fear that the pair will interfere with his swamp-draining project. Betty immediately jumps in and defends the new arrivals. Walsh storms out of the office, but after only a couple of exchanges between his niece and Halsey, he returns.

In the script, Halsey and Betty have a bit more time to get acquainted before Walsh comes stomping back in:

> *Walsh EXITS, Halsey watches the excitable man disappear from SCENE, then he turns back to Betty.*
>
> CLOSE TWO SHOT — HALSEY AND BETTY
>
> HALSEY: Thanks for helping us out ... but you shouldn't talk back to your boss like that.... You're liable to get fired...
>
> BETTY: *(lightly)* You mustn't mind Uncle Pat...
>
> HALSEY: *(reacting)* Your Uncle?
>
> BETTY: *(nods)* He isn't nearly as unpleasant as he appears to be.... It's only that we've been having so much trouble with native superstition...
>
> HALSEY: *(with a smile)* That's nothing new to us, is it, Ismail?...
>
> CMAERA TRUCKS BACK TO TAKE IN ISMAIL
>
> ISMAIL: *(curtly turns to her)* In archaeology, Miss Walsh ... one always experiences the same trouble...
>
> BETTY: *(after a slight pause; to Halsey)* Archaeology is a very interesting subject ... I took a year of it at college...
>
> HALSEY: *(immediately interested; draws closer to her)* Say, we have something in common, haven't we?
>
> *From o.s. they HEAR Walsh's voice:*
>
> WALSH'S VOICE O.S.: Dr. Halsey ... They turn and look.
>
> CLOSE SHOT — ON WALSH
>
> *He has just returned and is still wearing his hat.*
>
> WALSH: What makes you so sure that the Mummy Prince and Princess are buried here in the swamps?

It isn't so much that Walsh actually cares about the Mummy or Ananka, or even about the potential budding romance between his niece and this complete stranger, that induces him to barge back into the office. His question serves as a great excuse for the use of flashback footage from *The Mummy's Ghost*:

> HALSEY: Because, many years ago, the Mummy had run off with a girl. Pursued by the natives and sheriff's posse, he made for the swamps—right in this locale.

DISSOLVE OUT
DISSOLVE IN
EXT. INCLINE AND SHACK — (L.S.)
Men run up the incline as Kharis descends the ladder with Amina.
TRAVELING SHOT — ON INCLINE –(C.S.)
Showing a man running up. He EXITS.
LOWER PART OF STRUCTURE — (M.S.)
Kharis is at the foot of the ladder with Amina.
EXT. OPEN DOOR — (C.U.)
Walgreen comes on and EXITS inside. Sheriff and Deputies follow and EXIT inside.
EXT. ALONG BUSHY SLOPE — (C.S.)
Kharis carries Amina toward b.g.
EXT. EDGE OF MARSH — (C.S.)
Kharis carries Amina toward the ground, which is softening.
KHARIS' LEG — (C.U.) as it moves along, bringing more of his body INTO SCENE, Amina's withered arm swinging down. ALL EXIT.
EXT. MARSH — (C.S.)
Peanuts runs across thru the mire, barking.
EXT. RIVER BOTTOM — (C.S.)
Kharis moves across, carrying Amina.
ANOTHER ANGLE — (C.U.)
Kharis comes partly INTO SCENE, carrying the body of Amina, now an old woman with feet and legs withered and shrunken. He starts to EXIT with her.
EXT. RIVER BOTTOM — (C.S.)
Kharis carries Amina through slender saplings toward b.g.
EXT. RIVER BANK — (C.S.)
Kharis carries Amina toward b.g.
EXT. RIVER BOTTOM — (C.S.)
Kharis carries Amina toward b.g.
ANOTHER ANGLE — (M.S.)
Kharis carries Amina down into the water.
REAR VIEW OF KHARIS — (C.U.)
carrying Amina through the water.
EXT. RIVER — (C.S.)
Showing Kharis and Amina almost submerged.

> AMINA — (C.U.) her face shriveled and old.
>
> EXT. SIDE OF RIVER — (C.S.)
>
> Kharis and Amina are almost completely under water.
>
> AMINA'S FACE — (C.U.) Shriveled and old, as it disappears under water.
>
> EXT. RIVER — (C.U.)
>
> Showing no sign of life.
>
> INT. WALSH'S OFFICE — DAY — GROUP SHOT — CENTERING ON HALSEY with Betty listening eagerly, and Ismail nodding assent; Walsh has a look of disgust on his face.
>
> HALSEY: (to Walsh) And that, my friend, is a matter of record... (with a look to Betty) The newspaper files and the Bayou Times carried long, descriptive accounts of the event...

These flashback sequences were wisely cut from *Curse*. Its short running time of 62 minutes was already padded with flashback footage from *The Mummy's Hand*.

In the film, it isn't long before Goobie, one of the project workers, bursts into the office. He yells that they've discovered the body of one of the workers found in a pit in a recently drained section of the swamp. Walsh sends the excitable worker to Tante Berthe's Café to find Big Joe, who works as the foreman on Walsh's draining project.

Tante Berthe finishes singing and is now chatting with the patrons. The conversation quickly takes a turn to the macabre when the subject of the swamp is mentioned. But the very jolly Big Joe, with his think Cajun accent, fears nothing, including Kharis and his Princess. He further emphasizes this in the following deleted scene:

> CLOSE SHOT — BIG JOE (OTHERS SUGGESTED IN B.G.)
>
> BIG JOE: Wait... Stop... You listen to me... I know better from all of you ... I be pearl fishin' this place more than thirty year... Long ago there was a mummy like you say...
>
> The others react as he continues.
>
> BIG JOE: And he takes a girl in the swamp...
>
> Others look from one to the other, wondering whether to be frightened or whether this is just another one of Big Joe's famous jokes.
>
> BIG JOE: That'sa true ... I no foolin' ... but that been twenty-five year past...
>
> MED. ANGLE SHOT — CENTERING ON BIG JOE leaning over the bar, with Tante Berthe facing him across the bar. Others are suggesting in the b.g.
>
> BIG JOE: The Mummy's spirit he'sa never bodder me as I pass over his head hund'ed maybe t'ousan' times... And maybe even I tickla' his ribs when I dig for the oyster. Then he have a good laugh.

5. The Mummy's Curse 109

He laughs at his own joke. The others don't seem to appreciate his humor.

BIG JOE: Don' worry my fr'ens...

CLOSE SHOT — ON BIG JOE

BIG JOE: So you have not to be 'fraid from heem.

This is where Goobie comes in looking for Big Joe. The next scene has everyone congregating in the swamp at night near the body of the murdered man. Halsey finds a Mummy wrapping close by. Despite the fact that the victim was knifed, the wrath of Kharis is on everyone's mind — everyone except Walsh's. He instructs Big Joe to go into town and alert the authorities of the murder. In the script, Halsey has one extra line of dialogue before the scene dissolves to his tent where Betty pays him a visit. In this cut scene, flirting becomes more pertinent than the exchange of actual information between the two:

WALSH'S VOICE O.S.: Big Joe! ...Go into town and notify the authorities about Antoine's murder.

HALSEY: (*to Ismail*) Go along with him, and bring back the laboratory equipment.

During this dialogue, CAMERA DOLLIES IN to a CLOSE UP on the Mummy-wrapping in Halsey's hand.

DISSOLVE

INT. HALSEY'S LABORATORY TENT — DAY — CLOSEUP — ON MUMMY WRAPPING — ON A WORK TABLE

CAMERA DOLLIES SLOWLY BACK to disclose Halsey seated at a table, examining the Mummy-wrapping under a microscope. He is in intent on his study, when suddenly we hear BETTY'S O.S. VOICE behind him.

BETTY'S VOICE O.S.: May I come in?

Dr. Halsey is so intent, he doesn't hear it at first.

BETTY'S VOICE O.S.: (*calling again — louder*) Hello, there!... May I come in?

HALSEY: (*without looking up*) Yes ... Come in ... come in...

Betty ENTERS THE SCENE and approaches. When Halsey, looking up from the microscope discovers who it is, he quickly gets to his feet. CAMERA TRUCKS IN SLOWER.

HALSEY: Oh ... I'm sorry...

BETTY: I hope I'm not disturbing you ... I...

Halsey beckons her over to the microscope. CAMERA TRUCKS INTO A CLOSE TWO SHOT OF HALSEY AND BETTY

HALSEY: You're interested in archaeology... Take a look at that...

BETTY: (*looking into microscope*) What an interesting pattern! Looks like gorgeous lace...

HALSEY: The Egyptians knew their cotton … and how to weave it … thousands of years ago…

BETTY: (*looking up*) Thousands of years…

HALSEY: *That's Mummy cloth … found in the excavation…*

CAMERA PANS WITH HIM as he walks her to laboratory table, over to one side. There on the table before them is a piece of earthen clay, broken off into part of a mold.

HALSEY: Take a good look at this impression… What part of the Mummy's body would you say it is?

BETTY: I don't know … but it looks as if it might be the skull…

HALSEY: Right … the first time…

CLOSE SHOT — SHOOTING OVER HALSEY'S SHOULDER — ON BETTY

She is definitely interested in this young archaeologist.

BETTY: (*with admiration*) Wonderful, how quickly you've been able to find a clue…

CLOSE SHOT — ON HALSEY — BETTY SILHOUETTED IN B.G.

HALSEY: (*disappointedly*) We've certainly done alright… We find a clue … and lose the Mummy…

CLOSE TWO SHOT — ON HALSEY AND BETTY

BETTY: Isn't it the strangest thing how he could have disappeared?

HALSEY: Well, if it is old Kharis, he'll soon make his presence felt…

BETTY: Kharis?

HALSEY: That's the name of the Mummy… (*obviously changing the subject*) By the way, I never thanked you for talking your Uncle Pat into letting his workmen help me.

BETTY: (*modestly*) Aren't you exaggerating my influence?

HALSEY: (*looking at her intently*) You're gorgeously … beautifully…

BETTY: (*a little surprised*) I beg your pardon…

HALSEY: Noncommittal…

They both laugh… She walks around, looking over the laboratory, Halsey with her. CAMERA TRUCKS WITH THEM.

BETTY: You're very well equipped here aren't you… And everything is so neatly arranged…

HALSEY: Now you're giving me too much credit… (*waxing suddenly enthusiastic*) My assistant is a perfect pearl of reliability … and efficiency… (*calls out*) Ismail!!…

They turn to face the door. There is no answer.

5. The Mummy's Curse 111

> HALSEY: (*calling again*) Isamail!!!...
>
> *Receiving no answer, he walks toward the door and across toward Ismail's tent o.s.*
>
> HALSEY: Ismail!!! (*turns back to Betty*) That's what I get for bragging too much...
>
> *He walks back to Betty.*
>
> BETTY: You can't always expect him to be at your beck and call...
>
> HALSEY: That's strange ... I suppose I am spoiled ... but nothing like this ever happened before... (*turns to call again*) Ismail!!!...
>
> DISSOLVE
>
> EXT. MISTY SWAMP — NIGHT — CLOSE MOVING SHOT

The only part of the film hurt by the removal of the above scene was the love interest. I don't imagine many Mummy fans would concern themselves with these two.

The last few lines of the above scene, where Halsey calls out for Ismail, would have made a perfectly creepy segue. With Ismail nowhere to be found, Halsey is left to wonder where his assistant has gone. When the scene dissolves, we see Ismail rowing in a small boat in the swamp at night. He is off to meet his acolyte Abbas. Anyone who has seen the three previous Mummy films can deduce that these two are up to no good. It should come as no surprise that they turn out to be the recent inductees of the High Priests of Arkham.

Abbas leads his master down a path through the swamp to the ruins of an old monastery, which is really the temple set from James Whale's *Green Hell*. In the film, Abbas calls Ismail's attention to the long flight of steps from a distance. They climb the stairs quickly and are inside the monastery before you can say "Oh, mighty gods of Egypt." But in the script, there is a further exchange of dialogue between the two before they begin their ascent:

> EXT. BOTTOM OF MONASTARY STEPS — NIGHT — MED. CLOSE SHOT — ON ABBAS AND ISMAIL
>
> ABBAS: There it is, Master ... built by Spanish Padres centuries ago...
>
> ISMAIL: (*pointing off*) Wait ... until I summon you...
>
> *Abbas waits over to one side as Ismail walks to the first step. He then stops to look up prayerfully.*
>
> ISMAIL: To the great god, Amon-Ra... King of all the gods... Accept this prayer of thanks for leading us to this place ... where we may fulfill our tasks for thee... (*slight pause; then turns and calls*) Abbas...
>
> EXT. MONASTERY — NIGHT — LONG SHOT — (GLASS) — SHOOTING UP TEMPLE STEPS TO RUINS
>
> *Abbas joins Ismail.*

The above scene had to be clipped in the interest of keeping things moving along. Since Abbas is not yet a full-fledged High Priest, he has to be told of Kharis' fate, 3,000 years ago via *Mummy's Hand* flashbacks. Then, when Abbas asks why Kharis is in America, more flashbacks accompany Ismail's explanation — flashbacks that didn't make it to the release print:

> ABBAS: (*looking down at the Mummy*) Then why, Master is he here in America?
>
> ISMAIL: An American archaeologist, seeking the tomb of Princess Ananka, by accident, came upon and dared to desecrate the burial place of Kharis.
>
> DISSOLVE TO MONTAGE
>
> EXT. HILLSIDE — (F.S.)
>
> A TERRIFIC BLAST rocks an Egyptian pyramid, blowing open the stone door.
>
> ISMAIL'S VOICE: (*o.s.*) Because of it, Kharis has inflicted a horrible vengeance upon him and all his loved ones.
>
> THE ARCHAEOLOGIST — (M.F.S.) *being killed by the Mummy.*
>
> ANOTHER MUMMY KILLING — (M.S.)
>
> THE ARCHAEOLOGIST'S FRIEND — (M.F.S.) *being killed by the Mummy.*
>
> EXT. WOODS — (M.F.S.) SHOWING *the Mummy stalking through.*
>
> THE MUMMY — (C.S.) *strangling a man.*
>
> END OF MONTAGE
>
> DISSOLVE
>
> INT. MONASTARY CEREMONIAL ROOM — NIGHT — CLOSE SHOT — ON ISMAIL AND ABBAS — AT MUMMY CASE — X-ING OUT THE MUMMY
>
> ISMAIL: It is written in the sands of time that all who defile the secret resting place of Kharis and Princess Ananka shall die...
>
> ABBAS: I know, Master — but once Kharis had his revenge, why did he not go back to his tomb in Egypt?
>
> ISMAIL: Kharis desired to carry his Princess Ananka back with him, but non-believing infidels have driven them into these swamps...
>
> ABBAS: That, I have heard...

This additional flashback sounds intriguing. The quick cutaways to various Mummy murders generate memories of Lord Byron telling the tale of the monster's murder spree via flashback in *The Bride of Frankenstein*. But in a series already known for its flashback sequences, it was probably wise to make the last-minute snip and remove it.

Had it remained, viewers would have witnessed four Mummy killings within seconds of each other. According to the script, the victims were an archaeologist, his friend and two others. The only archaeologists Kharis ever killed were Dr. Petrie in *The Mummy's Hand* and Steve Banning in *The Mummy's Tomb*. The archaeologist's friend would have had to have been Babe, killed in *Tomb*. The other two victims could have been anyone from the previous three films, since it is unlikely anything new was shot specifically for use in flashback footage.

Back in the film, a quick dose of freshly brewed tana fluid gets the Mummy on his feet. Suddenly, Ismail, Abbas and Kharis have company. Michael, the self-ordained keeper of the monastery, identified as Sacristan in the script, couldn't have come in at a worse time. Kharis, awake for about a minute, uses the poor guy as a warm-up act and throttles the life from him.

All of Michael's lines from the script remained in the film, except for one. The script calls for Michael to speak to the oncoming Mummy just before his outstretched hand reaches his throat:

> SACRISTAN: I fear you not ... so go...

...To hell, perhaps? Silent film star William Farnum, who kicked off the body count in *Curse*, reportedly had trouble remembering his lines. This may have been the reason the line is missing.

Also missing is the shot of Ananka's hand, which was supposed to be seen protruding from the dried swamp bed. In the film, we see her hand appear very slowly as the camera pans from a moving bulldozer down to the mud. The mud starts to move, and within seconds, Ananka's half-human hand pushes through the caked mire. In the script, her hand is already visible when the scene begins:

> FADE IN
>
> EXT. NEAR SWAMP SHORE — DAY — LONG SHOT ON WORKMEN engaged in clearing the swamps, working with wagons, wheelbarrows, bulldozers, etc.
>
> MED. FULL SHOT — ON A WORKMAN riding a bulldozer. He sends the vehicle rumbling through a section of partly dried swamp.
>
> MED. SHOT — SHOOTING TOWARD REAR OF BULLDOZER
>
> As it moves away from CAMERA, we see a peculiar object which the bulldozer has uncovered, sticking up from the loose earth in f.g. It is a shriveled old hand. The bulldozer turns and heads out of scene.
>
> MED. LONG SHOT — ANGLE TAKING IN OTHER WORKMEN AND EQUIPMENT IN B.G.
>
> The bulldozer turns and heads back in direction of hand. OVER SCENE we suddenly HEAR the DISTINCT CLANG OF A BELL.

Soon after Ananka's spectacular return to the land of the living, Big Joe is strolling through the swamp on his way home. It isn't long before he sees Ananka wandering through the swamp in a trance-like state. In the script, animals near the edge of the swamp are aware that something is in the air beside mosquitoes.

Unlike Peanuts and King from *The Mummy's Ghost*, the animals from *The Mummy's Curse* had their scenes deleted:

> *Suddenly from O.S. we HEAR an animal's CRY OF FRIGHT. CAMERA TURNS QUICKLY toward a meadow near the swamp edge where HORSES WHINNY in terror and run; DOGS BARK and slink away.*
>
> *MED. MOVING SHOT — ON BIG JOE walking along the swamp edge, lunch pail in hand, his coat slung over his arm. His day's work is done and he is on his way home to his shack, when OVER SCENE he HEARS a continuation of the DOGS BARKING and the HORSES NEIGHING from the previous scene. He turns toward the o.s. dog and calls:*
>
> BIG JOE: Hey! Pettipas! What'sa ma weet you? (*imitating dog barking*) An' you, Marrianne — Cheetah?...
>
> *He neighs like a horse, laughing at himself. Suddenly, his laughter dies as he sees something o.s.*
>
> *MED. FULL SHOT — FROM BIG JOE'S ANGLE — ON PRINCESS ANANKA walking along the swamp edge toward the setting sun.*

Of course, Ananka just popped in for a quick rinse in an undrained portion of the swamp and emerged looking as though she just spent two hours in a Beverly Hills beauty salon. The script continues with the kindly Big Joe taking her back to Bayou's version of Florence Nightingale, Tante Berthe. Unbeknownst to them, Abbas is nearby and overhears Big Joe's plan. So he quickly dashes back to the monastery with the news. That night, Ismail turns Kharis loose in the direction of Tante Berthe's in the hope of retrieving the ancient Princess. In the film, omitting these next three lines shortened the scene:

> *INT. MONASTARY CEREMONIAL ROOM — NIGHT — CLOSE SHOT — ON TANA LEAVES BREWING*
>
> *CAMERA TRUCKS BACK, DISCLOSING Ismail brewing the magic potion.*
>
> ISMAIL: (*without looking up*) Is Kharis ready?
>
> ABBAS VOICE O.S.: Yes, Master...
>
> ISMAIL: Then let him approach.
>
> *CAMERA TRUCKS BACK to a WIDER ANGLE as Abbas and the Mummy come forward.*

In the film, Kharis and Abbas approach Ismail exactly as the script suggests. This is a clue that the three missing lines of dialogue were filmed, then cut.

One can play all kinds of guessing games and scrutinize various scenes in question to determine if and what has been cut at the last minute. Like the above scene, those that have been shortened are much easier to decipher than scenes that have been deleted entirely. If one cares enough to follow along with a complete script, and rewind and fast-forward videotape, the clues are there. The next cut scene would be virtually impossible to detect unless it presented itself through publicity stills or within a script, simply because it is an entire scene that has been removed. It appears immediately following the fade-out in Tante Berthe's room when her body is discovered:

> BIG JOE: Poor Tante Berthe... She'sa dead ... and the girl, she'sa gone... What 'appen to her?
>
> *As Dr. Cooper turns to look at him, completely baffled by the unexpected turn of events, Big Joe moves to the sorrowful Ulysses and tries to comfort him.*
>
> FADE OUT
>
> FADE IN
>
> EXT. ENTRANCE TO BETTY'S TENT — DAY — MED. CLOSE SHOT
>
> *Walsh ENTERS SCENE, followed by Big Joe.*
>
> WALSH: (*calling*) Betty! (*then a little louder and more impatient*) Betty!!!!
>
> BETTY: (*coming out; trying to quiet him*) Shhh!...shhh!
>
> *She leads the two men away from the entrance of the tent. CAMERA PANS WITH THEM.*
>
> WALSH: (*impatiently*) What's going on here?
>
> BETTY: Dr. Cooper's inside with that girl...
>
> CLOSE SHOT — ON WALSH
>
> WALSH: (*irritated*) Will you tell me what I'm running ... an Engineering Company, or a charity hospital?
>
> BETTY: Please, Uncle Pat...
>
> GROUP SHOT — BETTY, WALSH AND BIG JOE
>
> BIG JOE: You theenk maybe perhap' Miss Walsh, I might talk to her...
>
> *He indicates.*
>
> BETTY: Oh, not now ... while the Doctor's there...
>
> BIG JOE: I bring her to Tante Berthe ... and Berthe is killed ... with funny marks on her throat. Maybe this girl she can tell us something...
>
> BETTY: You couldn't talk to her now ... I don't think the doctor would allow it...
>
> WALSH: (*now aggravated*) Will you forget about this girl ... and let's get down to business. I need you over at the office...
>
> BETTY: Just as soon as I talk to Dr. Cooper, I promise you I'll be right over...

WALSH: (*cutting in; dolefully*)I should have known better than to let that college professor and his...

BETTY: He has nothing to do with this, Uncle Pat... so don't blame him...

Just at this point, HALSEY ENTERS THE SCENE brightly.

HALSEY: Good morning, Betty... 'Morning Mr. Walsh... Big Joe...

BETTY: (*sweetly*) Good morning...

WALSH: (*takes on look*) He had nothing to do with it, huh? (*disgustedly*) Come on, Joe.

He EXITS.

BIG JOE: Maybe see her later... yes?

He shrugs and EXITS.

HALSEY: (*looking toward tent*) How is she?

BETTY: Dr. Cooper just says she's ill and suffering from exposure... Frankly, I think she's just as puzzled as we are...

From o.s. we HEAR DR. COOPER'S VOICE: (*calling*) Miss Walsh!

They turn, CAMERA PANS WITH THEM TO THE TENT ENTRANCE, as the doctor comes out.

CLOSE GROUP SHOT — BETTY, HALSEY, DR. COOPER

DR. COOPER: Until such time as I can find accommodations for her at the camp infirmary, do you think the young lady could remain here in your tent?

BETTY: Of course, Doctor... (*nervously*) The only thing is, I can't be with her all the time... I have work waiting at the office...

DR. COOPER: All she needs is rest and nourishment...

Suddenly, they HEAR ANANKA'S STIFLED SCREAM. The three look at each other, then RUSH into the tent.

INT. BETTY'S TENT — DAY — MED. CLOSE SHOT — ON ANANKA sitting up on the cot. Her face is terrified. Betty, Halsey and Dr. Cooper rush in.

ANANKA: What has happened to me?... I woke up — and everything was so strange.

In the film, the scene fades in with Ananka waking up inside Betty's tent. Dr. Cooper, Halsey and Betty rush in when they hear her panic. There is no evidence this missing scene was ever shot. In the scene, Dr. Cooper suggests that Ananka room with Betty in her tent. Yet, later on in the film, Ananka runs to Betty's tent while attempting to escape from Kharis and asks if she can stay with her. According to script time, the scene should have run a little under three minutes but would not have advanced the story. (That is, unless one is a hopeless romantic and would

5. The Mummy's Curse

prefer to watch the scenes that Halsey and Betty share together rather than watch a good Mummy murder. The attention they give each other turn Ananka into a third wheel.)

But Ananka will have her opportunity to prove who the more interesting character is. After all, she has over 3,000 years of life experience behind her. Betty has some very stiff competition. Betty may have taken a course in archaeology in college, big deal. Ananka has *lived* it! In this next scene, Ananka starts flaunting her knowledge to Halsey. As Ananka examines a piece of Mummy wrapping under Halsey's microscope, she tells the good doctor quite a bit more than he expected to hear. In the film, the wrapping is from Kharis, but in the script, the wrapping is her own:

> EXT. HALSEY'S LABORATORY TENT — WIDE ANGLE — DAY — MED. SHOT
>
> *Ananka seated at a small desk, upon which is piled a number of research books and many old Egyptian vases and pottery fragments, all pushed aside to make way for microscope and a series of slides. Behind her, the tent flap above the sidewall is rolled. The sun pours down upon her and the desk, flooding everything with a glaring light. She is wearing a very attractive frock of Betty's. Anyone seeing her, thus engaged, would never suspect that there was anything wrong with the girl. She is at the moment looking into the microscope, quickly making notations on a pad beside her, when Halsey ENTERS through the tent entrance. He sees her there in the glaring sun, stops in surprise and calls:*
>
> HALSEY: (*cheerfully*) Hello … What are you trying to do … develop a fine case of sun stroke?
>
> ANANKA: (*looking up*) Oh, good morning, Dr. Halsey… I hope you do not mind me working out here… I had one of the men move the desk. I love the sun…
>
> HALSEY: O.K. …but does it love you that much? Or will you be shining like a boiled crawfish in an hour or two?
>
> ANANKA: (*smiling sweetly to him*) I can never get too much of the sun… By the way, if you'll excuse my saying so … I think you're wrong about this Mummy cloth…
>
> *Halsey crosses up to her, rather amused.*
>
> HALSEY: You do, huh?
>
> CAMERA TRUCKS IN TO A CLOSE SHOT OF HALSEY AND THE GIRL
> *He stands by the desk where she is seated.*
>
> ANANKA: This cloth is not part of the Mummy wrapping of Kharis…
>
> *He looks down at her quickly, completely surprised — his mouth opens wide … this is something he never expected.*

> ANANKA (cont'd): (*rises and steps away from chair*) See for yourself, Dr. Halsey.
>
> *Halsey sits down — looks into microscope.*
>
> ANANKA (cont'd): Notice the lacy net-work of the linen strands. If you count them you will find that they number more than three hundred and forty-four to the square inch, making a fine soft tightly woven material — almost silk-like...
>
> *Halsey looks up at her amazed as she continues.*
>
> ANANKA (cont'd): No, Doctor, a man's cloth would be more loosely woven and of coarser material.
>
> *He looks back into microscope.*
>
> ANANKA (cont'd): This is the fabric in which a woman might be wrapped...
>
> *Halsey looks up again, almost startled.*
>
> HALSEY: Did you say a woman?
>
> ANANKA: Yes, Dr. Halsey... (*glibly, almost mechanically*). I'd say a woman of royal blood ... of the Dynasty of King Amenophis... In fact, this piece was part of the shroud of the King's own daughter. The Princess Ananka...
>
> *Halsey gets up, stares at the girl.*
>
> HALSEY: How do you know all that?
>
> ANANKA: (*completely at a loss to explain*) I don't know how...

Later in the script, there is yet another lengthy scene between Halsey and Betty that never made it to the final print. In the film, Ananka falls into another trance-like state after seeing Ismail. She begins to call for Kharis until Halsey shakes her awake. In the script, the two are joined by Betty:

> HALSEY: What are you saying?
>
> *He shakes her so violently that Ananka suddenly snaps out of it.*
>
> ANANKA: I'm sorry... I don't know what possessed me ... I–
>
> HALSEY: What did you mean by calling Kharis?
>
> *He is still holding her by the shoulders.*
>
> ANANKA: Did I?
>
> *Just at this moment, we HEAR:*
>
> BETTY'S VOICE O.S.: Good morning...
>
> CAMERA TRUCKS BACK TO WIDER ANGLE *as Betty ENTERS THE SCENE. Halsey, unaware of it, is still holding Ananka by the shoulders close to him. Betty's eyes wander from the girl to Halsey and back again... Getting no immediate response, she calls to them.*

5. The Mummy's Curse

BETTY: (*meaningfully*) I hope I'm not intruding.

For the first time Halsey realizes his position.

HALSEY: (*quick dropping his hands*) Our young friend here has had another... (*gropes for a word*) spell...

Strangely, Betty is not too sympathetic ... there may be indications of jealousy.

BETTY: That's too bad...

ANANKA: Please forgive me, I can't understand...

CLOSE SHOT — ON ISMAIL — AT FLAP OF HIS TENT

He edges back as he hears:

HALSEY'S VOICE O.S.: Would you mind taking her over to Dr. Cooper's, Betty?

BETTY'S VOICE O.S.: Yes — I'll be glad to.

MED. CLOSE SHOT — ON HALSEY, BETTY AND ANANKA

ANANKA: (*to Betty*) No thanks ... But if you have no objection, I would rather go back to the tent with you ... I....

BETTY: If you need medical attention, Dr. Cooper...

ANANKA: (*cutting politely*) No ... I'm all right, really... It's just that I'm tired and need a little rest...

BETTY: (*starting toward tent*) Whatever you say...

HALSEY: See you later, Betty...

He watches the two EXIT FROM SCENE, then stands there, unable to figure out this strange creature ... her mysterious movements, her sudden attraction for Ismail... And it all doesn't seem to add up to anything but ... perplexity. Then he EXITS toward his tent. CAMERA SWINGS OVER to Ismail looking out of his tent flap and DOLLIES IN to a CLOSE SHOT of him. He glances about, then starts out.

FADE OUT

Again, this scene would only have contributed to the love interest, with a dash of jealousy for good measure.

After the fade-in, both script and film pick up where Ismail has another shot at instructing Kharis where to find Ananka. Again, Kharis comes close, but is eluded by his loved one. The Mummy does, however, strangle the life from Dr. Cooper, whose poor judgment in chivalry costs him his life. While attempting to protect Ananka, he attacks the advancing Mummy with a chair. What differentiates the film from the script is the good doctor's infirmary. In the script it is a building, not a tent. It also has enough glass in its construction to allow Kharis to make a spectacular, if not noisy, entrance. This certainly has to be an error, since in the script, it is clearly indicated that the scene should take place inside Dr. Cooper's tent:

> Dr. Cooper: You wait here. I'll get you something to quiet your nerves.
>
> *MED. CLOSE SHOT— ON THE TWO*
>
> *The Doctor turns to leave. Ananka grabs his arm.*
>
> Ananka: (*imploringly*) Please don't go— don't leave me–Please don't—
>
> *Then she tenses, as we HEAR the now familiar SOUND of the Mummy dragging his lame foot behind him, from outside.*
>
> Ananka: Listen, do you hear?
>
> *The Doctor immediately goes to the door, CAMERA TRUCKS BACK TO A MED. SHOT— TAKING IN THE ENTRANCE DOOR, as he opens it, we HEAR the approaching SOUND of the Mummy increase. The Doctor looks out, then seems to back away, and as he does, we suddenly HEAR a crash and the glass door opposite, that leads to the infirmary, falls to pieces as the Mummy ENTERS through this door... The girl, frightened, backs toward the door to which the Doctor had gone. The Doctor whirls around to face the Mummy. Protectively, he stands between the girl and the Mummy. Before he can escape, the Mummy reaches out and grabs him.*
>
> *EXT. CONSTRUCTION CAMP— NIGHT— MED. SHOT at the infirmary. Ananka, dressed in her white robe, RUNS OUT of the office, disappearing toward the swamp... The Mummy comes out and glancing about, lumbers away in another direction.*

The Mummy has claimed another victim. And again, the difference between script and film is great. In the film, it's Dr. Cooper's heroics that do him in. When he attempts to clobber Kharis with a chair, our Mummy simply perceives this as a blatant act of aggression and is forced to defend himself. In the script, Cooper attempts to run from the aggressor when Kharis grabs him. If this had in fact happened, Kharis probably would have let him off the hook and just walked off with the heroine.

Ananka seems to have won the battle, but will she win the war? Soon, newspapers are full of stories about the killings. Unlike *The Mummy's Tomb*, where headlines were constantly popping up to the cues of Hans J. Salter, *The Mummy's Curse* only had one, and it never made it to the film:

> FADE IN
>
> *INT. WALSH'S OFFICE— DAY— OF HEADLINES OF THE BAYOU TIMES reading: "MYSTERY SWAMP KILLINGS BAFFLE POLICE."*
>
> *CAMERA PULLS BACK from newspaper to MED. SHOT, TAKING IN Walsh at his desk, the newspaper in his hand. Betty is seated at her desk, watching silently. Walsh gets up and begins pacing the floor irritably, then whirls as Halsey opens the door and steps inside, followed by Ismail.*
>
> Halsey: You wish to see me?

5. The Mummy's Curse

> WALSH: Not with any pleasure, young man.
>
> BETTY: Please — Uncle Pat...
>
> *Halsey moves toward Walsh, saying:*
>
> HALSEY: That's frank — if not cordial.
>
> *CAMERA DOLLIES IN to a CLOSE TWO SHOT on Halsey and Walsh, who holds out the paper for Halsey to see.*
>
> WALSH: I suppose you've seen the morning paper — about Dr. Cooper being killed? — and that girl's strange disappearance?

Other than the headline, the first four lines of dialogue were also removed. In the film, the scene begins with Halsey already in the office and Walsh asking if he's seen the morning paper. Walsh insists there were no problems until Halsey and Ismail arrived. It makes you wonder where Walsh has been through this entire project. Or perhaps it's his nature to behave like an over-protective uncle when his niece has eyes for the local bone digger. In any event, the debate between Walsh and Halsey escalates. In the film, Walsh storms out of his office to send a telegram to the Scripps Museum, insisting that Halsey's permit be revoked. But in the script, before exiting:

> WALSH: (*to Halsey, as he crosses*) Good day to you, Dr. Halsey. That's all I wanted to say.
>
> *MED. SHOT — ON GROUP — OVERLAPPING WALSH'S DIALOGUE*
>
> *As he turns to EXIT, Halsey steps after him.*
>
> HALSEY: But that isn't all I have to say to you, Mr. Walsh.
>
> BETTY: (*pleading*) Please, Jim–
>
> *Halsey hesitates and Walsh continues on across the room and EXITS. Then, as Big Joe and Ismail move forward, CAMERA DOLLIES IN to a MED. CLOSE SHOT on group.*

Convinced that the strange girl can lead this ambitious group to Kharis, they take to the swamp. A fair idea, but how many times in the history of horror do we see groups disperse and individuals take off alone? In this instance, it is Big Joe who has the misfortune of crossing paths with the marauding Mummy. However, the script has different plans for the demise of Big Joe:

> *EXT. SWAMP — NIGHT — CLOSE MOVING SHOT — ON BIG JOE poling the swamp water in a dugout. With a smile of confidence on his face, he is a colorful, romantic figure as he stands, tall and unafraid, making his way through those eerie surroundings. He suddenly looks o.s.*
>
> *MED. LONG SHOT — FROM BIG JOE'S ANGLE — ON ANANKA running along shore of swamp.*

> *MED. CLOSE SHOT — ON BIG JOE*
>
> BIG JOE: (*waving o.s. and calling*) Wait ... wait...
>
> *LONG SHOT — ON ANANKA SHOWING the girl flitting through the dark, primeval swampland like a disembodied spirit.*
>
> *CLOSE MOVING SHOT — ON BIG JOE seeing the girl. He starts to pole faster, and as he does CAMERA PANS from him to the swampland behind him, catching in a MED. SHOT, the menacing form of the Mummy approaching along the shore.*
>
> *MED. SHOT — CENTERING ON A HUGE OLD SWAMP ASH OR CYPRESS TREE — AT EDGE OF SWAMP as Ananka breathlessly runs INTO SCENE, and looks back, sees herself pursued by Big Joe o.s. She climbs around and hides behind the trunk of this tree. She has hardly concealed herself when Big Joe poles his way INTO SCENE, nosing his dugout right in amidst the roots of the tree, while he scans in every direction for a sight of the girl. He can't figure it out.*
>
> BIG JOE: (*scratching his head*) That'sa funny...
>
> *He puts the pole across his dugout and looks to see what gives around the tree trunk. His back is to Camera.*
>
> *MED. SHOT — ON THE MUMMY as he moves INTO SCENE behind huge tree, then steps into the shallow water at the edge of the swamp and splashes to Big Joe in dugout, CAMERA PANNING with him. Big Joe whirls, and the gasp dies on his lips as the Mummy reaches out and grabs him.*
>
> *MED. SHOT — FROM A WIDE ANGLE*
>
> *Ananka, on the other side of the tree trunk, seeing what has happened, starts to run and splash away as fast as she can, in the opposite direction.*
>
> *MED SHOT — AT FOOT OF TREE*
>
> *We see the Mummy crushing the life out of the o.s. Big Joe in the stern of his dugout. Then, with scarcely a glance at his victim, the Mummy continues to make his way through the swamps in the direction taken by Ananka.*

The above scene underwent many changes before finally being filmed. The close moving shot of Big Joe poling in his dugout, completely unaware that the Mummy is advancing behind him, is a great touch. (The way Big Joe's death scene was handled in the film is also sufficiently effective.) It's too bad a scene of Kharis approaching behind his victim in the swamp wasn't utilized.

In the script, it's only a few pages later when Halsey discovers Big Joe's body, another scene that was written but not filmed:

> *EXT. SWAMP — NIGHT — MED. FULL SHOT — ON HALSEY making his way through the swampland, a lighted torch in his hand. He reaches f.g., and glances about, suddenly stares ahead in amazement.*

5. The Mummy's Curse 123

> *MED. SHOT— FROM HALSEY'S ANGLE— ON THE LIFELESS BODY OF BIG JOE huddled in a grotesque position in the stern of his dugout, the pole floating beside him. The light from Halsey's torch floods the scene. Halsey ENTERS SCENE and hurries to the dugout where he props up the torch and begins examining Big Joe.*
>
> *CLOSE SHOT— ON HALSEY examining Big Joe's body o.s., by the flickering light of the torch. He reaches down and feels Big Joe's throat, then picks up a small piece of tattered wrapping from the Mummy, which he holds up, his eyes widening understandingly. He puts the wrapping in his pocket; then, picking up an old blanket from the bottom of the dugout, starts putting it over Big Joe.*
>
> *MED. SHOT— OVERLAPPING ACTION OF ABOVE SCENE*
>
> *Halsey finishes covering Big Joe's body with the blanket; then, putting the torch in the bow of the dugout, he picks up the pole, gets into the boat and starts poling through the swamp in the general direction of the camp.*

In another draft of this script, Halsey calls out for Big Joe as the Mummy is strangling him, which indicates that Halsey comes a lot closer to a confrontation with the Mummy than he thinks:

> *MED. SHOT— AT FOOT OF TREE*
>
> *We SEE the Mummy crushing the life out of the o.s. Big Joe, in the stern of his dugout. From the distance we HEAR:*
>
> HALSEY'S VOICE (*o.s.*): (*calling*) Joe ... Big Joe!... re-echoing through the swampland.
>
> *The Mummy paying no attention to the call, and with scarcely a glance at his victim, continues to make his way through the swamp in the direction in which the girl has taken.*
>
> *MED. FULL SHOT— ON ANANKA*
>
> *She runs frantically away from CAMERA into swampland. She glances fearfully back; then, as she disappears, a menacing figure of the Mummy lumbers through and EXITS through SCENE after her. Then, we HEAR Halsey's VOICE again, CALLING from o.s., this time closer:*
>
> HALSEY'S VOICE: Joe— where are you?
>
> *CAMERA SWINGS OVER to PICK UP Jim Halsey making his way through swampland, a lighted torch in his hand. He reaches foreground and glancing about suddenly sees Joe's body o.s.*

Out of the two scripted versions of this scene, and the version which was filmed, for a total of three altogether, the scene described above is the best. We know Kharis hears Halsey calling for Big Joe, but we don't know how he will react.

Furthermore, knowing that Halsey is within spitting distance of the Mummy would have created much more suspense. What would Halsey have done if he actually saw the Mummy next to Big Joe's body, and vice versa? After all, for nearly an hour we've heard Halsey talk a good game, but he never really has a confrontation with Kharis. He always finds himself a couple of schleps behind him.

Meanwhile, back at camp, Ananka safely makes it back to Betty's tent to seek temporary refuge. Needless to say, Kharis is not far behind. In the script, the Mummy barges in and has a very rough confrontation with Betty before whisking Ananka into the night. Perhaps this was a little too violent for the censors at the Breen office. When the Mummy enters the tent in the version that was filmed, he just gives Betty a quick glance before simply passing her by on his way to the sleeping Ananka. This is further proof that if Dr. Cooper had minded his own business, he might have been around for the closing credits. The original script reads:

> *INT. BETTY'S TENT — NIGHT — MED. CLOSE SHOT ON BETTY*
>
> *As she finishes tying the tent flap, then turns and crosses to Ananka, CAMERA PANNING WITH HER. Ananka stands underneath a lantern, a pathetic, distraught looking creature.*
>
> BETTY: Why did you run away after Dr. Cooper was killed — and why are you afraid of the darkness?
>
> ANANKA: (*pathetically*) I don't know. (*then pleadingly*) If you'd only help me find myself.
>
> *Ananka sits down on the cot, huddled like a frightened animal, CAMERA DOLLIES IN TO CLOSE SHOT.*
>
> ANANKA (cont'd): I remember being brought here to this tent — and I was very happy. Then — he came to take me away.
>
> *CLOSE SHOT — ON BETTY*
>
> *She stares toward Ananka in amazement.*
>
> BETTY: Who — who came to take you away?
>
> *MED. CLOSE SHOT — ON ANANKA as Betty steps INTO SCENE with her.*
>
> ANANKA: (*emotionally*) The High Priest of Arkam. (*almost whimpering*) Three thousand years ago I died — a cursed death.
>
> *Betty stares toward Ananka in frightened wonderment.*
>
> ANANKA (cont'd): He said — I am the reincarnated spirit of the Princess Ananka. Now he has come to take me back — to Kharis —
>
> BETTY: (*suddenly understanding*) Kharis — the Mummy?
>
> *Ananka jumps to her feet, clinging to Betty's arm.*
>
> ANANKA: But it's not true — I'm not —
>
> *Ananka's words are halted by the sudden SOUND of the tent tearing and both whirl in terror.*

5. The Mummy's Curse

> *MED. CLOSE SHOT— REVERSE ANGLE— ON KHARIS the Mummy as he finishes tearing the side of the tent and steps inside.*
>
> *MED. SHOT— ON TENT INT.— OVERLAPPING ACTION OF ABOVE SCENE as the Mummy moves forward toward the two girls, Betty lets out a horrified gasp, but Ananka, with a little moan, collapses on the cot. The Mummy moves toward Ananka, and as Betty turns to run, he pushes her aside with such force that she falls to the tent floor, dazed. CAMERA DOLLIES INTO CLOSE SHOT as the Mummy picks up the inert body of Ananka and turning, heads back across the tent.*

Again, as is the case with Dr. Cooper, Betty is only attempting to escape when Kharis mercilessly tosses her aside. In the film, Betty does not attempt to escape, she merely recoils with fright after Kharis enters the tent. In the film, Kharis' attitude and disposition can probably best be compared to a swarm of bees. If you don't provoke them, there is usually no great danger. On the other hand, if you antagonize them, you'd better run.

In the script, Kharis is exceptionally more vicious. But in the film, his persona falls somewhere between Ismail, who is probably the most passive High Priest in the series, and Abbas, who closely resembles something one would expect to find under a wet rock. Whatever metaphor one wishes to use to describe Abbas, from this point on, he is the film's primary heavy, while Kharis' final moments within the script indicate a sympathetic side we really never see in the film. It's even a slight reminder of Karloff's Frankenstein Monster.

When Abbas shows up after quietly observing this entire escapade from a safe distance, he feigns concern to Betty and promises to lead her to Halsey. The somewhat gullible Betty trusts the secret acolyte, and together they head into the swamps:

> *MED. CLOSE SHOT— ON ABBAS, BETTY AND GOOBIE*
>
> BETTY: *(relieved)* Thank you, Abbas. *(then to Goobie)* I'll be back before long, Goobie. Don't say anything to alarm my uncle.
>
> *Goobie nods in open-mouthed awe and shakes his head as Betty turns and follows Abbas away from the camp, CAMERA PANNING WITH THEM.*

When Halsey shows up, once again a day late and a buck short, he finds Goobie underneath Betty's collapsed tent. The script indicates that just as Halsey exits the boat, Big Joe's covered body can be seen inside it. After careful scrutiny of Universal's crystal clear home video release of *The Mummy's Curse*, there *does* seem to be something covered in a blanket inside the boat. In the film, Halsey takes a curious pause for a moment to look inside before briskly walking off to the campsite. This would have to conclude that a scene of Halsey discovering Big Joe's body *was* definitely filmed and then deleted prior to the film's release.

In the script, when Halsey arrives at the campsite, he is approached by Goobie, who cues him in on the ruckus. Even Goobie, the limited laborer, knows what's going on before Halsey does:

> GOOBIE: Massah Halsey — de's jes gone lookin' fo' yo'!
> HALSEY: What are you talking about, Goobie? Who's looking for me — and where is Miss Walsh?
> GOOBIE: (*excitedly*) Dat's wha' I's tryin' t' 'splain! Dem feller, Abbas — take de boss' niece up do ol' road into de swamps to fin' yo' after she say de Mummy wreck' de tent and carry 'way de odder girl!!
> *Halsey reacts in grim understanding to this.*
> HALSEY: (*grimly*) I'm going after them. Wake up Walsh and tell him to follow ... Betty's probably in great danger.

Halsey's instructions contradict those of Betty, who did not wish to upset her uncle. At least Halsey is able to deduce that Betty is in danger. Having her go off alone through the swamp with Abbas is closely akin to having her go off with one of the FBI's ten most wanted. In any event, he is off like a prom dress to Betty's rescue:

> *INT. CEREMONIAL ROOM — NIGHT — MED. FULL SHOT as Ismail, dressed in his priestly robes, stands between the two mummy cases, as though in last minute inspection. The cases are on the floor ready for their destine occupants.*
> ISMAIL: (*calling o.s.*) Abbas!
> *He pushes both mummy cases a little further apart and makes his way toward the CAMERA as if surprised that his call is not answered.*
> ISMAIL: (*in sterner fashion*) Abbas!!
> *Again receiving no reply, he looks off greatly surprised. As he crosses the Ceremonial Room, he stops to look into the brazier, turns it over, and finds it is empty. He kneels to get box, finds tana leaves and puts them on to brew. As CAMERA DOLLIES into MED. CLOSE SHOT.*
> ISMAIL (*cont'd*): (*greatly upset*) Abbas!!!
> *Receiving no response, he starts hurrying OUT toward door, which leads toward the Monk's wing. CAMERA PANS WITH HIM AND HOLDS ON THE HEAVY DOOR as he EXITS FROM SCENE...*
> *As it holds, we suddenly HEAR from the opposite direction the familiar dragging SOUND of someone APPROACHING, CAMERA PANS OVER TO THE OPPOSITE SIDE, picks up the Mummy coming in the main entrance, still holding the girl, Ananka in his arms.*
> *MED. CLOSE SHOT — ON MUMMY HOLDING THE LIMP FORM OF ANANKA as he places her in one of the cases, he looks about as if seeking the High Priest Ismail, but neither the High Priest nor his disciple Abbas are*

5. The Mummy's Curse 127

there. He stands looking down upon this girl who, still mortal and alive cannot become his bride until she has been mummified like himself. Like a helpless automation, he looks about, not knowing what to do without his mentor, the High Priest. He leans over the girl.

CLOSE SHOT — ON ANANKA — SHOOTING DOWN UPON HER

The Mummy, leaning over her INTO THE PICTURE. Slowly she opens her eyes and then quickly whispers:

ANANKA: Kharis ... I am tired ... (*wearily*) Take me with you ... so that I may know ... rest....

She closes her eyes again, as though in sleep. CAMERA TRUCKS BACK STILL TILTED DOWN, as Kharis pulls himself up to his full height and looking around starts searching frantically for Ismail. CAMERA PANS him out a side door.

EXT. PATH NEAR MONASTERY — NIGHT — MED. SHOT — ON ABBAS AND BETTY as they hurry along the path and up to Monastery steps, CAMERA PANNING WITH THEM. Abbas starts up and Betty glances about her somewhat uneasily.

MED. CLOSE SHOT — ON THE TWO

BETTY: (*uneasily*) Why should Dr. Halsey be waiting here — in this old ruin?

ABBAS: (*with dignity*) If you wish to turn back —

Betty eyes the calm Abbas for a moment, then shakes her head, and turning starts up steps.

Abbas conceals his satisfaction and walks up the steps with Betty. CAMERA PANS WITH THEM.

EXT. MONASTERY ENTRANCE — NIGHT — MED. FULL SHOT — ON MUMMY as he comes out of the monastery apparently still looking for Ismail. He glances about, then makes his way around corner of building.

EXT. PATH NEAR MONASTERY STEPS — MED. FULL SHOT — ON HALSEY as he hurries in from b.g. and CAMERA PANS WITH HIM up to the steps where he halts in amazement and glances about. Then, as he glances up the steps, his eyes widen.

LONG SHOT — REVERSE ANGLE — SHOOTING UP MONASTERY STEPS showing Abbas and Betty disappearing from view.

MED. CLOSE SHOT — ON HALSEY as he takes out his revolver and makes sure it is in working condition, then puts out the torch and hurries up the steps.

INT. CEREMONIAL ROOM — NIGHT — MED. FULL SHOT as the door opens and Abbas ENTERS with the still uneasy Betty. He leads the way across the room and Betty halts in amazement as she sees the two mummy cases, *ceremonial paraphernalia and the brazier to brew the tana leaves. She glances toward the now smugly smiling Abbas, and she steps to the mummy cases, and slowly her eyes go to the form of Ananka inside. CAMERA DOLLIES slowly in to a MED. CLOSE SHOT on Betty and Abbas. Betty stares down in amazement at Ananka in the mummy case.*

MED. CLOSE SHOT— HER ANGLE— ON ANANKA

Apparently in the state of trance in the mummy case, her long hair around her beautiful face.

MED. CLOSE SHOT— ON BETTY AND ABBAS

Slowly Betty glances up towards Abbas, and her eyes widen understandingly.

BETTY: (*awed*) Now I understand why she said she died three thousand years ago. She's— she's Princess Ananka—

ABBAS: (*quietly*) The bride of Kharis... (then glancing down on Ananka in the case) ...In a fraction of life's moment Ismail will lift her mortal state— she will be sealed in this case— and, with Kharis, sent to Egypt, there to be embraced by the sands of the past!

BETTY: (*amazed*) Ismail?

ABBAS: Yes ... The High Priest of Arkam. I am his humble assistant.

BETTY: (*glancing somewhat fearfully about*) ...Where is Dr. Halsey? You told me he was here.

ABBAS: (*suggestively*) This monastery has been abandoned for nearly 100 years. Dr. Halsey has no idea of its existence.

Betty's eyes widen at Abbas' words; as Abbas moves toward her she recoils. Both halt at Ismail's calm voice o.s.

ISMAIL'S VOICE: You have nothing to fear, Miss Walsh.

MED. SHOT— ON ISMAIL

Standing inside the back doorway of the Ceremonial Room. His eyes gleam contemptuously as he moves across to Abbas and the frightened Betty, CAMERA PANNING WITH THEM.

ISMAIL: (*to Betty*) You will be allowed to return to the camp— on your promise to keep silent about what you have seen here!

In the script, Ismail is portrayed far more amiably than in the film. This is not behavior becoming a High Priest. Needless to say, Mummy experts familiar with the film know that Betty cannot be permitted to return to camp. She knows too much. Also in the script, Abbas actually goes through the trouble of explaining to her what the divine plan is for Kharis and Ananka, as if his priestly vows still meant something to this slimeball. And Betty, the trusting soul, still believes her Prince Charming, Halsey, is waiting for her in this abandoned monastery. By the time Abbas reveals what he really has up his sleeve, it's too late. There's nowhere to run until Ismail shows up and guarantees her safety back to camp if she keep mum, no pun intended, about the whole affair.

5. The Mummy's Curse

However, Abbas must pay the penalty for breaking his priestly vows. Taking issue with Ismail's threats, Abbas polishes him off just as Halsey shows up. But with all this human drama unfolding, what about poor Kharis? The Mummy races, figuratively of course, through the entire film, after the only woman he has ever loved. How does Ananka react? She flees at the very sight of him. Eventually, Kharis wins her over again. She sympathetically begs him to take her with him. These are words poor Kharis has waited over 3,000 years to hear. If that isn't enough, the poor Mummy searches like a lost dog for its master. But to no avail, Ismail, the only High Priest to maintain his loyalty to Kharis, has been murdered. Ironically, Abbas, his very own acolyte, killed him.

The final scene in the script differs greatly from the film:

> *MED. CLOSE SHOT— ON THE MUMMY as he moves into room, CAMERA PANNING WITH HIM. He halts at table where brew is steaming and sees the partly concealed body of Ismail on the floor. He becomes almost human in his grief, and then picking up the hot steaming brazier, drinks all of its contents, and as he drops the heavy utensil to the floor, CAMERA DOLLIES IN, TAKING IN Abbas, the terrified Betty and Halsey sprawled out on the floor. Abbas, who is moving toward Betty, halts at the sound of the brazier dropping. Then as the girl runs to Halsey's side, Abbas whirls and tries to escape from the enraged Mummy who moves toward him.*

In the film, Ismail does not give Betty a pardon before he is knifed to death. We do not hear Ananka ask Kharis if she can go with him, and we do not see the Mummy's sympathetic side. But in the film's closing scenes, Kharis is permitted to actually play the hero. For a moment as Halsey and Abbas duke it out, Abbas gets the best of Halsey and is about to finish him off. Abbas raises a metal torch and is about to bring it down on Halsey's skull when suddenly from behind Kharis stops him. The enraged Mummy catches on much faster to Abbas' treachery than Betty did, and pursues him through the monastery, eventually trapping him in one of the chambers. Using all his strength, Kharis crashes through a locked door, which brings the ceiling down, burying both of them under tons of stone. Soon after, Walsh arrives. In the film, he never does believe the goings-on in the swamp. But in the script, he is confronted with the truth:

> *As Halsey nods, his arm tightens around Betty. Walsh glances down toward Ismail o.s.*
>
> **WALSH:** (*perplexed*) Who's this?
>
> *CLOSE SHOT— ON WALSH, BETTY AND HALSEY*
>
> **HALSEY:** That's Dr. Ismail Farouk — my trusted assistant who happened to be the High Priest intent on stealing the mummies. (*then to Betty*) Where's the girl — Ananka?
>
> *Betty, without a word, turns and crosses to the mummy cases followed by*

Halsey and Walsh. CAMERA PANS WITH THEM, and they halt at the cases. They glance down inside and Halsey exclaims in amazement:

HALSEY: Look — here.

As all glance down at the case and their eyes widen, CLOSE SHOT — ON PRINCESS ANANKA IN THE MUMMY CASE

She has gone through a metamorphosis and has returned to the mummy state of an old decrepit hag.

MED. CLOSE SHOT — ON GROUP around mummy case. Halsey steps forward and puts the lid on the case and then turns to the others.

HALSEY: (*with a sigh of relief*) I never thought I'd get her ... (*then with genuine admiration*) And in such beautiful condition...

WALSH: I never would have believed it ... if I hadn't seen it with my own eyes...

Halsey closes the lid of the mummy case. CAMERA HOLDS ON WALSH, as he shakes his head in bewilderment.

CLOSE SHOT — ON MUMMY CASE as Halsey finishes fastening it ... CAMERA PANS TO THE OTHER MUMMY CASE, standing beside it empty, we HEAR:

HALSEY (*o.s.*): Now all we've got to do is put a crew of men to work digging Kharis out of the rubble and cart them both down to camp.

CAMERA PANS OVER TO TAKE IN HALSEY AND BETTY, as he puts his arm around her and starts walking with her toward entrance door.

HALSEY: (*smiling at Betty*) Well, the Scripps Museum should be satisfied...

BETTY (*smiling back*): And I hope you will be too...

HALSEY: (*noncommittal*) In a way, yes...

Betty looks up at him.

HALSEY (*cont'd*): After we're married ... I'd like to do some work in Yucatan...

BETTY: (*suspiciously*) More mummies?

HALSEY: Oh no ... Hidden temples...

BETTY: And do they kill people in them?

HALSEY: (*smiling at her*) No ... The ancient Mayans enjoyed a highly cultured civilization.

The rest is lost ... as they walk PAST CAMERA

WIPE TO EXT. MONASTERY STEPS — NIGHT — MED. FULL SHOT fascinatingly highlighted by the last rays of the fading moon. Halsey, Betty and party ENTER SCENE and start down the temple steps, CAMERA PANS WITH THEM

FADE OUT

"THE END"

5. The Mummy's Curse

It was inevitable that this closing scene be changed since a great deal of the romance between Halsey and Betty was deleted. In the film, there is no mention whatsoever of marriage between the two. Had all their scenes of making goo-goo eyes at each other remained, the script's finale might have been more justifiable. But what about Kharis, the Mummy? *The Mummy's Curse* was the *coup de grace* of the series and yet his demise was certainly the least destructive of the four films. After all, one has to assume if old Kharis could live though a roaring holocaust twice, and stay buried underneath a swamp for 25 years, certainly a few boulders from a decrepit monastery wouldn't keep him down. Unfortunately, his fate was in hands greater than that of the almighty Amon-Ra—studio executives.

Less than two years after the release of *The Mummy's Curse*, the studio was under new management. Along with the end of World War II came less need for escapist fare. The days of B Westerns, serials and, yes, horror films were numbered. The new regime was spearheaded by Leo Spitz, former president of RKO, and by former 20th Century–Fox executive William Goetz. They guaranteed, among other decrees, that no film was to run under 70 minutes. This applied to the majority of Universal's product, including most of the beloved horror flicks. Although production of this type of entertainment ceased, the monsters would soon be leased out to Jack Broder's Realart Pictures, a studio known more for borrowing other studios' work, changing the logos and distributing them back out to theaters for reissue during the late '40s and early '50s. By 1957, these films were making their debut on a brand new medium, television. They were winning over an entirely new generation of fans who would grow up with these now legendary heroes of folklore. Magazines such as Warren Publishing's *Famous Monsters of Filmland* were soon hitting the newsstands, thrilling youngsters with the re-telling of these classics, accompanied by enticing stills of their favorite monsters.

Meanwhile, in England, Hammer Films produced a slick series of Technicolor remakes of the old monsters, starring new horror sensations Peter Cushing and Christopher Lee. The best of the bunch was *The Mummy* in 1959. A couple of completely unrelated Mummy films followed, such as *Curse of the Mummy's Tomb* in 1964.

Others have tried to follow in Universal's footsteps by taking a crack at Mummy films, but they were never able to capture the atmosphere and all-around fun that the Universal series was able to provide.

Following are a few additional noteworthy facts from the *Mummy's Curse* script that were changed before the final release print:

- Abbas uses a knife instead of a torch to attack Halsey.
- Halsey is not knocked down. Abbas is the one temporarily knocked out cold.
- We never see Halsey's face scratched and bloodied from the fight with Abbas.
- The remainder of the fight scenes have Abbas giving Halsey a terrific beating.
- Betty's line from the script, "Now I understand why she said she died three thousand years ago. She's—she's the Princess Ananka," was actually spoken by Halsey.

- Abbas had a line in the script, "Ismail will lift her from her mortal state — she will be sealed in this case — and, with Kharis, sent to Egypt, there to be embraced by the sands of the past." In the film, the line was changed to, "The Princess Ananka shall be lifted from her mortal state — and sealed in this case…" and was actually spoken by Ismail.

6

The Heroes Who Saved the Day

Dick Foran

Steve Banning in *The Mummy's Hand* and *The Mummy's Tomb*

Dick Foran was the original singing cowboy, a major Saturday matinee draw and the quintessential good guy whose fan mail poured in with every picture he made.

He was born John Nicholas Foran on June 18, 1910, in Flemington, New Jersey, the son of former Senator and Mrs. Arthur F. Foran. He majored in Geology while attending Princeton University, where he also excelled as an athlete. He played baseball, football, hockey and lacrosse and was a member of the track team. During summer vacations, he was an able-bodied seaman on freighters, traveling to many South American countries and the West Indies. Dick expressed interest in acting but, curiously, never really considered it as a career.

After leaving Princeton, Dick was offered a professional football contract, but he turned it down. Instead, always one to prefer the outdoors, he worked on a Flemington farm owned by his father. Then he and his baritone voice studied music at the Leibling Studio in New York. This afforded him the opportunity to sing on live radio. He started his own orchestra but, due to a lack of gigs, had to disband it.

His next job was quite different. For whatever the reason, Dick became a special

Wallace Ford (left) and Dick Foran (right).

investigator for the Pennsylvania Railroad. This was the job that eventually led him to Hollywood. He met songwriter Lew Brown, who said he could get him a screen test. Lew talked Nick into it. Dick interviewed at Fox Studios with Winfield Sheehan. Then came the screen test. Before long, he was signed to a contract and given his first role. Dick's film debut came in 1934 under the name Nick Foran, in *Stand Up and Cheer* with Shirley Temple. He was an instant hit. The women went wild, despite the grime which covered his face in the film.

Dick appeared in several other Fox offerings such as *Change of Heart*, *Lottery Lover* and *One More Spring*. He even bounced from MGM and Paramount before signing a long-term contract with Warner Bros. in 1935.

He played his guitar, rode his horse and became quite comfortable around the endless miles of studio back lot, which in those days still very closely resembled the old West. A long, happy trail of Westerns would soon follow. Coupled with his guitar and baritone singing voice, Dick became one of Hollywood's first singing cowboys, kind of a strange occupation for a Jersey boy.

According to Dick's Fox Studio biography, "I'm amazed at the popularity of these so-called horse operas. Judging from my fan mail, adults are regular patrons as well as children. About fifty per cent of the letters come from men and women who prefer red-blooded action in their entertainment. It's a great audience to play

6. The Heroes Who Saved the Day

to, because if they think you're good, they say so. If they don't, they're just as quick to let you know about that, too."

By the time Dick's contract with Fox ended, producer Bryan Foy had seen much of Dick's work and asked the Western star to make a screen test. Just as at Fox, Dick was immediately signed to a long-term contract with Warner Bros., where he changed his name from Nick to Dick. Here he made nearly 40 films during the remainder of the '30s, opposite such esteemed stars as Humphrey Bogart and Bette Davis.

Then in 1939, Dick signed with Universal. Suddenly he found himself sort of an actor's version of a jack-of-all-trades. Between 1939 and 1942, Universal featured Dick in comedies such as *In the Navy*, *Keep 'Em Flying* and *Ride 'Em Cowboy*, all with Abbott and Costello. In *Cowboy*, Dick portrayed, of all things, a phony but likable cowboy named Bronco Bob Mitchell, who eventually wins the heart of Anne Gwynne. *My Little Chickadee* starred W.C. Fields and Mae West, and featured Dick as one of Miss West's gentleman suitors. He was featured in the Andrews Sisters musical *Private Buckaroo*, Westerns, Western serials like *Winners of the West* and *Riders of Death Valley* with Buck Jones, Noah Beery, Jr., and Leo Carrillo, and thrillers such as *The House of the Seven Gables* with Vincent Price and George Sanders, *Horror Island* with Peggy Moran and, of course, *The Mummy's Hand* and *The Mummy's Tomb* with his good buddy, Lon Chaney, Jr.

They were a tight bunch at Universal. Dick was great friends with Chaney, Andy Devine and Broderick Crawford, among others. When any combination of these guys got together, one had to allow extra time for retakes. During the filming of Damon Runyon's *Butch Minds the Baby* (1942), Dick and Broderick Crawford started really mixing it up. They were so convincing that director Al Rogell attempted to act as peacemaker. Needless to say, the joke was on him.

Dick's friends back east would write him letters kidding him about his occupation. In fact, Dick once said if he could go back and do it all over again, he would have skipped college and become a cowboy. He thoroughly enjoyed doing Westerns.

Many of Dick's interests were musical. In fact, he once stated that if he had not made a career in the dramatic arts, he would have pursued music. Besides playing the guitar and being quite the crooner, Dick was also well versed at the violin and accordion.

However, arts and entertainment were not his only fields of interest. He especially loved to fish, hunt, go boating and collect guns.

"Outdoor life is my meat," said Dick in his Warner Bros. biography. "On this series of westerns I'm on location most of the time. We work from daylight to dark and eat and sleep in the open. It gives you a great appetite, and I can eat my weight in flapjacks without a worry about picking up extra poundage. A fellow my size (a little over 6 feet) always has a tendency to gain unless he keeps a regular routine of exercise...."

Always trying to stay in shape, Dick boxed, played tennis and handball, went horseback riding, went camping, played squash and ping pong. On occasion he would take in a football game or boxing match. This was a lot safer than playing them.

Football is what made Dick superstitious. He wore the number 13 on his uniform three times and each time he left the game with an injury.

On the less physically demanding side, he was a self-proclaimed great cook, despite comments that salads and buttermilk were his favorite foods. He would occasionally diet, but his real secret was no starches. In his later years, he did quite a bit of fishing with *Psycho* novelist Robert Bloch.

Dick's outdoor activities were reflected in his choice of reading material. He liked the works of Zane Gray, Jack London, Joseph Conrad, Thorne Smith, Gene Fowler and Rafael Sabatini.

Dick also loved animals. In fact, one of his favorite four-legged friends made several appearances with him in his films: his horse, Smoke. Raising pheasants and breeding dogs were also among the star's vast array of hobbies.

Like anyone, Dick had his own pet peeves. Among them, unnecessary formality, insincere people and those who liked to throw around four-syllable words when a two-syllable word will do.

Of all the jobs that Dick has had in his life, the most important was raising his two boys on his own, John Michael and James Patrick. When Dick's marriage ended in divorce, he was awarded custody of the two boys.

"The first temptation was to rush out and buy a flock of books and bone up on the scientific care of children," Dick said in an interview. "I knew I had a big job and an important one on my hands, the kind of job at which I dare not fail. Sure I was scared, even a little panicky. Horses and cattle were a cinch, but kids—that was something else again!"

During the days at Universal, it was tough to give the kids all the attention he would have liked. So when his work at the studio was done for the day, Dick would almost literally fly through the gate to get home as fast as he could.

During the late '40s and '50s, Dick turned his attention to the New York stage where he appeared in *The Connecticut Yankee* and the road show of *The Rainmaker*. He also appeared in over 100 television shows, including *Perry Mason*, *Adam-12*, *Bonanza* and *Lassie*.

In 1951 while Dick and his family were back east, the star's San Fernando Valley house was vandalized. This was discovered when a neighbor called the police complaining there was a wild party going on at Dick's house. When they showed up, kids were the culprits, the oldest being 14.

Dick eventually remarried and had a third son. He made his last film in 1967, *Brighty of the Grand Canyon*. In his later years, he was not all that pleased at what had started to pass for entertainment in the movies, although he did take occasional roles on television throughout much of the '70s.

Dick Foran passed away on August 10, 1979, at the age of 69, in Panorama City, California. He left behind his wife Suzanne, four sons and a world of quality entertainment. While his name today may not be as widely remembered as his good friend John Wayne, and while "horse operas" were the films he liked making most, his fans continue to enjoy his company no matter what film genre he appears in. Dick Foran will always be one of the movies' "good guys," on stage and off.

6. The Heroes Who Saved the Day 137

DICK FORAN'S FILMS:

1934 *Stand Up and Cheer, Student Tour, Gentlemen Are Born, Change of Heart.*

1935 *One More Spring, It's a Small World, Accent on Youth, Shipmates Forever, Moonlight on the Prairie, Dangerous, The Lottery Lover, Ladies Love Danger, The Farmer Takes a Wife.*

1936 *The Petrified Forrest, Treachery Rides the Range, Song of the Saddle, The Golden Arrow, Sunkist Stars at Palm Springs, Trailin' West, California Mail, Earthworm Tractors, Black Legion, Public Enemy's Wife, The Big Noise.*

1937 *Guns of the Pecos, Land Beyond the Law, The Cherokee Strip, Empty Holsters, The Devil's Saddle Legion, Prairie Thunder, Sunday Night at the Trocadero, The Perfect Specimen, Blazing Sixes.*

1938 *Love, Honor and Behave; Over the Wall, The Cowboy from Brooklyn, Four Daughters, Boy Meets Girl, The Sisters, Heart of the North, She Loved a Fireman, Secrets of a Nurse.*

1939 *Inside Information, Daughters Courageous, I Stole a Million, Hero for a Day, Four Wives, Private Detective.*

1940 *The Fighting 69th, The House of the Seven Gables, My Little Chickadee, Winners of the West* (serial), *The Mummy's Hand, Rangers of Fortune.*

1941 *Four Mothers, Unfinished Business, Mob Town, Road Agent, Riders of Death Valley* (serial), *The Kid from Kansas, Keep 'Em Flying, In the Navy, Horror Island.*

1942 *The Mummy's Tomb, Behind the Eight Ball, Ride 'Em Cowboy, Private Buckaroo, Keeping Fit, Butch Minds the Baby.*

1943 *He's My Guy, Hi, Buddy.*

1945 *Guest Wife.*

1947 *Easy Come, Easy Go.*

1948 *Fort Apache.*

1949 *El Paso, Deputy Marshal.*

1951 *Al Jennings of Oklahoma.*

1955 *Treasure of Ruby Hills.*

1956 *Please Murder Me.*

1957 *Sierra Stranger, Chicago Confidential.*

1958 *Violent Road, Thundering Jets, The Fearmakers.*

1959 *The Atomic Submarine.*

1960 *Studs Lonigan, The Big Night.*

1963 *Donovan's Reef.*

1965 *Taggart.*

1967 *Brighty of the Grand Canyon.*

Wallace Ford

Babe Jenson in The Mummy's Hand *and Babe Hanson in* The Mummy's Tomb

He was an infant at the time he was separated from his parents in England. Wallace Ford was reared mostly in Canada.

Born Samuel Jones on February 12, 1899, Wally was brought to Canada while still a toddler, and placed in Dr. Bernardini's school. He remained in Canada until his early teens, when wanderlust began to take serious hold on him. After many failed attempts at running away, he finally succeeded at it at the age of 15, when he and a friend, who experienced the same desire to take to the road, quit school and explored all over Canada.

Then, tragedy struck. His friend accidentally fell underneath the wheels of an oncoming train and was killed. This horrible event affected Wally profoundly. Through this tragedy, two big decisions were born. First, he decided that it was time to leave "the road". Secondly, hating his own name (Sam), he decided to adopt his friend's name. So in 1914, Samuel Jones became Wallace Ford.

Along with this adoption came a clause, respectability. Wally tried to make his new name mean something. He went to Winnipeg and got an acting job. It wasn't long after that when the United States entered World War I. Using his new name, he enlisted in the Navy, where he served with distinction.

When the war ended four years later, Wally went to New York and soon became a name on Broadway. He was in several hit productions: *Abraham Lincoln*, *Seventeen*, *Broadway*, *Abie's Irish Rose*, *Gypsy*, *Bad Girl*, *Pigs* and *Young Sinners*.

Wally was "discovered" by a film scout in 1932 and was quickly signed to a seven-year MGM contract. That's when his film career really took off. He had leads, supporting roles and character parts in dozens of films for the studio. Perhaps the most popular of the bunch today is Tod Browning's *Freaks*.

Just prior to and during the years of the second World War, Wally made several films at Universal. Besides *The Mummy's Hand* and its sequel *The Mummy's Tomb*, he appeared in Alfred Hitchcock's *Shadow of a Doubt*. He also traveled quite a bit on USO tours and to the fighting fronts.

In 1944, while in England making a film at Gaumont, Wally located his real mother. Unfortunately, the two were not able to meet due to some red tape involving strict war-time regulations. His mother, then about 80 years old, was suffering from the combination of old age and war shock from the constant Nazi bombing raids. Sadly, by this stage of her life, she remembered little of Wally's father other than the fact that he died many years prior. Wally set up a trust fund for her to help her through her final years.

Back in the States, Wally returned to the stage and was a smash hit as George in Steinbeck's *Of Mice and Men*, among other shows. While *Of Mice and Men* toured, the idea of actually having some land, chickens and rabbits really started

6. The Heroes Who Saved the Day

to appeal to Wally. He purchased some 38 acres near Malibu; however, except for the sweet potatoes, he admitted in his RKO studio biography, "I'm a flop as a farmer."

Wally enjoyed playing tennis, swimming, horseback riding, sandlot baseball, smoking cigars and telling funny stories.

Wally and his wife Martha, whom he met at the Actor's Chapel in New York, remained happily married throughout. "The trick to staying happily married so long is to pamper them [women]", says Wally. "I feel like I'm still on my honeymoon."

Wallace Ford died of a heart attack on June 11, 1966, in Woodland Hills, California.

WALLACE FORD'S FILMS:

1930 *Fore, Absent Minded.*

1931 *Possessed, X Marks the Spot.*

1932 *The Beast of the City, The Wet Parade, Are You Listening?, Skyscraper Souls, Prosperity, Hypnotized, Freaks, Central Park.*

1933 *The Big Cage, Headline Shooter, Three-Cornered Moon, She Had to Say Yes, Night of Terror, My Woman, Goodbye Again, Employees Entrance, East of Fifth Avenue.*

1934 *The Lost Patrol, Men in White, Money Means Nothing, The Man Who Reclaimed His Head, A Woman's Man, I Hate Women.*

1935 *The Mysterious Mr. Wong, The Whole Town's Talking, In Spite of Danger, The Nut Farm, One Frightened Night, The Informer, Another Face, Swellhead, She Couldn't Take It, Men of the Hour; Mary Burns, Fugitive; Get That Man.*

1936 *Absolute Quiet, Two in the Dark, A Son Comes Home, The Rouges' Tavern.*

1937 *Stardust, O.H.M.S., Jericho, Exiled to Shanghai.*

1938 *Swing It, Sailor.*

1939 *Back Door to Heaven.*

1940 *Two Girls on Broadway; Love, Honor and Oh Baby!; The Mummy's Hand, Give Us Wings, Scatterbrain, Isle of Destiny.*

1941 *A Man Betrayed, Murder by Invitation, Blues in the Night, Roar of the Press.*

1942 *All Through the Night, Inside the Law, The Mummy's Tomb, Seven Days' Leave, Scattergood Survives a Murder.*

1943 *The Ape Man, Shadow of a Doubt, The Marines Come Thru, The Cross of Lorraine.*

1944 *Machine Gun Mama, Secret Command.*

1945 *Blood on the Sun, On Stage Everybody, Spellbound, They Were Expendable, The Great John L.*

- **1946** *The Green Years, Rendezvous with Annie, The Black Angel, Crack-Up, Lover Come Back, A Guy Could Change.*
- **1947** *Dead Reckoning, Magic Town, T-Men.*
- **1948** *Man from Texas, Coroner Creek, Shed No Tears, Embraceable You, Belle Starr's Daughter.*
- **1949** *Red Stallion in the Rockies, The Set-Up.*
- **1950** *The Breaking Point, Harvey, The Furies, Dakota Lil.*
- **1951** *He Ran All the Way, Warpath, Painting the Clouds with Sunshine.*
- **1952** *Rodeo, Flesh and Fury.*
- **1953** *The Nebraskan, The Great Jesse James Raid.*
- **1954** *Three Ring Circus, She Couldn't Say No, Destry, The Boy from Oklahoma.*
- **1955** *Wichita, The Man from Laramie, A Lawless Street, The Spoilers, Lucy Gallant.*
- **1956** *Johnny Concho, Thunder Over Arizona, Stagecoach to Fury, The Rainmaker, The Maverick Queen, The First Texan.*
- **1958** *Twilight for the Gods, The Matchmaker, The Last Hurrah.*
- **1959** *Warlock.*
- **1960** *Tess of the Storm Country.*
- **1962** *Bristle Face.*
- **1965** *A Patch of Blue.*

John Hubbard

John Banning in *The Mummy's Tomb*

John Hubbard was born in April 1914, in East Chicago, Indiana. He studied at the Goodman Theater of the Chicago Institute and was brought to Hollywood in 1937 after a talent scout spotted him.

Before he knew what hit him, John was under contract to Paramount Studios. His debut came in *Hold 'Em Navy* that same year. He stayed at Paramount until Hal Roach bought his contract. John was a suave, debonair leading man in films during the 1940s. He had a very successful film career until 1944. He, like many others, answered the call of Uncle Sam. He was drafted into the 88th Infantry Division in Italy where he won his sergeant's stripes. When he returned home, John found himself reduced to starring in B pictures such as *Fighting Mad* and *Linda Be Good*.

By the 1950s, John found that he was no longer a leading man. Instead, he portrayed second leads and filled character roles. However, the parts John had were solid and he was gracious enough to accept his newfound niche and stand out in

6. The Heroes Who Saved the Day

John Hubbard and Elyse Knox

films such as *Big Jim McLain*, *Soldier in the Rain* and *Fighting Mad*. He also toured England and Australia in the play *Mary Had a Little*.

In the '60s, John was very active on television, appearing on such popular shows as *Green Acres*, *Adam-12*, *The Munsters* and *Gunsmoke*. He was also a regular on *Family Affair* as Ted Gaynor and had two series of his own, *Hey Mulligan* with Mickey Rooney and *Don't Call Me Charlie*.

John enjoyed bowling and golf and remained happily married to his high-school sweetheart Lois for nearly 50 years. The couple and their three children (Jane, Lois and John Jr.) always called Sherman Oaks, California, their home. He died at a convalescent home in Camarillo, California, on November 6, 1988, at 74.

JOHN HUBBARD'S FILMS

1937   *Hold 'Em Navy.*
1938   *The Buccaneer, The Big Broadcast of 1938, Out West with the Hardy's, Dramatic School, Prison Farm, Men with Wings, College Swing, Coconut Grove.*
1939   *Fast and Loose, The Story That Couldn't Be Printed, Maisie, The Kid from Texas, The Housekeeper's Daughter, Happily Buried.*

1940   One Million B.C., Turnabout, Who Killed Aunt Maggie?
1941   Our Wife, You'll Never Get Rich, She Knew All the Answers, Road Show, Murder Among Friends.
1942   The Mummy's Tomb, Youth on Parade, Canal Zone.
1943   What's Buzzin', Cousin?; Whispering Footsteps, Secrets of the Underground, Dangerous Blondes, Chatterbox.
1944   Up in Mabel's Room, There's Something About a Soldier, The Cowboy and the Senorita, Beautiful But Broke.
1947   Linda, Be Good.
1948   Joe Palooka in Fighting Mad, An Old-Fashioned Girl, Mexican Hayride.
1951   Bullfighter and the Lady, The Sword of D'Artagnan, The Cimarron Kid.
1952   Big Jim McLain, Horizons West.
1953   Walking My Baby Back Home.
1957   The Tall T, Pal Joey.
1958   Escort West, The Buccaneer.
1963   Soldier in the Rain.
1964   Gunfight at Comanche Creek, Fate Is the Hunter.
1965   The Satan Bug, The Family Jewels.
1966   Duel at Diablo.
1969   The Love God?
1972   Justin Morgan Had a Horse.
1974   Herbie Rides Again.

Robert Lowery

Tom Hervey in *The Mummy's Ghost*

When Robert Lowery came to Tinsel Town, he was not faced with the usual struggles that plague thespians attempting to break into Hollywood's sometimes-unbreakable shell. In town a little over two months, he was offered a part in a film. Then a scant few months later, he was offered a long-term contract with 20th Century–Fox.

Robert Lowery was born Robert Lowery Hanks on October 20, 1913, in Kansas City, Missouri, a direct descendant of Abraham Lincoln. His grandfather, L.L.L. Hanks, was the freedom fighter's first cousin. His mother was a prominent concert pianist and his father a lawyer.

Bob was very athletic. At Paseo High School, he played baseball, football, basketball and tennis, swam and boxed, and was good at all of them.

6. The Heroes Who Saved the Day

Bob was always drawn to the entertainment industry, particularly the dramatic arts. With his fine singing voice, he began vocalizing his way into the front of orchestras, the most notable being Slats Randall's band.

When Bob's father died while only in his early forties, he and his mother decided to relocate. They came to California where, unfortunately, there was already an ample supply of singers; Bob found it difficult to stay employed as an entertainer. Working in a paper factory proved to bring in a much steadier paycheck. One day a family friend took Bob to a little theater in Hollywood. That day, he found a new direction.

He began his new career by taking parts in plays. It wasn't long before he

Robert Lowery

began getting offers from movie studios. Samuel Goldwyn was the first. The film was *Come and Get It*. A heftier part soon followed in *Great Guy* starring James Cagney. After this film was in theaters, Bob caught the attention of nearly every talent scout in town. He received offers from three studios. He chose 20th Century–Fox. After he signed, however, he was not cast in another film for about a year. The studio wanted Bob to go through dramatic training at the studio's stock school. But by 1937, Bob held a very desirable record: he was the only actor on the Fox lot to have kissed every actress under contract! It beat playing tennis, which along with swimming and reading, are what Bob liked to do for relaxation. He also liked to play bridge and go to the movies several times a week. Bob believed the best way to prepare for a day of filming was to get plenty of sleep (nine hours a night usually did the trick for him).

Friends and fans alike used to say that Bob bore a resemblance to Clark Gable in his later years. He was stopped in the street many times by fans actually seeking Mr. Gable's autograph.

Bob was married and divorced twice. His first marriage was to actress Jean Parker, who gave birth to a son, Robert Jr. His second marriage was to Barbara Farrell. After retiring from films in 1967, Bob ran a Hollywood acting school.

On the night of December 26, 1971, Bob was talking to his mother on the telephone when he began to complain of chest pains. Then, according to Bob's mother, Leah Hanks, the phone went dead. That night, Robert Lowery died of a heart attack at the age of 58. He was buried in Valhalla Memorial Park in North Hollywood, California.

Throughout his off-screen life, Bob was truly one of the good guys, well-loved by friends, family and fans.

ROBERT LOWERY'S FILMS:

1936 *Come and Get It, Great Guy.*

1937 *You Can't Have Everything, Wake Up and Live; Wife, Doctor and Nurse; Second Honeymoon, Life Begins in College, City Girl.*

1938 *Four Men and a Prayer, Alexander's Ragtime Band, Happy Landing, Josette, Always Goodbye, Submarine Patrol, Passport Husband, Kentucky.*

1939 *Tail Spin, Charlie Chan in Reno, Young Mr. Lincoln; Wife, Husband and Friend; Mr. Moto in Danger Island, Hollywood Cavalcade, Second Fiddle, Drums Along the Mohawk.*

1940 *Day-Time Wife, Four Sons, The Mark of Zorro, Star Dust, Shooting High, Murder Over New York, Maryland; Free, Blonde and 21; City of Chance, Charlie Chan's Murder Cruise.*

1941 *Great Guns, Ride on Vaquero, Private Nurse, Cadet Girl.*

1942 *My Gal Sal, Lure of the Islands, Criminal Investigator, Dawn on the Great Divide, Who is Hope Schuyler?, She's in the Army, Sex Hygiene.*

1943 *Immortal Sergeant, So's Your Uncle, Revenge of the Zombies, Campus Rhythm, Tarzan's Desert Mystery, Rhythm Parade, The North Star, December 7th.*

1944 *Hot Rhythm, The Mummy's Ghost, A Scream in the Dark, The Navy Way, The Mystery of the Riverboat* (serial), *Dark Mountain, Dangerous Passage.*

1945 *Fashion Model, Sensation Hunters, Thunderbolt, Road to Alcatraz, Prison Ship, The Monster and the Ape, High Powered.*

1946 *God's Country, Death Valley, Gas House Kids, They Made Me a Killer, Shep Comes Home, Lady Chaser, House of Horrors.*

1947 *I Cover Big Town, Killer at Large, Queen of the Amazons, Mary Lou, Jungle Flight, Danger Street.*

1948 *Highway 13, Heart of Virginia.*

1949 *The Dalton Gang, Call of the Forest, Batman and Robin* (serial); *Arson, Inc.*

1950 *Western Pacific Agent, Border Rangers, Train to Tombstone, I Shot Billy the Kid, Gunfire, Everybody's Dancin'.*

1951 *Crosswinds.*

1953 *Jalopy, The Homesteaders, Cow Country.*

6. The Heroes Who Saved the Day 145

1955 *Lay That Rifle Down.*
1956 *Two-Gun Lady.*
1957 *The Parson and the Outlaw.*
1958 *The Nine Lives of Elfego Baca* (TV movie)
1960 *The Rise and Fall of Legs Diamond.*
1962 *Young Guns of Texas, When the Girls Take Over, Deadly Duo.*
1963 *McLintock!*
1964 *Stage to Thunder Rock.*
1965 *Zebra in the Kitchen.*
1966 *Waco, Johnny Reno, The Undertaker and His Pals.*
1967 *The Ballad of Josie.*

Dennis Moore

Dr. Halsey in *The Mummy's Curse*

Dennis Moore had a promising career as a pilot until a tailspin at 3,200 feet put a premature end to his flying days. By the time he quit, he had several hundred miles to his flying credit. Having to surrender his first passion, Dennis decided to have a go at being an actor.

Dennis "Smoky" Moore was born on January 26, 1908, in Fort Worth, Texas. Being a native Texan, he learned to ride a horse almost as quickly as he learned to walk.

In his 1941 RKO studio biography, Dennis said, "I get my next greatest thrill outside of flying, when I am on the back of a speedy, spirited horse."

Dennis did quite a bit of traveling with his family. In fact, he saw nearly every part of the world before returning to the States and settling in El Paso, Texas. Against his parents' wishes, Dennis went to work as an usher in a theater. Not long after, he wanted to fulfill his desire to promote himself and become an actor. He performed on the road in stock companies for about five years, but his true desire was to fly. He enrolled in flying school and got his wings. Dennis became a transport pilot and flew planes all over Texas and the rest of the west until that fateful tailspin. The plane crashed; although Dennis survived by some miracle, he broke every bone in his body and was not expected to live. He spent over a year in the hospital and it took two more years before he made a complete recovery.

Dennis once said, "I never had to bail out, but always wanted to. If I could qualify, I sure would join the parachute troops."

After this disaster, Dennis still wanted to pursue flying. However, he could not pass the physical that would have enabled him to obtain another pilot's license. So it was back to acting.

Dennis Moore and Kay Harding

For decades, Dennis worked steadily in films, mostly Westerns, but his passion for flying could not be stifled. He would constantly show up on movie sets that had anything at all to do with aviation.

Dennis made a career out of playing heroes and heavies for over three decades, mostly in B westerns. He passed away on March 3, 1964. In nearly 150 films, Dennis Moore thrilled audiences by appearing with such esteemed talent as Ginger Rogers, Ray Milland, Bela Lugosi and Buck Jones.

Dennis Moore's Films:

1934 *West on Parade, Tailspin Tommy, The Red Rider.*

1935 *The Dawn Rider, Sagebrush Troubador.*

1936 *Valley of the Lawless, Silverspurs, The Lonely Trail, Too Much Beef, China Clipper, Down the Stretch, King of Hockey, Black Legion, Wildcat Saunders, Under Southern Stars, Two in the Dark, Here Comes Carter, Hair Trigger Casey, Desert Justice.*

1937 *Smart Blonde, Sing Me a Love Song, San Quentin; Ready, Willing and Able; Mountain Justice.*

1938 *Wild Horse Canyon, Rebellious Daughters.*

6. The Heroes Who Saved the Day 147

1939 *Trigger Smith, Across the Plains, Irish Luck, Mutiny in the Big House, Danger Flight, Overland Mail, The Girl from Rio, Fangs of the Wild.*

1940 *East Side Kids, Boys of the City, Rainbow Over the Range, Fugitive from a Prison Camp, Rocky Mountain Rangers, Know Your Money.*

1941 *Flying Wild, Pals of the Pecos, Cyclone on Horseback, Billy the Kid in Santa Fe, Arizona Bound, Bowery Blitzkrieg, Spooks Run Wild, Ellery Queen and the Murder Ring, Billy the Kid's Roundup, The Lone Rider Fights Back, The Sunset Murder Case, Roar of the Press, Pirates on Horseback, Law of the Wild, Dude Cowboy.*

1942 *Texas Manhunt, The Lone Rider and the Bandit, Below the Border, Raiders of the Range, The Lone Rider in Cheyenne, Rolling Down the Great Divide, The Lone Rider in Texas Justice, Riders of the West, Overland Stagecoach, Dawn on the Great Divide, Seven Sweethearts, Outlaws of Boulder Pass, Bandit Ranger.*

1943 *Tenting Tonight on the Old Camp Ground, Land of Hunted Men, Arizona Trail, Cowboy Commandos, Destroyer, Black Market Rustlers, Bullets and Saddles, Hitler's Madman, Frontier Law.*

1944 *Ladies Courageous, Lady in the Dark, Follow the Boys, Wells Fargo Days, Raiders of Ghost City* (serial), *The Imposter, Song of the Range, The Mummy's Curse, West of the Rio Grande, Weekend Pass; See Here, Private Hargrove; Oklahoma Raiders, Mr. Winkle Goes to War.*

1945 *The Frozen Ghost, The Purple Monster Strikes* (serial), *Frontier Feud, Springtime in Texas, The Master Key* (serial), *The Crime Doctor's Courage.*

1946 *Driftin' River, The Mysterious Mr. M* (serial), *Colorado Serenade.*

1947 *Rainbow Over the Rockies.*

1948 *Frontier Agent, The Tioga Kid, Range Renegades, The Gay Ranchero.*

1949 *Across the Rio Grande, Haunted Trails, Roaring Westward, Riders in the Sky, Navajo Trail Raiders.*

1950 *West of Wyoming, Gunslingers, Colorado Ranger, Arizona Territory, Hot Rod, West of the Brazos, Silver Raiders, Marshal of Heldorado, I Killed Geronimo, Hostile Country, Federal Man, Fast on the Draw, Desperadoes of the West, Crooked River.*

1951 *Abilene Trail, Man from Sonora, Blazing Bullets, King of the Bullwhip, I Was an American Spy, Fort Defiance.*

1952 *Canyon Ambush, Montana Belle, The Lusty Men.*

1955 *One Desire, Rage at Dawn, The Man from Bitter Ridge, I Died a Thousand Times.*

1956 *Perils of the Wilderness, Blazing the Overland Trail, Tribute to a Bad Man, Hot Shots, A Day of Fury.*

1957 *Chicago Confidential, Gunfight at the O.K. Corral, Utah Blaine.*

1958 *The Fearmakers.*

7

The Heroines Who Were Whisked Away

Peggy Moran

Marta Solvani in *The Mummy's Hand*

From the early days of her childhood, Peggy Moran knew she was going to be an actress.

Shortly after her arrival in Hollywood, someone asked Peggy if she had an agent. Her reply was, "What's an agent?"

Born Marie Jeanette Moran in Clinton, Iowa, on October 23, 1918, Peggy was determined to make her dream a reality. She graduated from high school in 1937 and moved west with her mother, who was a tremendous source of support and encouragement.

While Mrs. Moran was on jury duty, the judge told her that Peggy was so pretty she could be in pictures. He told the Morans he knew a talent scout. Soon after, Peggy had a screen test at Universal, but the studio elected not to sign the teenager. Peggy was devastated. Her mom convinced her that the road was full of disappointment and if she really wanted to be an actress, she would have to learn to handle rejection. So she pulled herself together and headed for the next studio, Warner Bros., where Peggy landed several bit parts in a variety of films.

Arguably her most interesting occurrence took place not in front of the camera but on the lot when she had a lunch date with Errol Flynn. She later described

Flynn as a perfect gentleman, and Flynn described her as "the girl he should have married."

Peggy never got big parts at Warner Bros. When she found out why, she couldn't believe it. She told me, "A gentleman friend who used to take me out from time to time told me that I was expected to show my gratitude. I knew just what he meant. You know, I always heard about the way actors and actresses had to sleep their way to the top in Hollywood, but I never believed it. So when my contract ended, they dropped me."

After becoming disillusioned with the business, she considered trying the New York stage; however, Peggy was talked into giving Tinsel Town one more chance by an acquaintance who wanted to introduce her to producer Joe Pasternak at Universal. Her response, "What if he wants to go to bed with me?"

Well, Peggy held her breath and went to meet Mr. Pasternak. She was immediately cast in a film and was whisked off to wardrobe to be fitted. Later, she returned to Joe's office. Seeing that the producer was in a meeting, she decided to just leave word with his secretary. "She told me to go on in anyway and that it is no trouble. Now, I started to get nervous."

Peggy went into Joe's office. Henry Koster, the film's director, was in the room. He and Joe kidded Peggy a bit and made her feel very welcome. Her career at Universal had begun, complete with an exhausting schedule.

To say Peggy Moran worked her tail off would be a gross understatement. From 1940 to 1942, she was featured in over 20 films for Universal. Her perky, no-nonsense persona in films won her great popularity. She relentlessly pursued Robert Cummings in Abbott and Costello's first film, *One Night in the Tropics*. She accompanied Dick Foran, Leo Carrillo and Fuzzy Knight to *Horror Island*, and flirted with Franchot Tone in *Trail of the Vigilantes*. In 1942, she had a chance to play the heavy in *Drums of the Congo*.

At the time, Peggy was attracted to Henry Koster, who was in an unhappy marriage. That and the fact that he was over a decade her senior induced her to keep her feelings to herself. Then one night a dream changed the direction of her career.

"I dreamt about Mr. Koster last night," Peggy said to her mother.

"It wasn't an erotic dream or anything like that. But I still did not want to mention it to him because I thought it might embarrass him. Then when I showed up for work, he walked over to me and said, 'I dreamt about you last night!' I remember thinking, he's interested in me too."

Henry (Bobby to Peggy) Koster was soon divorced and, on October 30, 1942, Peggy Moran became Peggy Moran Koster. By mutual agreement with Bobby, she gave up acting, her reason being that the work was far too grueling. His reason was that he didn't want the members of the crew pinching her on the behind anymore. However, that was not Peggy's biggest pet peeve. "I just always hated the way they would make up my hair!"

Besides directing Deanna Durbin in films like *It Started with Eve*, *Spring Parade* (with Peggy) and *First Love*, Bobby continued directing classics such as *Luck*

7. The Heroines Who Were Whisked Away

of the Irish with Tyrone Power, *Harvey* with Jimmy Stewart, *The Robe* with Richard Burton and *Flower Drum Song*. Peggy stayed home and raised two children, Nicholas, a San Francisco psychiatrist (now deceased) and Peter, a Los Angeles probation officer.

Among Peggy's favorite films are those directed by her husband. She also enjoys the films of Billy Wilder and Martin Scorsese.

Until Bobby's death on September 21, 1988, the Kosters were inseparable, doing everything together, from taking walks to lunching on the set of one of Bobby's pictures.

"Like people always say today, we were real

Peggy Moran

soulmates. And when he died, it was the faith I had in my religion [Science of the Mind] and my passion for life that helped me through it. I really believe that there is a power out there and we are all a part of it."

Peggy claims she is really starting to slow down these days, but when she noticed a refrigerator magnet of Lon Chaney as the Mummy in my kitchen, she quickly glanced at it and said, "That's not *my* Mummy" (meaning Tom Tyler).

Today Peggy lives in Woodland Hills, California, and remains active in mind and body. Her motto, "If you don't use it, you lose it," has served her well both physically and spiritually. She continues to go for walks, is an active member of her church and has even taken a computer class in an attempt to get a handle on some of today's new technology. She receives fan mail regularly and is always being invited to film and memorabilia shows and conventions.

Looking back at her life, Peggy says she would not have done a single thing differently. "When I read about all the heartache and tragedy that seems to go with being a star, especially today, I don't regret not becoming a big star at all. I've had a great life."

"Do you mind if I say I think you are a swell person?" A line from Peggy Moran to Dick Foran in *The Mummy's Hand* in 1940, and to me in 1994. Peggy Moran (right) with the author.

Peggy Moran's Films:

1938 *Gold Diggers in Paris, Boy Meets Girl, The Sisters, Rhythm of the Saddle, Girls' School, Campus Cinderella.*

1939 *Ninotchka, First Love, The Big Guy, Winter Carnival, Little Accident.*

1940 *Oh Johnny, How You Can Love; Alias the Deacon, The Mummy's Hand, Slightly Tempted, Argentine Nights, One Night in the Tropics, West of Carson City, Trail of the Vigilantes, Spring Parade; I Can't Give You Anything But Love, Baby; Hot Steel, Danger on Wheels.*

1941 *Horror Island; Hello, Sucker; Flying Cadets, Double Date.*

1942 *Drums of the Congo, Treat 'Em Rough, There's One Born Every Minute, Seven Sweethearts.*

1943 *Stage Door Canteen, King of the Cowboys.*

7. The Heroines Who Were Whisked Away

Elyse Knox

Isobel Evans in *The Mummy's Tomb*

As a New York model, she smiled and flirted with readers through thousands of magazine ads. Her wholesome girl-next-door looks were the envy of women and the desire of men.

Elyse Knox was born in Hartford, Connecticut, on December 14, 1917. Her father, Frank Knox, was Secretary of the Navy under Franklin D. Roosevelt. Unlike most young, attractive models, Elyse never aspired to become an actress until she received an offer from 20th Century–Fox. She received some training in school as an artist but her professional goal was to become a fashion illustrator or designer.

One day, production head Darryl F. Zanuck was sitting in his projection room looking at some of the recent newsreels and fashion shorts turned out by the Fox studios in New York. Suddenly Miss Knox sashayed across the screen in Vyvian Donner's Technicolor *Fashion Forecasts*.

Zanuck was quite impressed with the poise and charm Miss Knox possessed and wasted no time in wiring the New York office to have her tested for the screen. Her test wowed the studio head. Not only did Elyse photograph well, she also had the ability to feel and display deep emotions. Within 24 hours, she was on a train headed for Hollywood.

Elyse's film career began to take off in 1940 when she was featured opposite Alice Faye, Don Ameche and Henry Fonda in *Lillian Russell*. From then on, the young actress worked steadily. She usually played the love interest opposite such stars as Patric Knowles in *Hit the Ice*. She was occasionally seen portraying Anne Howe in the popular

Elyse Knox

Joe Palooka series for Monogram. At the end of the decade, Elyse retired to marry and raise a family with Michigan football star Tom Harmon.

Elyse had no problem adjusting to a life out of the limelight. She settled down to become a homemaker and a mother to three children. She also returned to her true love, painting. While most call it "her hobby," Elyse insists it is much more than that. Her style bears a resemblance to the French impressionists Monet, Manet and Renoir. In fact, Elyse's older daughter Kristin went on to become a serious painter herself. Kristin later married pop singer Rick Nelson and was seen regularly on *The Ozzie and Harriet Show*. But perhaps Elyse's most famous child is Mark Harmon, a veteran television actor and star of *St. Elsewhere* and *Chicago Hope*.

Knox's husband Tom died in 1990. Today Elyse lives in Encinitas, California.

Elyse Knox's Films:

- **1937** *Wake Up and Live.*
- **1940** *Lillian Russell, Youth Will Be Served, Star Dust, Girl in 313, Girl from Avenue A.*
- **1941** *Tanks a Million, Sheriff of Tombstone, Hay Foot, Footlight Fever.*
- **1942** *The Mummy's Tomb, Arabian Nights, Top Sergeant.*
- **1943** *So's Your Uncle, Mister Big, Keep 'Em Slugging, Hit the Ice; Hi 'Ya, Sailor; Don Winslow of the Coast Guard* (serial).
- **1944** *Follow the Boys; A Wave, a WAC and a Marine; Moonlight and Cactus, Army Wives.*
- **1946** *Joe Palooka, Champ; Sweetheart of Sigma Chi.*
- **1947** *Linda, Be Good; Black Gold.*
- **1948** *Joe Palooka in Fighting Mad, I Wouldn't Be in Your Shoes, Joe Palooka in Winner Take All.*
- **1949** *Forgotten Women, Joe Palooka in the Counterpunch, There's a Girl in My Heart.*

Ramsay Ames

Amina Monsouri in *The Mummy's Ghost*

She was nicknamed "body beautiful" before even setting foot in front of a motion picture camera. The nickname was certainly befitting as she went on to seduce moviegoers throughout her career.

Born in New York on March 30, 1924, Ramsay Phillips certainly was a feminine beauty. Ironically though, anyone today unfamiliar with her work in films may regard her name to be somewhat masculine. However, Ramsay was anything but.

7. The Heroines Who Were Whisked Away

Dorothy Vaughan (left), Ramsay Ames and Robert Lowery.

Ramsay began to display a preference for the dramatic arts during her early schoolgirl days. She entered the Walter Hillhouse School for Dancing and took center stage in a rumba band in Miami, Florida. As Ramsay Del Rico, she made up half of a moderately successful dance team in some of New York's hottest dance clubs (La Conga, Beachcombers and the Stork Club). She even worked with the king of rumba, Xavier Cugat. These career decisions did not sit well with Ramsay's parents, who encouraged their daughter to become a lawyer or doctor. However, her mother eventually sided with Ramsay due in part to her own unfulfilled professional aspirations.

Still in her teens, the singer and leader of her own rumba band was noticed not only by half the men in New York, but by Hollywood as well. In 1943, Ramsay appeared in Columbia's *Two Senoritas from Chicago*, but was quickly signed by Universal and debuted with Lon Chaney as his unfaithful wife in *Calling Dr. Death*.

This was a very tough time for Ramsay. It was about now when she lost both of her parents. She also admitted to being in love, which was unrequited. But these chapters in one's life either make or break a person. Ramsay appeared to toughen a bit, although these events may have contributed to her fiery temperament, which would occasionally erupt.

Ramsay had the opportunity to display her singing, dancing and maraca playing a couple of times for Universal. She appeared in Olsen and Johnson's psychotic comedy *Crazy House*, and the next year she gave Universal's queen of Technicolor, Maria Montez, some on-screen competition in *Ali Baba and the Forty Thieves*. Ramsay was also featured among the obligatory cast of thousands in *Follow the Boys*. Maracas and rumba records aside, Ramsay also liked to dance for pleasure, collect unusual costume jewelry and sunbathe at the beach. Ramsay stated, "I like to go to the beach and sun-tan, and when I do that I go to bed at about ten o'clock. If I'm at the studio I follow a work schedule which is too strenuous to permit partying." She claimed she is not the party animal that everyone thinks she is. "I went to a café six nights running once, but it was to learn a song."

Ramsey lost her battle with lung cancer on her 74th birthday in 1998. In her later years, Ramsay placed Hollywood behind her, regarding it as part of her past. She had been very active in fighting for animal rights, declaring, "There are things in life far more important than making movies."

RAMSAY AMES' FILMS:

1943 *Two Senoritas from Chicago, Calling Dr. Death.*
1944 *Ali Baba and the Forty Thieves, Hat Check Honey, Follow the Boys, The Mummy's Ghost; A Wave, a WAC and a Marine.*
1945 *Mildred Pierce, Too Young to Know, The Gay Cavalier.*
1946 *Below the Deadline, Beauty and the Bandit, The Time, the Place and the Girl.*
1947 *Green Dolphin Street, The Vigilante, Philo Vance Returns, The Black Widow* (serial).
1948 *G-Men Never Forget* (serial).
1953 *Vicki.*
1956 *Alexander the Great.*
1961 *At Five in the Afternoon.*
1963 *Tal Dulcinea, Una, The Running Man.*

Virginia Christine

Princess Ananka in *The Mummy's Curse*

For two decades, she was the matronly Mrs. Olson, spokesperson for Folger's Coffee. This is how a new generation of TV watchers came to know her. However, she is familiar to film fans for her appearances in *Judgment at Nuremberg*, *Guess Who's Coming to Dinner* and, of course, *The Mummy's Curse*, where she starred as the thoroughly mud-caked Egyptian Princess Ananka who rose from the murky mire.

7. The Heroines Who Were Whisked Away

Virginia Christine was born Virginia Kraft of Swedish decent on March 5, 1920, in Stanton, Iowa, to musician parents. Her father, who died when she was just nine, was a cellist, and her mother, a pianist. Attempting to follow in her parents' footsteps, Virginia studied the piano at an early age. She found herself drawn to acting; when she was 17, her family relocated to Los Angeles.

In 1939, Virginia met accomplished stage and film actor Fritz Feld at a dinner held by L.A. City College. In their initial meeting, she snubbed him. However, this did not last long. By 1940, the two were married. They remained together until Fritz's death in 1993.

Fritz cast Virginia in his stage production of *Hedda Gabler*. Soon Warner Bros. offered her a contract, and by 1942, she had a bit part in Lewis Milestone's *Edge of Darkness* starring Errol Flynn and Ann Sheridan. Virginia's film career was underway. She acted in every film genre for four decades. While juggling both careers, the Felds had two sons, Steven and Danny.

During the '50s, Virginia continued her film career but also accepted numerous television roles on everything from *Twilight Zone* to *The Fugitive*. The only work Virginia turned down was commercials. "When television became popular, actors looked down at commercials," said Virginia in a 1985 *Los Angeles Times* interview. "They were beneath us. I

Virginia Christine

turned down anything that was offered, until one day in 1966, a casting director at Universal told me about the Mrs. Olson part." As soon as Virginia auditioned, she got the gig. However, it was still a commercial and, although she was glad to have the work, Virginia was not jumping up and down with joy.

As the Folger's spokesperson, Virginia made over 100 commercials. Looking back, she felt it was a very good working relationship. "I was proud to be associated with [Folger's]). I'm certainly glad I didn't spend 20 years selling feminine hygiene products." If there was any disappointment at all resulting in her long-running stint as Mrs. Olson, it was the lack of offers to return to the big screen. "It's time for me to put down my cup of coffee and get off my duff." Mrs. Olson was parodied by the best in the business— Bob Hope, Jackie Gleason, Carol Burnett and even Johnny Carson, the king of late night, all took their shots.

Mrs. Olson notwithstanding, one of Virginia's personal favorite roles was *Hedda Gabler*, where she made her stage debut. The others were television appearances: "Mary, Queen of Scots" from the series *You Are There*, *Tales of Wells Fargo*, and two TV movies, *Daughter of the Mind* and *Woman of the Year*.

Virginia was made honorary mayor of Brentwood, California, where she lived with Fritz for so many years. It was a position previously held by Fred MacMurray, Phyllis Diller and Lorne Greene. Virginia did volunteer work for Planned Parenthood and even judged the American College Theatre Festival.

In her later years, Virginia suffered from heart problems, and on July 24, 1996, she was reunited with her husband of 53 years: She passed away, at home, in her sleep, at the age of 76.

VIRGINIA CHRISTINE'S FILMS:

1942 *Edge of Darkness.*

1943 *Truck Busters, Mission to Moscow, Raiders of Ghost City* (serial).

1944 *The Mummy's Curse, The Old Texas Trail.*

1945 *Phantom of the Plains, Girls of the Big House, Counter-Attack.*

1946 *Murder Is My Business, The Wife of Monte Cristo, The Killers, The Scarlet Horseman* (serial), *The Mysterious Mr. Valentine, The Inner Circle, Idea Girl, House of Horrors.*

1947 *Women in the Night, The Invisible Wall, The Gangster.*

1948 *Night Wind.*

1949 *Special Agent, Cover-Up.*

1950 *The Men, Cyrano de Bergerac.*

1952 *High Noon, Never Wave at a WAC, The First Time.*

1953 *The Woman They Almost Lynched.*

1954 *Dragnet.*

1955 *Not As a Stranger; Good Morning, Miss Dove; The Cobweb.*

7. The Heroines Who Were Whisked Away

1956 *Invasion of the Body Snatchers, The Killer Is Loose, Nightmare.*
1957 *The Spirit of St. Louis, Three Brave Men, Johnny Tremain, The Careless Years.*
1960 *Flaming Star.*
1961 *Judgment at Nuremberg.*
1962 *Incident in an Alley.*
1963 *Cattle King, The Prize, 4 for Texas.*
1964 *One Man's Way, The Killers.*
1965 *A Rage to Live.*
1966 *Billy the Kid Versus Dracula.*
1967 *Guess Who's Coming to Dinner?*
1968 *In Enemy Country.*
1969 *Daughter of the Mind* (TV); *Hail, Hero!*
1970 *The Old Man Who Cried Wolf* (TV), *Woman of the Year* (TV).

Kay Harding

Betty Walsh from *The Mummy's Curse*

She didn't act in pictures for long. In fact, her screen credits begin and end in 1944. However, she is certainly remembered by fans of the horror genre for her roles as the ill-fated Marie Journet in the Sherlock Holmes classic *The Scarlet Claw*, and for her role in the final entry into Universal's Kharis series, *The Mummy's Curse.*

Jacqueline Lou Harding was born on January 5, 1924, in Cushing, Oklahoma. Kay, as she was later known, always dreamed of becoming an actress. Fortunately, she had the support of both her parents as well as her high school drama teacher. She worked as a theater usher while attending Whittier High School in California. It was there where she really shined, acting and singing in several productions. Kay portrayed Agnes in *David Copperfield*, Mrs. Faulkner in *The Night of January 16* and Erna in *Letters to Lucerne*. Later, with Whittier's Community Players, she performed in *The Male Animal* and *Green Stockings* and played the title role in *M'Liss*.

After graduating high school in 1943, Kay got her driver's license and took a job at a rubber company. This was not just any old rubber company. This rubber company made the mask worn by Claude Rains in *Phantom of the Opera*. Guess who was assigned to deliver the mask to Universal? This brunette beauty with sparking brown eyes and trim figure caught the attention of *Phantom*'s director, Arthur Lubin. He recommended that Kay take a screen test and, within a few weeks, she was cast in a bit role in Robert Siodmak's *Phantom Lady*. Her next role had a bit more substance. She played opposite Basil Rathbone and Nigel Bruce in arguably the most memorable of the great sleuths' adventures, *The Scarlet Claw*.

Kay Harding with Basil Rathbone

Kay was thrilled. Her desire to become an actress no doubt stemmed from her love for movies (she went to them regularly). However, Kay also loved to sing, dance and meet people. In fact, she enjoyed meeting one particular Navy man a little more than most. That summer, Kay married Aviation Machinist's Mate L.N. Patterson, the son of an Oklahoma City magistrate.

At only 5'2½", Kay liked to dress in very high heels. She also liked bright colors and spoke a little French, which may have helped her win the role of Marie in *The Scarlet Claw*. Kay also liked classic literature (Lloyd C. Douglas was one of her favorites), poetry and philosophical fiction.

Shortly after her brief stint at Universal, Kay (Jackie Lou) Harding dropped out of sight. One thing's for certain — being remembered a half century later for appearing in a mere half dozen pictures is quite an accomplishment.

KAY HARDING'S FILMS:

1944 *Phantom Lady, Weird Woman; Hi, Good Lookin'; Follow the Boys, The Scarlet Claw, The Mummy's Curse*

8

Who Were the High Priests?

Eduardo Ciannelli

The High Priest in *The Mummy's Hand*

He had one of those faces that you looked at and said, "I know him, what's his name?", perhaps because his name was not the easiest to recall.

Eduardo Ciannelli was born in Naples, Italy, on August 30, 1888, to an Italian father and a British mother. He sometimes went by Edward Cianelli or by virtually any variation of spelling to his last name.

Eduardo attended the University of Naples with the goal of becoming a physician, but it was the opera that enticed him away from medicine into a singing career.

Eduardo's amazing career as an opera singer began in 1910 and lasted for nearly six decades. In the beginning, he toured professionally throughout Europe. Then in 1914, he visited the United States. One of his burning ambitions was to see Niagara Falls. While in New York, Eduardo came to New York City and was equally impressed with its man-made wonders, namely the subways and skyscrapers.

Completely enthralled at all the New World had to offer, Eduardo decided to stay in the U.S. He understood only a little English; however, he grasped the rest of the language so quickly that within a few years he had written two plays that he

Eduardo Ciannelli

managed to get produced on Broadway, *Puppets* and *Foolscap*. He soon gained a reputation there as a stage actor. When he met producer Henry W. Savage at the Metropolitan Opera Company, he was given a contract that launched his acting career. He performed on Broadway in *Rose Marie*, *The Front Page* and *Reunion in Vienna*, among others.

In 1935, Eduardo segued from Broadway into motion pictures in Noël Coward's The Scoundrel. He quite often portrayed sinister villains or criminals, which is ironic, because off-screen, Eduardo was an extremely warm, friendly man.

Some of Eduardo's most memorable films are *Gunga Din*, *Foreign Correspondent*, *Kitty Foyle* and *For Whom the Bell Tolls*. Eduardo worked continually in Hollywood and abroad right up until his death from cancer in Rome on October 8, 1969. His last film, *Boot Hill*, was released posthumously.

EDUARDO CIANNELLI'S FILMS:

1917 *The Food Gamblers.*

1933 *Reunion in Vienna.*

1935 *The Scoundrel.*

1936 *Winterset, Criminal Lawyer.*

1937 *Marked Woman, The Girl from Scotland Yard, Hitting a New High, Super Sleuth, On Such a Night, The League of Frightened Men.*

1938 *Blind Alibi, The Saint in New York, Law of the Underworld.*

8. Who Were the High Priests? 163

1939 *Risky Business, Gunga Din, Bulldog Drummond's Bride, Society Lawyer, Criminal Cargo, The Angels Wash Their Faces.*

1940 *Strange Cargo, Zanzibar, Foreign Correspondent, The Mummy's Hand, Outside the Three-Mile Limit, Mysterious Doctor Satan* (serial), *Kitty Foyle, Forgotten Girls.*

1941 *Ellery Queen's Penthouse Mystery, They Met in Bombay, Sky Raiders* (serial), *Paris Calling, I Was a Prisoner on Devil's Island.*

1942 *Cairo, You Can't Escape Forever, Dr. Broadway.*

1943 *They Got Me Covered, Flight for Freedom, For Whom the Bell Tolls, The Constant Nymph, Adventures of the Flying Cadets* (serial).

1944 *The Mask of Dimitrios, The Conspirators, Passage to Marseille, Storm Over Lisbon.*

1945 *Dillinger, Incendiary Blonde, Crime Doctor's Warning, A Bell for Adano.*

1946 *Gilda, Perilous Holiday, The Wife of Monte Cristo; Joe Palooka, Champ; Heartbeat, California.*

1947 *Seven Keys to Baldpate, Rose of Santa Rosa, The Lost Moment, Crime Doctor's Gamble.*

1948 *On Our Merry Way, I Love Trouble, To the Victor, The Creeper.*

1949 *Volcano, Fugitive Lady, Prince of Foxes.*

1950 *Sangue Sul Sagrato, The Fighting Men.*

1951 *The People Against O'Hara, E l'Amore Che Mi Rovina.*

1952 *Il Tenente Giorgio, Sul Ponte dei Sospiri, The Stranger's Hand, The City Stands Trial, Prigionieri delle Tenebre, Voice of Silence.*

1953 *Youth and Perversion.*

1954 *Uomini Ombra, La Tua Donna, Forbidden, The Ship of Condemned Women, Mambo, Atilla.*

1955 *New Moon.*

1956 *Helen of Troy.*

1957 *Il Ricatto di un Padre, Monster from Green Hell, Love Slaves of the Amazon.*

1958 *Houseboat.*

1963 *40 Pounds of Trouble.*

1964 *The Visit.*

1966 *The Chase.*

1968 *The Brotherhood.*

1969 *Mackenna's Gold, Stiletto, The Secret of Santa Vittoria, Colpo Rovente, Boot Hill.*

George Zucco

Prof. Andoheb in *The Mummy's Hand* and *The Mummy's Tomb*;
High Priest in *The Mummy's Ghost*

If you are a fan of George Zucco—and most true horror film fans are—you are undoubtedly familiar with the rumor that George Zucco died insane, a raving madman, in the infamous padded cell. It is simply not true.

In front of the camera, George's sinister demeanor usually surpassed and upstaged that of the monsters in which he shared the screen. Off-screen, he was as gentle as they come, a quiet, soft-spoken, mild-mannered individual who disliked big parties and loved animals. In fact, George's ranch at the end of Mandeville Canyon, high above Los Angeles, was home to several rabbits, chickens, horses, turkeys, pigs and two German Shepherds, Benjy and Helen.

George Desylla Zucco was born on January 11, 1886, in Manchester, England, to a Greek father and an English mother. He was educated at Kent where he excelled in math. George also enjoyed playing cricket and soccer. After traveling to Canada, his love for animals guided him to farm work.

George Zucco

While in Winnipeg, George worked in a bank and then joined a touring company where he discovered an interest in acting. He soon became a leading man. George's stage debut came when he appeared in *What Happened to Jones* in 1908. By 1913, he was in New York's *The Suffragette*. After World War I broke out the following year, George put his career on hold and returned to England to join the army as a Private. It was due to an injury suffered in 1916 that George lost part of his right arm due to shrapnel damage. He also suffered tendon damage and lost the use of two fingers on his right hand.

After the war, George

8. Who Were the High Priests?

attended the Royal Academy of Dramatic Arts. He acted in a string of productions, including *The Taming of the Shrew*, *A Midsummer Night's Dream* and *Journey's End*. George then married fellow stage actress Stella Francis and the two settled down in a small house in a London suburb. Besides their common interest in acting, they both enjoyed classic literature, particularly the works of Dickens. They also played quite a bit of tennis and had a daughter, Frances.

While Stella retired to keep house and raise a family, George continued working in theater, film and radio.

In 1935, George came to New York to play Disraeli in *Victoria Regina* on Broadway. This resulted in an offer from MGM, which George accepted. The following year, George and his family migrated to Southern California.

At MGM, George's talents contributed to several of the studio's extravagant productions such as *The Firefly*, *Three Comrades* and *Marie Antoinette*. By the end of the decade, George began to reveal talents on-screen that would ensure his screen immortality.

He pleaded to have Maureen O'Hara's character tortured in RKO's *The Hunchback of Notre Dame*. At Fox, he portrayed one of fiction's most infamous criminals, Prof. Moriarity, battling opposite Basil Rathbone's Sherlock Holmes and attempting to make off with England's crown jewels in *The Adventures of Sherlock Holmes*. George's presence was so evil and so lecherous at times in 1940, he upstaged the Mummy in Universal's *The Mummy's Hand*. One could see him practically drooling over Peggy Moran as he plotted to eliminate all other members of the archaeological expedition. A couple of films later, George practically repeated the role of Andoheb, again donning the Egyptian fez for Universal in *Dark Streets of Cairo*. No Mummy this time, only jewels.

Not much changed throughout the war years. At Universal, he again matched wits with Sherlock Holmes, as a master jewel thief in *Sherlock Holmes in Washington*. He also subjected medical student David Bruce to an ancient deadly gas as the two-faced Dr. Morris in *The Mad Ghoul*.

Unlike many character actors, George's career continued to flourish long after World War II. Then in 1951, Stella received a call from 20th Century–Fox where George was making *The Desert Fox*. He was having a terrible time remembering his lines. Thinking this condition was only temporary, filming was scheduled to continue around the actor until he recovered. He never did. It was later learned that George had suffered a stroke. Two years later, at the request of the family doctor, George entered a nursing home. As an actor, he was still very much in demand, but he was unable to make films.

George Zucco passed away at the San Gabriel Monterey Sanitarium from pneumonia on May 31, 1960. He was 74. He left behind his wife Stella and their daughter, Frances.

Stella Zucco outlived her husband by nearly four decades, but lost her daughter Frances in March 1962 after she accidentally received an overdose of radiation. Frances had a brief career in films, which included appearances in *Top Secret* (uncredited) and *Never Wave at a Wac* (both 1952).

George Zucco's Films:

1931 *The Dreyfus Case.*

1932 *There Goes the Bride, The Midshipmaid.*

1933 *The Roof, The Man from Toronto, The Good Companions.*

1934 *Something Always Happens, What's in a Name?, What Happened Then?, Road House, The Lady Is Willing, Autumn Crocus.*

1935 *It's a Bet.*

1936 *The Man Who Could Work Miracles, After the Thin Man.*

1937 *Parnell, Saratoga, Souls at Sea, Sinner Take All, The Bride Wore Red, Conquest, Madame X, The Firefly, Rosalie, London by Night.*

1938 *Three Comrades, Lord Jeff, Arsene Lupin Returns, Fast Company, Marie Antoinette, Vacation from Love, Suez, Charlie Chan in Honolulu.*

1939 *Arrest Bulldog Drummond, The Adventures of Sherlock Holmes, Here I Am a Stranger, The Cat and the Canary, The Magnificent Fraud, The Hunchback of Notre Dame, Captain Fury.*

1940 *New Moon, The Mummy's Hand; Arise, My Love.*

1941 *Topper Returns, A Woman's Face, Dark Streets of Cairo, Ellery Queen and the Murder Ring, The Monster and the Girl, International Lady.*

1942 *Dr. Renault's Secret, The Mummy's Tomb, Half Way to Shanghai, My Favorite Blonde, The Mad Monster, The Black Swan.*

1943 *Dead Men Walk, Sherlock Holmes in Washington, Never a Dull Moment, The Mad Ghoul, Holy Matrimony, The Black Raven.*

1944 *The Mummy's Ghost, House of Frankenstein, Voodoo Man, Shadows in the Night, The Seventh Cross, Return of the Ape Man.*

1945 *Fog Island, Sudan, Confidential Agent, Week-End at the Waldorf, One Exciting Night, Hold That Blonde, Having Wonderful Crime.*

1946 *The Flying Serpent.*

1947 *Scared to Death, Where There's Life, Captain from Castile, Moss Rose, Lured, The Imperfect Lady, Desire Me.*

1948 *Tarzan and the Mermaids, Joan of Arc, Who Killed Doc Robbin?, Secret Service Investigator, The Pirate.*

1949 *The Barkleys of Broadway, The Secret Garden, Madame Bovary.*

1950 *Let's Dance, Harbor of Missing Men.*

1951 *David and Bathsheba, Flame of Stamboul, The First Legion.*

8. Who Were the High Priests? 167

Turhan Bey

Mehemet Bey in *The Mummy's Tomb*

When Turhan Bey came to America in 1938, women just loved him. The dark-skinned, deep-eyed, soft-spoken actor was soon dubbed "The Turkish Delight" by his fans. And despite being cast as the heavy most of the time, his popularity soared.

Turhan Selahettin Schultavey was born on March 30, 1922, in Vienna, Austria. Turhan came from a very affluent family. His father was a Turkish diplomat and his mother a wealthy Czechoslovakian. Although his parents divorced when Turhan was very young, he was never deprived of the comforts customarily found among the wealthy. His main field of interest as a child was photography, an interest and hobby that continues to this day.

The political atmosphere of Vienna began to change rapidly as clouds of war descended over Turhan's homeland and the rest of Europe. So in 1939, Turhan boarded a ship for America with his mother and grandmother. Their journey first

Turhan Bey with Evelyn Ankers

led them to the east coast where Turhan's uncle worked with Albert Einstein. Their next stop would be Hollywood. Ironically, Turhan had absolutely no aspirations of becoming an actor — yet. He enrolled in Ben Bard's School of Dramatic Arts, but his only aim was to improve his English. In fact, it was Bard who came up with the name Turhan Bey. One day, he asked Turhan to play the role of someone 30 years his senior in a stage production. Turhan accepted and was seen in the audience by talent scouts from Warner Bros., who quickly signed him for a role in the Errol Flynn film *Footsteps in the Dark*. Turhan's grandmother was astounded at the money he was bringing home. He continued to get calls for work at regular intervals. Then he signed with Universal. His roles varied considerably from Axis spies in *Danger in the Pacific* and *Junior G-Men of the Air* to voiceover work in *Captive Wild Woman*. He also beat out both George Zucco and David Bruce for the affection of Evelyn Ankers in *The Mad Ghoul*. Turhan shared the screen with Jon Hall and Maria Montez in several of Universal's Technicolor escapist pictures, including *Arabian Nights* and *Ali Baba and the Forty Thieves*.

After his last Universal film, *A Night in Paradise*, Turhan was drafted into the Army, where he spent about a year and a half. While he was gone, Universal merged with International Pictures and everything changed. Turhan told *Filmfax* magazine, "Before, we were treated like family." Turhan said. While the studio may have upgraded the quality of their pictures, the family atmosphere was missing.

In 1947, Turhan went to Eagle-Lion where he made *Out of the Blue* with George Brent and Virginia Mayo, and *The Amazing Mr. X*. In typical Turhan fashion, he felt his performance could have been "stronger."

Turhan returned to Europe and tried his hand at producing. Unfortunately, *Stolen Identity* did not do well at all but taught him a valuable lesson — "Always use someone else's funds."

Turhan began to refocus on photography. For years he was a successful photographer of portraits, landscapes and nudes. "I love to photograph scenes of cities. I use filters to enhance the mood or the effect. There is one picture that is very special. It is the statue of Alexander the Great which I took in Vienna."

Turhan returned to Hollywood in 1989 to appear in the American Cinema Awards. From then on, he began receiving offers to return to work. He accepted some roles, such as that of the Centauri Emperor in *Babylon Five*.

Today, Turhan commutes between Europe and the United States. In Los Angeles, he occasionally attends movie conventions, memorabilia shows and revivals of his old films. He is gracious and witty, claiming at a revival of *The Amazing Mr. X* at Hollywood's Egyptian Theatre, "I'm now at the age where I only buy ripe bananas." He would also like to continue acting. "I still love it, and will continue to perform when I am wanted. I want to thank all the fans who remember me, both as a young man in the '40s, and as I am today."

TURHAN BEY'S FILMS:
1941 *Footsteps in the Dark, Raiders of the Desert, Shadows on the Stairs, The Gay Falcon, Burma Convoy.*

1942	*The Falcon Takes Over, Drums of the Congo, Destination Unknown, The Mummy's Tomb, Arabian Nights, Yank on the Burma Road, Unseen Enemy, Junior G-Men of the Air* (serial), *Danger in the Pacific, Bombay Clipper.*
1943	*White Savage, The Mad Ghoul, Captive Wild Woman, Background to Danger, Adventures of Smilin' Jack* (serial).
1944	*Ali Baba and the Forty Thieves, Follow the Boys, Dragon Seed, The Climax, Bowery to Broadway.*
1945	*Sudan, Frisco Sal.*
1946	*A Night in Paradise.*
1947	*Out of the Blue.*
1948	*The Amazing Mr. X, Adventures of Casanova.*
1949	*Song of India; Parole, Inc.*
1953	*Prisoners of the Casbah.*
1994	*Possessed by the Night, Healer.*
1995	*The Skateboard Kid 2.*
1996	*Virtual Combat.*

John Carradine

Yousef Bey in *The Mummy's Ghost*

Of the thousands of screen personalities who have appeared in films through the decades, it is difficult to produce a name that has had a more diverse roster of screen credits than John Carradine, perhaps because he could do it all. He could be an understanding preacher in *The Grapes of Wrath*, or completely without conscience as Bob Ford in *Jesse James*. He appeared in the classics *The Hound of the Baskervilles* and *Western Union*, and slummed in the bottom-of-the barrel "C" pictures *Vampire Hookers* and *Mary, Mary, Bloody Mary*. One never knew where John Carradine would show up next.

Born Richmond Reed Carradine on February 5, 1906, in Greenwich Village, New York, John attended private schools in Peekskill and Kingston, New York. As a boy, John loved the arts. He excelled at painting, sculpting and singing but, oddly, his ambition was to be a lawyer. That all changed one day while John was in Philadelphia attending a stage performance of *The Merchant of Venice*. He was mesmerized by the performance of Robert Mantell as Shylock. From that day forward, John had his sights set on the stage.

As a teenager, John worked as a summer camp counselor and as an assistant librarian in New York's Public Library at Lincoln Center. Just prior to his twentieth birthday, he made his move. His debut as a thespian came while in New Orleans

John Carradine

in a 1925 production of *Camille*. Acting jobs came steadily, but in order to pay the rent, John sketched portraits. This was the routine that literally kept him alive through the years as he eventually made his way west. The artist arrived in Hollywood in 1927. He continued as a portrait painter and artist to keep food on the table until 1929, when he began to find work as an actor. Among the roles he portrayed was Shakespeare's Richard III.

In 1930, things were tighter than ever. John began to wash dishes to avoid eviction from his room. But his landlady knew of the artist's plight. Her son-in-law was a director at Columbia and she told her son about John, who was quickly cast in *Tol'able David*. His celluloid career had begun.

Throughout the early '30s, John accepted small roles and bit parts at various studios. Probably the most memorable of these were his appearances in Universal horror films. He telephoned the police giving his advice on how to catch *The Invisible Man*. He was Karloff's organ-playing disciple at the Black Mass in Edgar G. Ulmer's *The Black Cat*. He also crashed the party between the monster and the blind hermit in James Whale's *Bride of Frankenstein*.

By 1935, John began using John Carradine as his screen name, rather than Richmond Carradine. That same year, he married Ardanelle McCool Cosner, whom he met at a party. The following year, the couple had a son, David, and adopted another, Bruce. However, the happiness would be short-lived for John and his bride. By 1938 she had filed for divorce, but the couple did not separate. It was only the beginning of a rocky relationship that would continue for another six years.

In 1939, John appeared in what he termed, "the definitive Western," John Ford's *Stagecoach*. In the film, John played opposite John Wayne, Donald Meek, George Bancroft, Andy Devine and Claire Trevor as the mysterious southern gambler Hatfield. Soon to follow would be *Drums Along the Mohawk* and *The Grapes of Wrath*. By now, John was such a box office attraction that 20th Century–Fox stopped lending him out to other studios.

8. Who Were the High Priests?

The string of Fox hits continued throughout the early '40s with *The Return of Frank James*, *Western Union*, and one of John's personal favorites, *Blood and Sand*.

In 1941, John and Ardanelle divorced, ending nearly six years of belligerence. By 1942, John's Fox contract had expired. At the salary of $2,500 per week, he chose to freelance. The first nibble came from MGM but he soon found himself bouncing everywhere from Warner Bros. to Universal, appearing in virtually every genre from western to horror. He was at film studios and soundstages by day while moonlighting on stage as Hamlet by night.

Some of John's most notable horror outings came in 1944 and 1945. Besides playing the Mummy's mentor in *The Mummy's Ghost*, he provided a transparent escape for wanted criminal Jon Hall in *The Invisible Man's Revenge*. He had the title role in *Bluebeard*, he also delivered a true Shakespearean version of Count Dracula in *House of Frankenstein* and *House of Dracula*.

During the summer of 1944, John and actress Sonia Sorel were married in Las Vegas. The two continued as man and wife, through thick and thin, mostly thin. There were alimony demands from John's first wife, and two more kids to support — Christopher (born in 1947) and Keith (born in 1949). By the end of the decade, the Carradines were living in a two-room apartment in Greenwich Village.

By 1953, John and Sonia were back in Hollywood, but the good times would not last. John was jailed for failure to pay alimony and the government bagged him for thousands of dollars in back taxes. John again became a father when Robert was born In 1954. John, always a fair man with the bottle, began to drink heavily, and by 1957, he and Sonia were in divorce court. John won custody of his sons and was not too particular with the roles he chose. A good many of them were bottom-of-the-barrel grade "Z" exploitation flicks. At least the money was coming in.

That same year, John was married for a third time to fashion show commentator Doris Rich. The Carradine name kept a good many lawyers employed through the decades. John's second wife sued him for custody of their children, and in 1960, his agent sued for back commission. By year's end, John had filed for bankruptcy.

Continuing to sink himself into his work, John found a new medium to explore. Television provided him with fresh opportunities. During the 1960s, his television appearances became as diverse as his big screen appearances. John was seen in *Gunsmoke*, *Bonanza*, *The Twilight Zone*, *Thriller*, *The Munsters*, even *Starsky and Hutch*.

John managed to stay a bachelor until 1975 when he took on wife number four, Emily Cisneros.

In 1978, John's close call with an apartment fire almost claimed his life. Firemen carried him and his grandson down a ladder to safety. But his home was gutted and all of the actor's movie memorabilia was lost.

He continued working in ultra low-budget films and, in the 1980s, acted in many direct-to-video features.

Shortly after climbing 328 steps to the top of Milan Italy's famous gothic cathedral, the Duamo, in 1988, the 82-year-old actor died of heart failure. He left behind nothing short of a legacy. Besides his three actor sons, David, Keith and Robert, there are hundreds of film and television performances to remember John Carradine by. His personal favorite roles were in *The Grapes of Wrath*, *Captains Courageous* and *Stagecoach*. His favorite director was John Ford and favorite actor and actress, Spencer Tracy and Katharine Hepburn.

Whether looking to satisfy the most sophisticated cinema palate or just the need for a cheap thrill, John Carradine will always be equal to the task.

JOHN CARRADINE'S FILMS:

1930 *Tol'able David.*
1931 *Heaven on Earth, Bright Lights.*
1932 *Forgotten Commandments, The Sign of the Cross.*
1933 *To the Last Man, The Invisible Man, This Day and Age, The Story of Temple Drake.*
1934 *The Meanest Gal in Town, The Black Cat, Cleopatra.*
1935 *Les Miserables, Bride of Frankenstein, Alias Mary Dow, Bad Boy, Clive of India, Transient Lady, She Gets Her Man, The Man Who Broke the Bank at Monte Carlo, The Crusades, Cardinal Richelieu.*
1936 *The Prisoner of Shark Island, Under Two Flags, Half Angel, Mary of Scotland, Ramona, A Message to Garcia, Daniel Boone, The Garden of Allah, Winterset, White Fang, Dimples, Captain January, Anything Goes.*
1937 *This Is My Affair, Captains Courageous, The Hurricane, The Last Gangster; Thank You, Mr. Moto; Nancy Steele Is Missing!, Love Under Fire, Laughing at Death, Danger — Love at Work, Ali Baba Goes to Town.*
1938 *Four Men and a Prayer, Kentucky Moonshine, International Settlement, Alexander's Ragtime Band, Kidnapped, Of Human Hearts, I'll Give a Million, Submarine Patrol, Gateway.*
1939 *Jesse James, Mr. Moto's Last Warning, Stagecoach, The Three Musketeers, Five Came Back, The Hound of the Baskervilles, Frontier Marshal, Drums Along the Mohawk, Captain Fury.*
1940 *The Grapes of Wrath, The Return of Frank James, Chad Hanna, Brigham Young — Frontiersman.*
1941 *Western Union, Blood and Sand, Man Hunt, Swamp Water.*
1942 *Son of Fury, Whispering Ghosts, Reunion in France, Northwest Rangers.*
1943 *I Escaped from the Gestapo, Isle of Forgotten Sins, Revenge of the Zombies, Silver Spurs, Hitler's Madman, Gangway for Tomorrow, Captive Wild Woman.*
1944 *The Mummy's Ghost, The Adventures of Mark Twain, Bluebeard, Alaska, House of Frankenstein, Waterfront, Voodoo Man, Return of the Ape Man, The Invisible Man's Revenge, The Black Parachute, Barbary Coast Gent.*

8. Who Were the High Priests?

1945 *Fallen Angel, It's in the Bag!, House of Dracula, Captain Kidd.*

1946 *The Face of Marble, Down Missouri Way.*

1947 *The Private Affairs of Bel Ami.*

1949 *C-Man.*

1954 *Casanova's Big Night, Johnny Guitar, The Egyptian, Thunder Pass.*

1955 *Stranger on Horseback, The Kentuckian, Desert Sands.*

1956 *The Court Jester, The Ten Commandments, Around the World in 80 Days, Hidden Guns, Female Jungle, Dark Venture, The Black Sleep.*

1957 *The Unearthly, The True Story of Jesse James, The Story of Mankind, Half Human: The Story of the Abominable Snowman.*

1958 *Showdown at Boot Hill, The Proud Rebel, The Last Hurrah, Hell Ship Mutiny.*

1959 *Invisible Invaders, The Oregon Trail, The Cosmic Man.*

1960 *The Adventures of Huckleberry Finn, Tarzan the Magnificent, Sex Kittens Go to College, The Incredible Petrified World.*

1962 *Invasion of the Animal People, The Man Who Shot Liberty Valance.*

1964 *The Patsy, Cheyenne Autumn.*

1965 *Curse of the Stone Hand, House of the Black Death, The Wizard of Mars.*

1966 *Munster Go Home!, Billy the Kid Versus Dracula, Night Train to Mundo Fine.*

1967 *Hillbillys in a Haunted House, Dr. Terror's Gallery of Horror, The Death Woman.*

1968 *Pacto Diabolico, They Ran for Their Lives, The Astro-Zombies, The Hostage, Autopsy of a Ghost, Genesis.*

1969 *Blood of Dracula's Castle, The Good Guys and the Bad Guys, The Trouble with Girls, The Vampires, The Mummy and the Curse of the Jackals, Daughter of the Mind* (TV).

1970 *Cain's Way, Hell's Bloody Devils, The McMasters, Myra Breckinridge, Horror of the Blood Monsters, Five Bloody Graves, Blood of the Iron Maiden, Crowhaven Farm* (TV).

1971 *Shinbone Alley, The Seven Minutes, Bigfoot.*

1972 *Boxcar Bertha, The Gatling Gun, Blood of Ghastly Horror, Moon Child, Portnoy's Complaint, Richard, Everything You Always Wanted to Know About Sex But Were Afraid to Ask, Decisions! Decisions!* (TV).

1973 *Hex, Legacy of Blood, The House of Seven Corpses, Superchick, Terror in the Wax Museum, Bad Charleston Charlie, The Night Strangler* (TV), *The Cat Creature* (TV).

1974 *Silent Night Bloody Night.*

1975 *Mary, Mary, Bloody Mary; Stowaway to the Moon* (TV).

1976 *The Shootist, The Last Tycoon; Won Ton Ton, The Dog Who Saved Hollywood; The Killer Inside Me, Death at Love House* (TV).

1977 *The Sentinel, The White Buffalo, Crash, Satan's Cheerleaders, Shock Waves, Golden Rendezvous, Journey into the Beyond, Dr. Dracula, Tail Gunner Joe* (TV); *Christmas Miracle in Caufield, U.S.A.* (TV).

1978 *Vampire Hookers, Sunset Cove, The Bees, The Mouse and His Child, Greatest Heroes of the Bible* (TV).

1979 *Monstroid, Americathon, Teheran Incident, Nocturna, The Seekers* (TV).

1980 *The Boogey Man.*

1981 *The Nesting, The Monster Club, The Scarecrow, The Howling, Klynham Summer, Golaith Awaits* (TV).

1982 *The Secret of NIMH, Satan's Mistress.*

1983 *Frankenstein Island.*

1984 *The Ice Pirates, House of the Long Shadows, Evils of the Night.*

1986 *Peggy Sue Got Married, The Tomb, Hollywood Ghost Stories* (TV).

1987 *Monster in the Closet.*

1988 *Star Slammer, the Escape.*

Peter Coe

Dr. Ilzor Zaandab in *The Mummy's Curse*

Peter Coe is yet another of yesteryear's stars who remembers a different kind of Hollywood—the kind of Hollywood that encouraged and nurtured nervous newcomers like Peter, regardless of how wet behind the ears they were.

Born Peter Knego on Armistice Day, November 11, 1918, in Yugoslavia, he was the only member of his family who ever wanted to be in show business. His father, a captain in the Yugoslavian Navy, wanted Peter to continue the family's long military tradition, but Peter had other ideas. Even as a child, Peter would try his hand at writing plays, putting on shows and designing costumes.

Peter was smart enough to realize that his passion for acting was not enough to get him where he wanted to be. So when he was old enough, he enrolled in England's Royal Academy of Dramatic Arts. Upon graduating, Peter came to America and was hired as Johnny Weissmuller's understudy in the 1939 *World's Fair*. After managing to secure several small roles on Broadway, Peter was cast as a Nazi lieutenant in *A Man in the Shadow*. It was this performance that caught the attention of Hollywood agent Charles K. Feldman. When Feldman offered him $150 a week, Peter thought he was dreaming. Then, true shock hit him when Universal signed him for $350 a week!

Peter's first film had him taking commands from Randolph Scott in 1943's *Gung Ho!* In the film, he was a member of "Carlson's Raiders," a special division

8. Who Were the High Priests?

Peter Coe with Anne Gwynne

of Marines chosen for the 1942 raid on the Japanese-infested Makin Island. After dying on screen in that film, Peter came back to be part of the victory committee in *Follow the Boys*. The "cast of thousands" featured George Raft, Marlene Dietrich, Orson Welles and an endless list of Universal contract players.

Of course, few Universal actors during the early '40s avoided being cast in a horror film. Peter was no exception. Besides appearing in *The Mummy's Curse*, he was not about to give up Anne Gwynne to Dracula without a fight in *House of Frankenstein*. It's interesting to note that these two films were released by Universal as a double feature in December 1944, giving audiences a double-dose of the diverse Peter Coe, both as the hero who saves his wife from Dracula's clutches and as an evil High Priest. By now, Peter was earning $500 a week, but that would soon drop to less than $10.

Impressed by what he learned about the Marines while filming *Gung Ho!*, he enlisted. After receiving an honorable discharge, Peter returned to stage work. He beat out Marlon Brando for a role in *The Greatest of Ease*, but it was Brando who had the last laugh as he accepted the role in *A Streetcar Named Desire*, a role that Peter Coe was offered by Tennessee Williams, but turned down.

Peter returned to Hollywood, and throughout the 1950s he accepted a wide range of roles. He played a Frenchman in *Rocky Mountain* with Errol Flynn and Gung in the Hope-Crosby vehicle *Road to Bali*. In 1965, he returned to his hometown of Dubrovnik, Yugoslavia, with Roger Corman for *The Secret Invasion*.

Those who knew Peter Coe throughout his career acknowledge that he was one of the nicest guys in Hollywood. This was certainly a great part of why he was so welcomed into the business when he began back in 1943. Peter was always sensitive and empathetic to the plight of others, and he was particularly appalled while on location in New Mexico for *Rocky Mountain*. There he witnessed first-hand the plight of the American Indian. Peter told *Hollywood Studio Magazine*, "They even searched the garbage cans they were so hungry. It was unbelievable that this was happening in this country."

Coe passed away in June 1993. He left behind his wife Tomasa, her daughter Rebecca and grandson Erick; and sons, Brian, Vince, Peter Jr., and Alexander.

Peter Coe's Films:

1943 *Gung Ho!*
1944 *Follow the Boys, Gypsy Wildcat, House of Frankenstein, The Mummy's Curse.*
1945 *Frontier Gal.*
1948 *My Own True Love.*
1949 *Sands of Iwo Jima, Sword in the Desert.*
1950 *Rocky Mountain.*
1951 *The Wild Blue Yonder.*
1952 *Road to Bali, Hellgate, Diplomatic Courier.*
1953 *Desert Legion, Flight to Tangier, Captain Scarface, Arrowhead.*
1954 *Sabaka, Alaska Seas, Passion.*
1955 *Escape to Burma, Smoke Signal, Shotgun.*
1956 *The Ten Commandments.*
1957 *Hell Ship Mutiny.*
1958 *The Buccaneer.*
1959 *Okefenokee, The Louisiana Hussy.*
1960 *Can-Can.*
1961 *Snow White and the Three Stooges.*
1963 *The Prize.*
1964 *The Secret Invasion.*
1967 *Tobruk.*
1976 *Vigilante Force.*

8. Who Were the High Priests?   177

Martin Kosleck

Ragheb in *The Mummy's Curse*

During his day, he personified screen treachery with many portrayals of vicious Nazis. He played SS troopers, concentration camp officials and Hitler's propaganda minister, Joseph Goebbels, several times.

Martin Kosleck was born in Germany on March 24, 1907. Always drawn to the arts, he left the small village where he lived to study acting in Berlin before he was a teenager. He invested six years of his life in the trade before eventually becoming known in Europe as a Shakespearean actor.

As Hitler began his rise to power, Martin came to America at the age of 26 in 1933. He came directly to Hollywood and was invaluable in translating American film dialogue into German. Other than his native language, Martin also spoke Russian, Polish and Bohemian. He became an American citizen in 1938.

Martin was an accomplished artist and opened a small art studio where he painted and exhibited his work. On more than one occasion, Marlene Dietrich was his subject. He later left Hollywood to open a studio in New York while attempting

to act on the New York stage. Before long, he not only created stage designs but was playing Lancelot Gobbo in a Broadway production of *The Merchant of Venice*.

Martin's time was equally divided between art and acting. His first New York exhibit featured work he had completed while in California. His work included portraits of Dietrich, Bette Davis and the beautiful California landscape.

At that time, director Anatole Litvak came to New York specifically to look for Martin. He was about to direct *Confessions of a Nazi Spy* and believed Martin would be the "perfect" Joseph Goebbels. In fact, his impersonation of the German propaganda minister was so good, it enraged the Fascists. Fearing repercussion, whenever the actor was asked his name, he didn't chance disclosing his true identity. Instead he used his uncle's name, Nicoli Yoshkin.

Between films, Martin continued to have friends and celebrities pose for him. He also rarely missed an opening night at art exhibits, concerts, the theater and ballets. However, one of his most important roles came off-screen as an active member of the European refugee movement. He despised the Nazis for what they had done to his homeland. Portraying them on screen gave him a great deal of satisfaction because this enabled him to reveal just how evil the Nazis really were. But Martin also confessed, "I would not always choose to play spies, play Goebbels, and play sneaky killers, but at least the parts are dramatic, and I have been told that I am a dramatic actor."

His piercing stare continued to win him roles as psychotics, killers, scoundrels, henchmen and other undesirable characters in films like *The Mad Doctor*. He attempted to match wits with Sherlock Holmes opposite his good friend Basil Rathbone in *Pursuit to Algiers*. He appeared in *The Frozen Ghost* with Lon Chaney and also in *House of Horrors* where he used a homicidal maniac, the Creeper (Rondo Hatton), to knock off art critics who stood in the way of his success.

In a letter to the author, Martin wrote, "*House of Horrors* I liked best." He also felt Hollywood's "best director was Alfred Hitchcock," whom he worked with in *Foreign Correspondent*. Without doubt, the most gratifying passage in Martin's letter was the very first sentence. He wrote, "Dear Tom, Thank you very much for your letter. It is the best birthday present I could think of." At the time, I had no idea that Martin was turning 84. Small compensation indeed for all the thrills he has given film audiences since he made his screen debut over 70 years earlier.

Martin Kosleck was married in 1947 to German actress Eleonor von Mendelssohn, who came to America because she was banned from performing due to her political beliefs. She died from an accidental overdose of sleeping pills in 1951.

Martin passed away in Los Angeles on January 16, 1994, less than 24 hours before the Northridge earthquake shook Los Angeles residents awake the following morning. Although he left no immediate survivors, he did leave many wonderful performances to fans and friends who remember his screen persona as "the character you love to hate."

8. Who Were the High Priests?

MARTIN KOSLECK'S FILMS:

- 1929 *Napoleon auf St. Helena.*
- 1930 *Daughter of Evil, The Singing City.*
- 1939 *Confessions of a Nazi Spy, Nurse Edith Cavell, Espionage Agent, Nick Carter — Master Detective.*
- 1940 *Calling Philo Vance, Foreign Correspondent.*
- 1941 *Underground, The Mad Doctor, International Lady, The Devil Pays Off.*
- 1942 *All Through the Night, Nazi Agent, Berlin Correspondent, Manila Calling, Fly-By-Night.*
- 1943 *The North Star, Chetniks, Bomber's Moon.*
- 1944 *The Hitler Gang, The Mummy's Curse, Secrets of Scotland Yard, The Great Alaskan Mystery* (serial).
- 1945 *The Frozen Ghost, The Spider, Pursuit to Algiers, Gangs of the Waterfront.*
- 1946 *The Wife of Monte Cristo, Strange Holiday, She-Wolf of London, Just Before Dawn, House of Horrors, Crime of the Century.*
- 1947 *The Beginning or the End.*
- 1948 *Smuggler's Cove, Half Past Midnight, Assigned to Danger.*
- 1956 *Spion fur Deutschland.*
- 1961 *Something Wild.*
- 1962 *Hitler.*
- 1964 *The Flesh Eaters, 36 Hours.*
- 1965 *Morituri.*
- 1966 *Agent for H.A.R.M.*
- 1969 *Wake Me When the War Is Over* (TV).
- 1970 *Which Way to the Front.*
- 1971 *Longstreet* (TV).
- 1980 *The Man with Bogart's Face.*

9

Getting to Know the Victims

Charles Trowbridge

Dr. Petrie in *The Mummy's Hand*

Charles Trowbridge was born on January 10, 1882, in Vera Cruz, Mexico.

Before becoming an actor, Charles tried his hand at several different jobs, among them architecture and coffee grower in Hawaii.

He made his way to Broadway and was featured in the stage production of *Craig's Wife* in 1925. During the Depression, Charles headed to Hollywood where he achieved success playing a wide array of character roles in over 200 films. His scholarly-looking features won him many roles as lawyers, doctors, judges and high-ranking military officers. He even portrayed the President of the United States, Martin van Buren, in *The Gorgeous Hussy* (1936) featuring Lionel Barrymore, Joan Crawford, Robert Taylor and James Stewart.

In 1940, Charles had the distinction of being the very first victim of Kharis, the Mummy, in Universal's *The Mummy's Hand*.

Trowbridge died on October 30, 1967, at the age of 85. Perhaps the saddest aspect of his death was that it went almost entirely unnoticed. There was not even a mention of him in local trade papers.

CHARLES TROWBRIDGE'S FILMS INCLUDE:

1910s   *The Fight, Sunday, The Siren's Song, Prohibition, Thais, The Eternal Magdalene.*

1920s   *The Fortune Hunter, Island Wives.*

1930s   *I Take This Woman, The Secret Call, Operation 13, Rendezvous, It's in the Air, Mad Love, The Great Ziegfeld, The Garden Murder Case, The Gorgeous Hussy, We Went to College, A Day at the Races, Captains Courageous, Alcatraz Island, Reported Missing, The Invisible Menace, Crime School, Little Tough Guy, The Last Express, Angels with Dirty Faces, Nancy Drew — Detective, Crime Ring, Tropic Fury, The Man They Could Not Hang, The Angels Wash Their Faces, Café Society.*

1940s   *The Fatal Hour, The Fighting 69th, The House of the Seven Gables, Virginia City, Johnny Apollo, The Man with Nine Lives, Andy Hardy Meets Debutante, The Mummy's Hand, Trail of the Vigilantes, Mysterious Doctor Satan* (serial), *Dr. Kildare Goes Home, Charlie Chan at the Wax Museum, Before I Hang, The Great Lie, Meet John Doe, Sergeant York, Too Many Blondes, Wake Island, Over My Dead Body, The Amazing Mrs. Holliday, The Falcon in Danger, Action in the North Atlantic, The Fighting Seabees, The Story of Dr. Wassell, Mildred Pierce, They Were Expendable, Valley of the Zombies, Shock, Tarzan and the Huntress, The Secret Life of Walter Mitty, Buck Privates Come Home, The Paleface.*

1950s   *A Woman of Distinction, Unmasked, The Last Hurrah.*

Leon Belasco

Ali in *The Mummy's Hand*

Leon Belasco was born Leonid Simeonovich in Odessa, Russia, on October 11, 1902. He was educated in North Manchuria and Yokohama, Japan, where he attended St. Joseph's College.

During the early 1920s, Leon began a career as a musician. While in Japan, he performed as first violinist with the Tokyo Symphony. After moving to Los Angeles, his career began to accelerate. He performed with his own quartet on radio and on cruises. He also played with Russ Columbo and the Andrew Sisters.

While music was his main focus, Leon's screen career blossomed in 1926 with a small role in *The Best People*. It was not until 1938 that film work became the center of his attention.

Leon usually portrayed high-strung, excitable types, and was often cast as waiters, landlords and other comedic characters. His acting career lasted until the mid–70s. He was also seen on Broadway in *Silk Stockings* and *Once More, with Feeling.*

Leon passed away at the age of 85 on June 1, 1988, in Orange, California, from complications resulting from a stroke.

LEON BELASCO'S FILMS INCLUDE:

1930s *Dramatic School, Topper Takes a Trip, I Take This Woman, Broadway Serenade, Legion of Lost Flyers.*

1940s *The Mummy's Hand, It's a Date, Comrade X, Never Give a Sucker an Even Break, Nothing But the Truth, Yankee Doodle Dandy, Holiday Inn; Give Out, Sisters; Road to Morocco, Casablanca, Over My Dead Body; Henry Aldrich, Editor; It Comes Up Love, She's for Me, Hers to Hold, Pin-Up Girl, Storm Over Lisbon; San Diego, I Love You; Suspense, Philo Vance Returns, Adventures of Don Juan, Bagdad.*

1950s *Abbott and Costello in the Foreign Legion, Love Happy, Bomba and the Hidden City, Son of Ali Baba, Gobs and Gals, The Fabulous Senorita.*

1960s *Can-Can, My Six Loves.*

1970s *Playmates, Woman of the Year.*

Frank Lackteen

Temple Priest in *The Mummy's Hand*

Frank Lackteen was born on August 29, 1894, in Kubber-Ilias, Asia Minor, today known as Lebanon. He was one of the industry's most notable heavies during the silent film and early-talkie era, mostly in serials and Westerns. He appeared with silent film sensation Mary Pickford in *Less Than the Dust* in 1916. His work in film spanned six decades.

Frank died on July 8, 1968, in the Motion Picture Country Home of cerebral and respiratory illness. He was 73.

FRANK LACKTEEN'S FILMS INCLUDE:

1910s *The Yellow Menace, Woman.*

1920s *The House Without a Key, The Warning, Hawk of the Hills, The Black Book.*

1930s *Heroes of the West* (serial), *Jungle Mystery* (serial), *Tarzan the Fearless, Perils of Pauline* (serial), *Mummy's Boys, The Charge of the Light Brigade, I Cover the War, Arrest Bulldog Drummond, Union Pacific.*

1940s *Strange Cargo, The Mummy's Hand, The Sea Hawk, Meet the Wildcat, The Sea Wolf, Half Way to Shanghai, Arabian Nights, For Whom the Bell Tolls, Above Suspicion, Sahara, Action in Arabia, Can't Help Singing, Lost City of the Jungle* (serial).

1950s *The Prince Who Was a Thief, The Big Sky, Phantom of the Rue Morgue, The Ten Commandments.*

1960s *Requiem for a Gunfighter.*

Murdock MacQuarrie

Temple Priest in *The Mummy's Hand*

Murdock MacQuarrie was born on August 28, 1878, in San Francisco, California. For decades he was one of many actors who made a living as a bit player. He also wrote and directed various silent films including *Where Brains Are Needed* (1915) and *Nancy's Birthright* (1916).

He continued to appear in films through the early 1940s until his death on August 22, 1942.

Murdock MacQuarrie's Films Include:

1910s *The Trap, Bloodhounds of the North, The Embezzler, The Tragedy of Whispering Creek, The Forbidden Room, The Great Universal Mystery* (short), *Richelieu, The Finest Gold, The Stain of Blood, The Kingdom of Love, Fear Not, Loyalty, The Little Diplomat.*

1920s *The Silver Horde, Sure Fire, The Unfoldment, The Only Woman, The High Hand, The Jazz Girl, Hair Trigger Baxter, Black Jack, The Apache Raider.*

1930s *Captain of the Guard, Dr. Jekyll and Mr. Hyde, One Man Law, Daring Danger, Fighting Hero, The Man from Hell, The Return of Chandu, Les Miserables, The Dark Angel, Pinto Rustlers, Stormy Trails, Fighting Texan, Western Trails, Zorro Rides Again* (serial), *The Phantom Stage, Tower of London.*

1940s *The House of the Seven Gables, The Mummy's Hand, Man from Montana, Cat People, Arabian Nights.*

Dick Foran

Steve Banning in *The Mummy's Tomb*

See Chapter 6: The Heroes Who Saved the Day.

9. Getting to Know the Victims 185

Paul E. Burns

Jim the Caretaker in *The Mummy's Tomb*

Paul E. Burns was born on January 26, 1881. He made a career out of playing bit parts and small supporting roles in films spanning four decades, usually as a hotel clerk, a bartender or some kind of manual laborer.

Paul was a farmer in Alfred Hitchcock's *Saboteur* (1942) as well as a bum in 1967's *Barefoot in the Park*.

Television presented more opportunity for Paul. He appeared in a variety of shows in virtually the same types of roles.

The veteran of nearly 150 features and numerous TV shows died at age 86 in Van Nuys, California, on May 17, 1967.

PAUL E. BURNS' FILMS INCLUDE:

1930s *Hell Harbor, Jesse James, The Saint Strikes Back, Young Mr. Lincoln, Return of the Cisco Kid, Another Thin Man.*

1940s *Lillian Russell, Seventeen, Wild Bill Hickok Rides, Men of the Timberland, Belle Starr, Saboteur, Timber, The Mummy's Tomb, Mystery of Marie Roget, The Ox-Bow Incident, Sweet Rosie O'Grady, Dragon Seed, The Clock, State Fair, San Quentin, My Pal Trigger, Framed, Unconquered, Exposed, The Paleface, Belle Starr's Daughter, I Married a Communist.*

1950s *Young Man with a Horn, It's a Small World, Hot Lead, Santa Fe, Son of Paleface, The Lusty Men, The Man with the Golden Arm, Love Me Tender.*

1960s *Spartacus, Pocketful of Miracles, The Adventures of Bullwhip Griffin, Barefoot in the Park.*

Mary Gordon

Jane Banning in *The Mummy's Tomb*

Mention the name Mary Gordon to anyone familiar with films of the 1940s and they will immediately conjure up memories of the maternal Mrs. Hudson from Baker Street. She was the landlady and friend to Basil Rathbone's Sherlock Holmes, and for years she had a reputation as one of the best-known mothers in Hollywood.

Mary Gordon was born Mary Gilmour in Glasgow, Scotland, on May 16, 1882. This was also where she began her career as a performer, singing on the concert stage in Glasgow. After being widowed at the very young age of 35 (her husband was killed in the first World War), she came to North America to try and make a new start for herself. Hoping to find a more suitable climate than that of her homeland, her first stop was Canada, but she found it to be far too cold. Hearing about the good California weather, she headed for San Francisco, but that still was not to her liking. Her next stop was Los Angeles. Deciding to stay, she got a job as a cook in the café at RKO Studios, formerly Robertson-Cole Studios. When word of possible work as an extra reached Mary's ears, she took a stab at it, believing her stage experience abroad might help her get work. But her interest was purely financial. "I knew I'd have to start at the bottom," she said in her Universal Studio biography. "I went to work in the restaurant for $5 a week, so I didn't think $3 a day as an extra player would be too bad."

Then Mary was presented with the opportunity to make $10 a day after she lost a tooth. It so happened that a close-up shot of a toothless woman was needed. Mary fit the bill to a T.

Mary's professional aura, coupled with her masterful delivery of Scottish dialect, gave her the chance to further her budding career as a character actress. Her roles gradually became larger and more significant. She appeared in *Blonde Venus* with Marlene Dietrich, *She Done Him Wrong* with Mae West and James Whale's *Bride of Frankenstein*. Then in 1936, after nearly every character actress in Hollywood had been tested for the role of James Cagney's mother in *The Irish in Us*, she mailed a photo of herself along with a letter to the film's director, Lloyd Bacon, which said, "I'm terribly Scotch, but I'd like to try for the part. I believe I could do it." After receiving her photo, he quickly telephoned her, had her pick up the script and test for the part. The role was hers and Mary's future as a cinema mom was born.

Mary was now earning in the neighborhood of $2,500 per week. But Hollywood's fame and fortune had no ill effect on her. She continued to enjoy many of the activities she did prior to life in the spotlight (gardening, doing her own housework, baking scones which she usually brought to the set of whatever film she happened to be working on). "Everyone's been so sweet to me. It's the only way I can repay them," she said.

During the Second World War, Mary contributed her time to veteran hospitals and the Hollywood Canteen where she did what most "mothers" would do, volunteer to work in the kitchen.

After the war, she continued to work in films for another five years until she retired in 1950. In all, she appeared in nearly 250 feature films spanning four decades. She passed away on August 23, 1963, in Pasadena, California at the age of 81.

MARY GORDON'S FILMS INCLUDE:

1920s *Tessie, The People vs. Nancy Preston, Black Paradise, Naughty Nanette, Clancy's Kosher Wedding, The Old Code, Dynamite, Is Everybody Happy?*

1930s *When the Wind Blows, Dancers in the Dark, Blonde Venus, She Done Him Wrong, Vanessa: Her Love Story, Bride of Frankenstein, The Irish in Us,*

9. Getting to Know the Victims

Great Guy, Way Out West, Double Wedding, One Man Justice, Her Husband Lies, Kidnapped, Code of the Streets, Racketeers of the Range, The Hound of the Baskervilles, The Adventures of Sherlock Holmes, Mr. Smith Goes to Washington, Captain Fury.

1940s *The Invisible Man Returns, Brother Orchid, The Invisible Woman, When the Daltons Rode, The Man Who Talked Too Much, Unfinished Business, How Green Was My Valley, Sealed Lips, Appointment for Love, It Started with Eve, The Pride of the Yankees, Four Jacks and a Jill, The Strange Case of Dr. Rx, The Mummy's Tomb, Half Way to Shanghai, Sherlock Holmes and the Voice of Terror, Sherlock Holmes and the Secret Weapon, Bombay Clipper, Sherlock Holmes Faces Death; You're a Lucky Fellow, Mr. Smith; Keep 'Em Slugging, Hat Check Honey, The Spider Woman, The Pearl of Death, Hollywood Canteen, The Body Snatcher, The Woman in Green, See My Lawyer, Kitty, Dressed to Kill, Little Giant, The Secret Life of Walter Mitty, Exposed, Fort Apache, Mighty Joe Young.*

1950s *West of Wyoming.*

Wallace Ford

Babe Jenson/Hanson in *The Mummy's Hand* and *The Mummy's Tomb*

See Chapter 6: The Heroes Who Saved the Day.

Frank Reicher

Prof. Norman in *The Mummy's Tomb* and *The Mummy's Ghost*

His father was the idol of the German stage and his mother one of Germany's most famous opera singers, and yet Frank Reicher felt that his family's name was actually a burden. Frank Reicher was born on December 2, 1875, in Munich, Germany, where he trained in the German theater and studied drama and voice. At the age of 20, he decided it was time to begin his career as an actor. However, when he completed an acting job, he was always compared to his father. When he sang, it was his mother everyone compared him to. The pressure was too much. So his goal was to get as far away from his parents as he could.

Frank came to America in 1889 and divided his time between acting and directing in Hollywood and stage acting in New York, where he joined the Theatre Guild as a director. He accepted an offer to direct Jane Cowl's production of *Romeo and Juliet*. He also directed Ethel Barrymore more than once, then returned to acting where he became one of the first stage actors ever to cross over into films.

Frank returned to Hollywood in 1926 and for many years played mostly authoritative characters. Among his more popular roles were Captain Englehorn in *King Kong* and Dr. Pfeiffer in *The Story of Louis Pasteur*.

Reicher died on January 19, 1965, in Playa del Rey, California, at the age of 89. His impressive career included appearances in over 200 features as an actor and nearly 50 as director, including the 1920 version of Jack London's *The Sea Wolf*, which he co-directed with George (Spanish *Dracula*) Melford in 1931.

Frank Reicher's Films as an Actor Include:

1920s *Wise Husbands, The Masks of the Devil, Strange Cargo, Black Waters, Mister Antonio.*

1930s *The Grand Parade, Suicide Fleet, King Kong, A Bedtime Story, The Son of Kong, The Count of Monte Cristo, Let's Talk It Over, Secret of the Chateau, Rendezvous, Charlie Chan in Egypt, The Great Impersonation, Remember Last Night?, The Lone Wolf Returns, Life Returns, The Invisible Ray, Anthony Adverse, The Devil-Doll, The Gorgeous Hussy, The Story of Louis Pasteur, Night Key, Torchy Gets Her Man, Ninotchka, Mystery of the White Room.*

1940s *Typhoon, Dr. Cyclops, The Face Behind the Mask, To Be or Not to Be, Night Monster, The Mummy's Tomb, Mystery of Marie Roget, Above Suspicion, The Song of Bernadette, Background to Danger, The Hitler Gang, The Mummy's Ghost, The Adventures of Mark Twain, House of Frankenstein, Captain America* (serial), *Voice of the Whistler, The Shadow Returns, My Pal Trigger, The Secret Life of Walter Mitty, Joe Palooka Is Fighting Mad, Samson and Delilah.*

1950s *Superman and the Mole Men, The Lady and the Bandit.*

Frank Reicher's Films as a Director Include:

The Clue, Pudd'nhead Wilson, Public Opinion, The Storm, The Trap, The Black Circle, The Sea Wolf, Idle Hands, Wise Husbands, Mister Antonio.

Eddy Waller

Jim Evans in *The Mummy's Ghost*

Eddy Waller was born in Wisconsin on June 14, 1889. He had an active career in theater and vaudeville prior to making the move to celluloid in 1936.

Eddy spent a good part of his film career as a character actor, mostly for Republic Studios, where he appeared in many B Westerns with Tim Holt. He might best be remembered as Allan "Rocky" Lane's sidekick Nugget Clark in several films.

9. Getting to Know the Victims

However, like so many actors who make their living in B Westerns, Eddy's career began to peter out in the '50s as the popularity of the genre declined, thus bringing his career to an end. He died on August 20, 1977, in Los Angeles, California from a stroke.

EDDY WALLER'S FILMS INCLUDE:

1930s *One-Way Ticket, Poppy, Meet Nero Wolfe, Wild Bill Hickok, Out West with the Hardys, State Police, Jesse James, Young Mr. Lincoln, Return of the Cisco Kid, Mutiny on the Blackhawk, Geronimo.*

1940s *The Grapes of Wrath, The Man from Montreal, You're Not So Tough; Love, Honor and Oh Baby!; The Devil's Pipeline, Enemy Agent, The Cisco Kid and the Lady, Sergeant York, In Old Colorado, Double Date, Don't Get Personal, Night Monster, The Mummy's Tomb, Sin Town, Junior G-Men of the Air* (serial), *A Lady Takes a Chance, Raiders of Ghost City* (serial), *The Mummy's Ghost, The Adventures of Mark Twain, Under Western Skies, The Missing Corpse, Lady on a Train, Little Giant, In Old Sacramento, Boston Blackie and the Law, Nightmare Alley, River Lady, The Return of the Whistler, Desperadoes of Dodge City, Black Bart, Ma and Pa Kettle.*

1950s *Code of the Silver Sage, Rustlers on Horseback, California Passage, Montana Territory, It Happens Every Thursday, 99 River Street, The Far Country, Foxfire, The Man from Laramie, Man Without a Star, The Restless Breed.*

Oscar O'Shea

Night Watchman in *The Mummy's Ghost*

Oscar O'Shea was born on October 8, 1881, in Peterboro, Canada.

Oscar appeared in nearly 100 films since beginning his career in 1937, usually playing authoritative, dignified characters.

His screen debut was in *Captains Courageous*. After that he appeared in *The Roaring Twenties* with James Cagney and Humphrey Bogart, *Of Mice and Men* with Betty Field and Lon Chaney Jr., both in 1939, and *Stranger on the Third Floor* with Peter Lorre in 1940. He retired from acting in 1953 and passed away in Hollywood, California at the age of 78 on April 6, 1960.

OSCAR O'SHEA'S FILMS INCLUDE:

1930s *Captains Courageous, Rosalie, Mannequin, Racket Busters, Angels with Dirty Faces, The Roaring Twenties, Of Mice and Men, She Married a Cop, Missing Evidence.*

1940s *Zanzibar, Stranger on the Third Floor, Four Mothers, The Riders of the Purple Sage, Mutiny in the Arctic, Accent on Love, Half Way to Shanghai, Sin Town, The Postman Didn't Ring; Henry Aldrich, Editor; Good Morning, Judge; Corvette K-225, Her Primitive Man, South of Dixie, The Mummy's Ghost, The Mystery of the Riverboat* (serial), *Here Come the Waves, The Brute Man, It Had to Be You, My Wild Irish Rose.*

1950s *The Daughter of Rosie O'Grady, Thy Neighbor's Wife.*

John Carradine

Yousef Bey in *The Mummy's Ghost*

See Chapter 8: Who Were the High Priests?

William Farnum

Michael the Caretaker in *The Mummy's Curse*

At $10,000 a week, he was once Tinsel Town's highest paid star, yet at the time of his death, he was almost broke.

William Farnum was born exactly 100 years to the day after the birth of America, July 4, 1876, in Boston, Massachusetts. He made his stage debut at the age of 16 with a Shakespearean group, and eventually became well-known as a great tragedian. His first major success was playing the title role in *Ben Hur*, which kept him on tour for five years.

Besides Shakespeare, William enjoyed mixing it up in the occasional Western. In 1914, he put on a rarely seen physical display when he and actor Tom Santchi came out swinging in an adaptation of Rex Beach's *The Spoilers*. During the brawl, no stunt doubles were used. The result was something more than a few skinned knees and scraped elbows. After the scene, both actors had to be hospitalized for their injuries. William's performance was so good that, years later, he was used as a fight consultant during a remake of the film.

History repeated itself in 1925 when William was making a film ironically titled *The Man Who Fights Alone*. While filming another fight scene, William was so seriously injured, it almost finished his career. As a result, he was reduced to playing minor roles and bit parts.

In 1940, William was honored with the Veterans of Foreign Wars Citizenship Award for inspiring the sale of $37,000,000 worth of Liberty Bonds.

While William was raising money for worthy causes, his own personal funds were evaporating at an alarming rate. During his life, he was married three times, to Mabel Eaton, Olive White and Isobel Major. His lavish Hollywood lifestyle included an extravagant home, automobiles, stables and horses. He could have easily retired earlier, but now was forced to keep working.

William's final film appearance was with Abbott and Costello in *Jack and the Beanstalk* (1952). He passed away at age 76 from cancer on June 5, 1953. The Hollywood elite attended his funeral, reflecting how much Farnum meant to the film industry. Two of his pallbearers were Cecil B. DeMille and Frank Lloyd.

WILLIAM FARNUM'S FILMS INCLUDE:

1910s *The Redemption of David Corson, The Spoilers, The Sign of the Cross, A Wonderful Adventure, The Broken Law, A Soldier's Oath, Samson, The Bondman, A Tale of Two Cities, American Methods, When a Man Sees Red, Les Miserables, The Heart of a Lion, True Blue, For Freedom, Riders of the Purple Sage, The Rainbow Trail, The Man Hunter, The Jungle Trail, The Lone Star Ranger, The Last of the Duanes, Wings of the Morning.*

1920s *If I Were King, The Orphan, His Greatest Sacrifice, Moonshine Valley, Brass Commandments, The Man Who Fights Alone.*

1930s *The Painted Desert, A Connecticut Yankee, Mr. Robinson Crusoe, The Drifter, Supernatural, Cleopatra, The Scarlet Letter, The Count of Monte Cristo, The Crusades, Custer's Last Stand* (serial), *Hollywood Boulevard, Undersea Kingdom* (serial); *Git Along, Little Doggies; The Secret of Treasure Island* (serial), *The Lone Ranger* (serial), *South of the Border.*

1940s *Kit Carson, Adventures of Red Ryder* (serial), *The Spoilers, Deep in the Heart of Texas, Frontier Badmen, The Mummy's Curse, Captain Kidd, God's Country, The Perils of Pauline, Samson and Delilah.*

1950s *Jack and the Beanstalk.*

Holmes Herbert

Dr. Cooper in *The Mummy's Curse*

Having appeared in over 200 feature films, Holmes Herbert was highly familiar to movie audiences.

Holmes Edward Herbert was born Edward Sanger on July 30, 1878, in Dublin, Ireland. His stage debut was with London's William Lane Stock Company in 1886. Soon after, he enjoyed a long string of appearances in a variety of England's most successful stage productions and tours. Holmes came to America in 1912 as a leading man, starring in the play *Mind the Paint Girl*. He stayed in the States until World War I, when he served a four-year stint in the British military.

After the war, Holmes appeared on the screen in *The Man Without a Country*.

The sole reason for accepting the role was free time while waiting for his next stage opportunity, never realizing that that decision would set his career off in a new direction. His performance was impressive enough to entice producers to extend further offers. Embracing the new medium, Holmes moved to Hollywood in 1924. The offers continued until he was signed by Paramount the following year.

In 1930, Holmes married Mrs. Elinor Kershaw Ince, the widow of film director Thomas Ince. By marrying Holmes, Elinor Ince forfeited her interest in her late husband's estate, valued at $2,000,000.

Those well acquainted with the horror and mystery genre are more than familiar with Holmes Herbert. He is a fixture in the Rathbone-Bruce Sherlock Holmes films of the '40s. During the '30s and '40s he also appeared in *Dr. Jekyll and Mr. Hyde* with Fredric March, *Mystery of the Wax Museum* and *Mark of the Vampire* with Lionel Atwill, *Tower of London* with Basil Rathbone and Boris Karloff, *The Ghost of Frankenstein* with Bela Lugosi and Lon Chaney, Jr., and *Invisible Agent* with Jon Hall and Peter Lorre.

Holmes reached his sixtieth year as an entertainer with his portrayal of Jesse in 20th Century–Fox's *David and Bathsheba* in 1950. He was married twice. He passed away in December 1956 in Santa Monica, California, at the age of 78.

Holmes Herbert's Films Include:

1910s *The Man Without a Country, His Wife, A Doll's House, The Rough Neck, The Market of Souls.*

1920s *The Right to Love, Lady Rose's Daughter, Dead Men Tell No Tales, The Wild Goose, Her Lord and Master, Toilers of the Sea, Her Own Free Will, Sinners in Heaven, Up the Ladder, A Woman of the World, The Wanderer, The Honeymoon Express, The Fire Brigade, Heart of Salome; East Side, West Side; Gentlemen Prefer Blondes, The Terror, The Charlatan, Madame X, Say It with Songs, The Thirteenth Chair, The Kiss, Her Private Life.*

1930s *Dr. Jekyll and Mr. Hyde, Miss Pinkerton, Mystery of the Wax Museum, The Invisible Man, The House of Rothschild, The Count of Monte Cristo, Captain Blood, Mark of the Vampire, Cardinal Richelieu, Charlie Chan at the Race Track, The Charge of the Light Brigade, Lloyds of London, House of Secrets, Lancer Spy, The Adventures of Robin Hood, Marie Antoinette, Kidnapped, The Black Doll, Mr. Moto's Last Warning, The Mystery of Mr. Wong, The House of Fear, The Adventures of Sherlock Holmes, Tower of London, The Sun Never Sets, Mystery of the White Room.*

1940s *Foreign Correspondent, Boom Town, The Letter, British Intelligence, Scotland Yard, The Ghost of Frankenstein, Invisible Agent, Strictly in the Groove, Sherlock Holmes and the Secret Weapon, Lady in a Jam, Danger in the Pacific, Sherlock Holmes in Washington, Sherlock Holmes Faces Death, Corvette K-225, Calling Dr. Death, The Pearl of Death, The Uninvited, The Mummy's Curse, Enter Arsene Lupin, The Strange Affair of Uncle Harry, The House* *of Fear, Dressed to Kill, Love Laughs at Andy Hardy, Bulldog Drummond Strikes Back; Sorry, Wrong Number; Jungle Jim.*

1950s   *David and Bathsheba, The Son of Dr. Jekyll, The Wild North.*

Ann Codee

Tante Berthe in *The Mummy's Curse*

Ann Codee was born on March 5, 1890, in Belgium and represented the seventh generation of her family to act in European theater.

Ann came to America in 1909 and appeared with her future husband Frank Orth on the New York stage. The two were fixtures in vaudeville for many years.

During the late 1920s, Ann aided Warner Bros. Studios in Brooklyn by pioneering the first talkie comedy shorts such as *Stranded in Paris* (1929).

With talkies being the new rage, Ann's unique Belgian accent helped create demand for her as a character actress. She appeared in many well-known classics such as *The Roaring Twenties* with James Cagney and Humphrey Bogart, *Mr. Skeffington* with Claude Rains and Bette Davis, *The Clock* with Judy Garland and Robert Walker, *The War of the Worlds* with Gene Barry and Ann Robinson, *Daddy Long Legs* with Fred Astaire and *Kings Go Forth* with Frank Sinatra and Tony Curtis.

Shortly after celebrating her fiftieth wedding anniversary, she died of a heart attack on May 18, 1961, at age 71.

ANN CODEE'S FILMS INCLUDE:

1920s   *Stranded in Paris, Music Hath Charms, A Bird in the Hand.*

1930s   *Imagine My Embarrassment, On the Job, Under the Pampas Moon, Jezebel, The Roaring Twenties, Charlie Chan in City in Darkness.*

1940s   *Arise, My Love; Charlie Chan in Rio, Woman of the Year, Dr. Renault's Secret, Mr. Skeffington, Bathing Beauty, The Mummy's Curse, The Clock, Johnny Angel, Secret Agent X-9* (serial), *Hangover Square, Kitty, It's Great to Be Young, Till the Clouds Roll By.*

1950s   *When Willie Comes Marching Home, On the Riviera, An American in Paris, Detective Story, What Price Glory, The War of the Worlds, Kiss Me Kate, The Last Time I Saw Paris, So This Is Paris, Daddy Long Legs, Kings Go Forth.*

1960s   *Can-Can.*

Kurt Katch

Cajun Joe in *The Mummy's Curse*

Kurt Katch was yet another actor who came to America after the rise of Hitler.

Kurt was born Isser Kac on January 28, 1896. He was a popular Yiddish actor who toured the stages of Europe. Kurt arrived in America in 1937 and continued his stage career on Broadway after being exiled from Germany by the Hitler regime. He portrayed Uncle Chris in *I Remember Mama*.

Kurt was extremely adept at learning languages and dialects. He spoke fluent German, Russian and Polish, and without any knowledge of the English language whatsoever, he mastered enough of it in just two weeks to win a role as a German consul in the comedy *Margin for Error*.

In 1941, Kurt made his Hollywood debut. He played a bit part as a gypsy with a bear that wrestled Larry Talbot in *The Wolf Man*. Unfortunately, the scene found its way to the cutting room floor. During his Hollywood career, Kurt usually portrayed heavies. He was "The Scorpion" in the serial *Don Winslow of the Navy* in 1942; and Maria Montez fans recall Kurt giving the Technicolor diva a particularly difficult time as Hulaga Khan in Universal's *Ali Baba and the Forty Thieves* in 1944.

Kurt Katch died at 62 on August 14, 1958, in Los Angeles, California.

KURT KATCH'S FILMS INCLUDE:

1940s *Secret Agent of Japan, Don Winslow of the Navy* (serial), *The Strange Death of Adolph Hitler, They Came to Blow Up America, Background to Danger, Ali Baba and the Forty Thieves, The Mummy's Curse, The Seventh Cross, The Purple Heart; Salome, Where She Danced; Song of Love*.

1950s *The Secret of the Incas, The Adventures of Hajji Baba, Abbott and Costello Meet the Mummy, Pharaoh's Curse, The Beast of Budapest*.

Martin Kosleck

Ragheb in *The Mummy's Curse*

See Chapter 8: Who Were the High Priests?

10

The Mummies

Tom Tyler

Kharis, the Mummy in *The Mummy's Hand*

For decades dating back to the silent days of the '20s, the name Tom Tyler was synonymous with only one thing, Westerns. He was in enough of them to rival anyone, including the star who is most identified with the Hollywood Western, John Wayne.

Tom Tyler was born Vincent Markowski on August 9, 1903, in Port Henry, New York, where, as a teenager, he proved to have tremendous athletic ability. Throughout school his favorite sports were baseball, basketball, hockey and weightlifting. Expressing no interest in film, Tom's first job after leaving school was as water boy in the mines where his father worked.

Since being a water boy was not going to keep Tom in shape, he joined the Y.M.C.A. That is where his interest in weightlifting began to take off. It all started when Tom witnessed a man considerably shorter than himself lifting weights. When the man was through, Tom attempted to lift the same weights. He became furious when he could not even budge them, let alone lift them above his head. From that day on, Tom was determined to develop his muscles. His determination was so strong that by 1928, he qualified for the Olympics. He became a world heavyweight champion, a title he held for 14 years.

Since being a water boy held little promise for a future, Tom became a realtor, a tile manufacturer, a merchant seaman and a lumberjack. Then he turned his eyes toward the skies. Tom began notching several hours of flying time to his

Tom Tyler

credit, but his desire to be airborne went into an unexpected tailspin during a vacation. He went to Hollywood to see what Tinsel Town was all about. The word around town was that men with a physique like Tom's were in demand. About 6'2", he was very athletic. There was a "cattle call" for men to be cast in *Three Weeks*. Tom showed up and immediately landed his first bit part. He was chosen by FBO Studios to star as a leading man in a string of B westerns. At this time, he replaced the name Vincent Markowski with Tom Tyler.

Tom was married in the fall of 1937 to actress Jeannie Martel, who worked with him on a couple of his films. She also had a small handful of credits during the mid-30s. The couple resided in the Hollywood Hills where Tom turned the basement of his home into a workshop to satisfy his hobby for making cabinets. While upstairs, he enjoyed spending time in the kitchen as a chef, with sirloin tips being his specialty.

After over a decade of playing the quintessential good guy in white, Tom asked to play an occasional heavy. His request was granted, especially by Universal. The studio cast him as the bandaged bad guy seeking vengeance on tomb defilers in *The Mummy's Hand*.

However, the overall decision to have Tom on the opposite side of the law did not sit well with his fans. They enjoyed seeing the star catching the boys in black just prior to the closing credits. The result was a deluge of letters from fans who wanted their hero back. So it was Republic Pictures who presented Tom with not just another gallant persona, but arguably the role for which he is most remembered, 1941's *Adventures of Captain Marvel*. The only differences between this

15–chapter Republic serial and Tom's previous heroic stints in horse operas is that this time out, he did not need his steed to travel from point A to point B. Tom literally flew around every week helping the heroines and thwarting the thugs. Week after week, audiences returned to see their caped hero in the latest action-packed chapter, regardless of what double feature it was playing with.

In 1942, Tom was voted the Motion Picture Herald Fame Poll's biggest moneymaking Western star. Only a few years later, the ravages of rheumatoid arthritis began to plague the burly star. Clearly unable to meet the physical demands that Westerns call for, he soon found himself reduced to supporting roles.

By the early 1950s, Tom won even more popularity with a new generation of fans who watched him in reissued films and on TV. However, he never secured a financial future for himself because he never purchased the television rights to any of his hundreds of films. With his starring days as a major box office draw now behind him and his physical condition worsening, Tom moved to Hamtramck, Michigan, near Detroit, to live with his sister.

However, the rheumatoid arthritis that virtually crippled Tom in his later years proved to be too great a strain on the star's heart, and on May 1, 1954, Tom died from a heart attack at the far too young age of 50.

Tom once said that if he hadn't been an actor, he would have become a pilot. As his legion of admirers continue to grow and as films of Hollywood's golden age gain renewed popularity, I'm certain I speak for many when I say I'm glad Tom made the career choice that he did.

TOM TYLER'S FILMS:

19?? *Valley of Superstition.*

1924 *Galloping Gallagher, Leatherstocking.*

1925 *Let's Go Gallagher, Wild Horse Mesa, The Wyoming Wildcat, The Only Thing, The Cowboy Musketeer, Ben-Hur.*

1926 *Born to Battle, The Arizona Streak, Wild to Go, The Masquerade Bandit, The Cowboy Cop, Red Hot Hoofs, Tom and His Pals, Out of the West.*

1927 *Lighting Lariats, The Sonora Kid, Cyclone of the Range, Splitting the Breeze, Tom's Gang, The Flying U Ranch, The Cherokee Kid, The Desert Pirate.*

1928 *When the Law Rides, Phantom of the Range, The Texas Tornado, Terror, The Avenging Rider, Tyrant of Red Gulch, Terror Mountain.*

1929 *Trail of the Horse Thieves, Gun Law, Idaho Red, The Pride of Pawnee, Law of the Plains, The Phantom Rider, The Sorcerer, Pioneers of the West, The Man from Nevada, The Lone Horseman.*

1930 *Call of the Desert, The Canyon of Missing Men, 'Neath Western Skies, Half-Pint Molly.*

1931 *The Phantom of the West* (serial), *West of Cheyenne, God's Country and the Man, Rider of the Plains, Partners of the Trail, The Man from Death Valley,*

Two-Fisted Justice, Battling With Buffalo Bill (serial), *Galloping Thru, 99 Wounds.*

1932 *Single-Handed Sanders, The Man from New Mexico, Vanishing Men, Honor of the Mounted, Jungle Mystery* (serial), *The Forty-Niners.*

1933 *When a Man Rides Alone, Clancy of the Mounted* (serial), *The Phantom of the Air* (serial), *Deadwood Pass, War on the Range.*

1934 *Ridin' Thru, Mystery Ranch, Fighting Hero, Riding the Lonesome Trail.*

1935 *The Unconquered Bandit, Tracy Rides, Silver Bullet, The Laramie Kid, Powdersmoke Range, Terror of the Plains, Silent Valley, Rio Rattler, Coyote Trails, Born to Battle.*

1936 *Fast Bullets, Ridin' On, Roman Wild, Pinto Rustlers, The Last Outlaw, Santa Fe Bound, Rip Roarin' Buckaroo, Phantom of the Range, Trigger Tom.*

1937 *Cheyenne Rides Again, The Feud of the Trail, Mystery Range, Orphan of the Pecos, Brothers of the West, Lost Ranch.*

1938 *King of Alcatraz.*

1939 *Stagecoach, The Night Riders, Gone with the Wind, Frontier Marshal, Drums Along the Mohawk.*

1940 *The Grapes of Wrath, Brother Orchid, The Westerner, The Mummy's Hand, Cherokee Strip, The Texas Rangers Ride Again, The Light of Western Stars.*

1941 *Buck Privates, Riders of the Timberline, Gauchos of El Dorado, West of Cimarron, Outlaws of Cherokee Trail, Border Vigilantes, Bad Man of Missouri, Adventures of Captain Marvel* (serial).

1942 *Raiders of the Range, Code of the Outlaw, The Talk of the Town, Valley of the Sun, Westward Ho, Valley of Hunted Men, Shadows on the Sage, The Phantom Plainsman.*

1943 *Wagon Tracks West, Thundering Trails, Santa Fe Scouts, Riders of the Rio Grande, The Phantom, The Blocked Trail.*

1944 *Gun to Gun, Boss of Boomtown, The Princess and the Pirate, The Navy Way, Ladies of Washington.*

1945 *Sing Me a Song of Texas, They Were Expendable, San Antonio.*

1946 *Badman's Territory, Never Say Goodbye.*

1947 *Cheyenne.*

1948 *The Golden Eye, Red River, The Three Musketeers, Return of the Bad Men, The Dude Goes West, Blood on the Moon.*

1949 *Masked Raiders, Lust for Gold, She Wore a Yellow Ribbon, Samson and Delilah, Square Dance Jubilee, The Younger Brothers, I Shot Jesse James, The Beautiful Blonde from Bashful Bend.*

1950 *Rider of the Range, Colorado Ranger, West of the Brazos, Trail of Robin Hood, Rio Grande Patrol, Marshal of Heldorado, Hostile Country, Fast on the Draw, The Daltons' Women, Crooked River.*

10. The Mummies

1951   *The Great Missouri Raid, Best of the Bad Men.*

1952   *Outlaw Women, What Price Glory, Road Agent, The Lion and the Horse.*

1953   *Crossroad Avenger: The Adventures of the Tucson Kid, Cow Country.*

Lon Chaney, Jr.

Kharis, the Mummy in *The Mummy's Tomb, The Mummy's Ghost* and *The Mummy's Curse*

With the aid and assistance of home video, horror films of the '30s and '40s are enjoying another run of immeasurable popularity. A lot has been written about those who will always remain the embodiment of the genre. Names like Lon Chaney, Sr., Bela Lugosi, Boris Karloff and Basil Rathbone have all been the subject of authors who have enlightened us and brought us closer to them. One man who belongs to that very exclusive list of horror immortals is Lon Chaney, Jr. However, little has been written about him. Much of the Chaney legacy still remains shrouded in mystery, and at least for the time being, historians and fans will have to remain content with what we already know. It would not be useful to try to write a complete bio-

Lon Chaney, Jr.

graphical sketch on someone as popular as Lon Chaney, Jr., in just a few pages. Considering that he was the main character for about 75 percent of this book, a modest look at his outstanding career and life is in order at the very least.

The chilling birth of Creighton Tull Chaney came on February 10, 1906, in a cabin near Oklahoma City, Oklahoma. Cleva, his 16-year-old mother, gave birth to a baby who was not breathing. Creighton's 23-year-old father, Chaney, Sr., grabbed the baby, ran outside to the frozen waters of Belle Isle Lake, smashed through the ice and dunked his son. The sudden shock brought life to the baby (but probably would have killed the mother if she had witnessed the event).

His father introduced young Creighton to show business when he was three. Ironically, in the years to come, it was Chaney, Sr., who tried, in vain to prevent his son from pursuing a career in film.

While Chaney, Sr., was reveling in front of the camera, the scenes taking place behind it were clearly not as bright. Creighton's youth was besieged with heartache. His mother Cleva, was an alcoholic who also attempted suicide by poisoning herself. The poison succeeded in damaging her vocal chords, which ended her singing career — a career that eclipsed that of her husband's. She inevitably wound up in an asylum and when young Creighton asked about his mother, the senior Chaney told his son that she was dead. That was hardly the worst of it. Little Creighton Chaney endured many wicked beatings from his father, sometimes for no reason at all. Yet, Creighton remained in awe of his father and his career.

Lon Chaney, Sr., died of throat cancer at the age of 47 on August 30, 1930. All activity at every studio closed for a five-minute tribute. By this time, Creighton had married Dorothy Hinckley and the couple had two sons, Lon and Ronald. Although the great silent screen star was now gone, and Creighton had a life of his own, the specter of his father was still alive and well in his mind. Creighton attempted to surpass his late father in a competition that began when he signed an RKO contract in 1932. His screen debut came in *Bird of Paradise*. By the time Creighton made it over to Paramount in the mid–30s, alcohol had wormed its way into his life.

As time went on, it became painfully evident that offers would not come to Creighton as easily as they would if he shared his father's name. Studio executives believed that the name Lon Chaney, Jr., would be much more bankable. So by 1935, Creighton reluctantly took his father's name.

But a name change was not going to help his marriage. In June 1936, Dorothy filed for divorce, citing her husband's excessive drinking as the chief reason.

On October 1, 1937, Lon married for a second time, this time to model Patsy Beck, who quickly became familiar with her husband's demons. By the late '30s, Lon still had no substantial acting offers, only criticism which came with the stigma of being the son of the once great Lon Chaney, Sr. In fact, the only caller was the repo company after his possessions.

Then, a little over a month later, Lon auditioned for the stage role of Lennie in John Steinbeck's *Of Mice and Men*. Coached by good friend Wallace Ford, he received rave reviews and nearly 30 curtain calls. Lon reprised the role in 1939 for

10. The Mummies

United Artists' film release. His success was overwhelming, perhaps because of all the similarities between Lon and Lennie. Lon loved to play with animals, was big and boisterous, and in many ways was a child living in a man's body. But there was also the dark side that was not always visible, memories of cruelty, abuse and the increasing signs of alcoholism.

If Lon Chaney, Jr., was going to continue to work in film, an offer from Universal was inevitable. After all, this was the studio that gave Lon's father his big break decades ago. With the second horror cycle now under way, studio executives had to wonder if lightning could strike twice. "The Electric Man" was a story intended to metamorphose into *The Man in the Cab* for icons Karloff and Lugosi during the first horror cycle, but was shelved in favor of *The Invisible Ray*. However, it was dusted off, punched up and served to the public in March 1941 as *Man Made Monster*.

In this great little B flick, Lon makes his horror debut as Dynamo Dan, the electrical man opposite top-billed Lionel Atwill. Lon literally lights up the screen as a subject of Atwill's experiments in electrobiology. It was a great opportunity for Lon. During the opening reels of the film, he is a sweet, lovable sideshow performer. He is given the chance to show versatility when Atwill's "treatments" begin to take their toll, eventually transforming him into a superhuman dynamo whose touch means death. Released on a double-bill with *Horror Island*, producer-director George Waggner's *Man Made Monster* proved to be a hit with audiences.

Later that year, Lon also appeared in other Universal features, including *San Antonio Rose* and the all-star serial *Riders of Death Valley* with Dick Foran and Buck Jones. Although Lon was now working fairly steadily, stardom evaded him, at least until late the following year.

During the summer of 1941, George Waggner had another idea for a horror film. He enlisted the services of skilled horror writer Curt Siodmak, who only weeks later created the script that would make a star of Lon. *The Wolf Man* was released a scant few days after the bombing of Pearl Harbor. Universal was fearful that releasing a horror film now would not only be distasteful, but that the real-life horrors of World War II would deter the public from fictitious horrors. The studio was wrong on both counts. Theaters were packed with a public who wanted a distraction from newspaper headlines and the more unrealistic the topic, the better. This public opinion inspired a relentless output of horror films by Universal; most featured Lon, who would go on to portray the Wolf Man four more times for Universal in *Frankenstein Meets the Wolf Man*, *House of Frankenstein*, *House of Dracula* and *Abbott and Costello Meet Frankenstein*.

During the war years, the studio saw fit to squeeze Lon into as many horror roles and outfits as possible. Besides his three appearances as Kharis in *The Mummy's Tomb*, *The Mummy's Ghost* and *The Mummy's Curse*, he was Karloff's successor as the Monster in *The Ghost of Frankenstein* and was Universal's choice over Bela Lugosi to play the Count in *Son of Dracula*.

However, he did lose out to Claude Rains that same year for the role of Erique in Universal's Technicolor extravaganza *Phantom of the Opera*. This is the same character his father immortalized nearly two decades earlier.

In late 1943, Lon was presented with a series of his own, minus the heavy monster make up. Universal's Inner Sanctum series was comprised of six *very* B programmers. The films were popular with fans but they were small compensation for the loss of the Phantom role.

By 1946, Universal merged with International Pictures. Many of the former Universal "family" was let go, among them Lon. He went on to freelance almost everywhere. He did *My Favorite Brunette* with Bob Hope at Paramount, *High Noon* at United Artists and *Only the Valiant* at Warner Bros. He was even back at Universal for *The Black Castle* with Boris Karloff.

Lon did a lot of television during the '60s. He appeared on an array of television shows such as *Wagon Train, The Rifleman, Rawhide; Have Gun, Will Travel;* and *The Monkees*. He even reprised some of his monsters on *Route 66*.

Back in the horror genre, he appeared with Vincent Price in American-International's *The Haunted Palace*. In his final years, Lon appeared in films with budgets so small that if they were made today would have gone straight to video.

Lon's final curtain call came in 1969 when he starred with another screen great, J. Carrol Naish, in *Dracula vs. Frankenstein*. Compounding the atrocious production values was that fact that Lon did nothing but groan through the entire film. By now, Lon was stricken with throat cancer, the very disease that killed his father four decades earlier. However, it was actually a heart attack that took the life of Lon Chaney, Jr., on July 12, 1973 in his home in San Clemente, California. It was Lon's request that his wife of 36 years, Patsy, donate his remains to be used as a specimen by the University of Southern California School of Medicine.

As the Wolf Man and the Mummy, Lon Chaney, Jr., provided audiences with much needed escapism during a very difficult time. He reached those same patrons with his touching portrayal of Lennie.

Did Lon Chaney, Jr., ever achieve the status of his famed father? Maybe not, but he did succeed in establishing and immortalizing his own identity. It's only too bad he didn't recognize it.

Lon Chaney, Jr.'s Films:

1932   *Bird of Paradise, Girl Crazy, The Last Frontier* (serial).

1933   *Lucky Devils, Scarlet River, Son of the Border, The Three Musketeers* (serial).

1934   *Sixteen Fathoms Deep, The Life of Vergie Winters, Girl o' My Dreams.*

1935   *Accent on Youth, The Shadow of Silk Lennox, Scream in the Night, The Marriage Bargain, Hold 'Em Yale, Captain Hurricane.*

1936   *Singing Cowboy, Rose Bowl, Killer at Large, Undersea Kingdom* (serial).

1937   *Cheyenne Rides Again, Born Reckless, Wild and Woolly, Love Is News, Slave Ship, Thin Ice; Wife, Doctor and Nurse; That I May Live, Secret Agent X-9* (serial), *Second Honeymoon, One Mile from Heaven, Midnight Taxi, Love*

10. The Mummies

and Hisses, Life Begins in College, City Girl, Charlie Chan on Broadway, Angel's Holiday.

1938   Sally, Irene and Mary; Mr. Moto's Gamble, Alexander's Ragtime Band, Happy Landing, Josette, Walking Down Broadway, Submarine Patrol; Straight, Place and Show; Speed to Burn, Road Demon, Passport Husband.

1939   Jesse James, Union Pacific, Of Mice and Men, Frontier Marshal, Charlie Chan in City in Darkness.

1940   One Million B.C., North West Mounted Police.

1941   Man Made Monster, Too Many Blondes, The Wolf Man, San Antonio Rose, Riders of Death Valley (serial), Billy the Kid, Badlands of Dakota.

1942   North to the Klondike; The Ghost of Frankenstein; Overland Mail (serial); The Mummy's Tomb.

1943   Eyes of the Underworld, Frankenstein Meets the Wolf Man, Frontier Badmen, Son of Dracula, Crazy House, Calling Dr. Death.

1944   Weird Woman, Follow the Boys, Cobra Woman, The Mummy's Ghost, House of Frankenstein, Dead Man's Eyes, The Mummy's Curse, Ghost Catchers.

1945   Here Come the Co-Eds, The Frozen Ghost, The Daltons Ride Again, Pillow of Death, Strange Confession, House of Dracula.

1947   My Favorite Brunette.

1948   Albuquerque, The Counterfeiters, Abbott and Costello Meet Frankenstein, Sixteen Fathoms Deep.

1949   There's a Girl in My Heart, Captain China.

1950   Once a Thief.

1951   Only the Valiant, Flame of Araby, Inside Straight, Bride of the Gorilla, Behave Yourself!

1952   High Noon, Thief of Damascus, Springfield Rifle, The Bushwhackers, The Black Castle, Battles of Chief Pontiac.

1953   Raiders of the Seven Seas, A Lion Is in the Streets.

1954   Jivaro, Casanova's Big Night, Passion, The Boy from Oklahoma, The Black Pirates, The Big Chase.

1955   Not as a Stranger, The Silver Star, The Indian Fighter, I Died a Thousand Times, Big House U.S.A.

1956   Indestructible Man, Pardners, Manfish; Daniel Boone, Trail Blazer; The Black Sleep.

1957   The Cyclops.

1958   The Defiant Ones; Money, Women and Guns.

1959   The Alligator People, The House of Terror.

1961   Rebellion in Cuba.

1962   The Devil's Messenger.

- **1963** *The Haunted Palace.*
- **1964** *Law of the Lawless, Stage to Thunder Rock, Witchcraft.*
- **1965** *Black Spurs, Young Fury, Town Tamer, House of the Black Death.*
- **1966** *Apache Uprising, Johnny Reno.*
- **1967** *Welcome to Hard Times, Hillbilly in a Haunted House, Dr. Terror's Gallery of Horror.*
- **1968** *Buckskin, Spider Baby.*
- **1969** *A Stranger in Town, Fireball Jungle.*
- **1971** *The Female Bunch*; *Dracula vs. Frankenstein.*

11
Behind the Scenes

The Directors

CHRISTY CABANNE

The Mummy's Hand—He was born William Christy Cabanne in St. Louis, Missouri, on April 16, 1888. He went on to an education at the Naval Academy at Annapolis. Following a stint in the Navy, he began his career as an actor in several productions for film pioneer D. W. Griffith. In 1910, he became Griffith's assistant. Three years later, he began directing, and in 1915, he directed Douglas Fairbanks, Sr., in *The Lamb*. Other stars that worked under his directorial guidance were Wallace Reid, Lillian Gish and Frances X. Bushman.

Virtually a pioneer in his own right, Christy was also a writer and producer and could perform any job needed on a set. His talent and ability afforded him the chance to begin his own production company. He also hired himself out to direct for an array of companies such as FBO, Tiffany-Stahl, Pathé and others.

During the '30s and '40s, Christy directed many low- to medium-budget pictures, usually adding style and atmosphere to otherwise hopeless fare (although the 1947 *Scared to Death* was beyond repair).

During the span of his career, Christy directed nearly 150 films, wrote nearly another 40 and acted in over a dozen. He passed away from a heart attack in Philadelphia, Pennsylvania, on October 15, 1950, at the age of 62.

CHRISTY CABANNE'S FILMS AS WRITER INCLUDE:

1910s *An Adventure in the Autumn Woods, A Chance Deception, The Adopted*

Brother, The Failure, The Lamb, Flirting with Fate, Miss Robinson Crusoe, Fighting Through.

1920s   Burnt Wings, What's a Life Worth?, Live and Let Live, Till We Meet Again.

1940s   Scatttergood Pulls the Strings, The Man Who Walked Alone, Robin Hood of Monterey, King of the Bandits.

CHRISTY CABANNE'S FILMS AS DIRECTOR INCLUDE:

1910s   By Man's Law, The Adopted Brother, The Suffragette's Battle in Nuttyville, The Saving Grace, Moonshine Molly, The Gangsters of New York, For Those Unborn, The Better Way, The Lost House, The Failure, The Lamb, Daphne and the Pirate, Flirting with Fate, Miss Robinson Crusoe, National Red Cross Pageant, The Pest, God's Outlaw, The Pleasant Devil.

1920s   Burnt Wings, What's a Life Worth?, Live and Let Live, Till We Meet Again, The Sixth Commandment, The Midshipman, The Masked Bride, Nameless Men, Annapolis, Restless Youth.

1930s   Conspiracy, Graft, The Sky Raiders, The Midnight Patrol, The Unwritten Law, Hotel Continental, The Eleventh Commandment, Jane Eyre, Rendezvous at Midnight, One Frightened Night, The Last Outlaw, We Who Are About to Die, The Westland Case, Everybody's Doing It, Smashing the Spy Ring, Tropic Fury, Mutiny on the Blackhawk, Legion of Lost Flyers.

1940s   The Man from Montreal, Alias the Deacon, Hot Steel, Black Diamonds, The Mummy's Hand, The Devil's Pipeline, Danger on Wheels, Blonde Menace, Top Sergeant, Drums of the Congo, Timber, Scattergood Rides High, Keep 'Em Slugging, Dixie Jamboree, The Man Who Walked Alone, Scared to Death, Robin Hood of Monterey, Silver Trails.

HAROLD YOUNG

The Mummy's Tomb—Harold Young was born on November 13, 1897, in Portland, Oregon. He began his career in 1920 as a film editor. Only a few years later, he went to France as supervising cutter for Paramount Pictures European Productions. There, he performed the same duties for producer-director Alexander Korda. Harold's directorial debut came in 1934 in Korda's *The Scarlet Pimpernel*.

During the '30s and '40s, Harold directed numerous films for Universal, usually B pictures like *Little Tough Guy* with the Dead End Kids and *There's One Born Every Minute* (Elizabeth Taylor's screen debut).

Harold's career began to fizzle out during the late '40s after starting his own production company, Harold Young Productions. He passed away at the age of 74 in 1970, a victim of heart failure.

Harold Young's Films Include:

1930s   *The Scarlet Pimpernel, My American Wife, Little Tough Guy, The Storm, Hero for a Day.*

1940s   *Bachelor Daddy, There's One Born Every Minute, The Mummy's Tomb, Jukebox Jenny, I Escaped from the Gestapo; Hi, Buddy; Hi'ya, Chum; Machine Gun Mama, I'll Remember April, The Frozen Ghost, The Jungle Captive.*

1950s   *Roogie's Bump.*

Reginald Le Borg

The Mummy's Ghost—Out of the four directors that shared creative duties in the Universal Mummy series of the '40s, Reginald Le Borg was the only one who could legitimately be called a horror film director.

    Born in Vienna, Austria, on December 11, 1902, he was an economics major in school and eventually entered his father's banking business. In 1929, Reginald worked at Max Reinhardt's school. Reinhardt was Europe's most powerful stage producer-director during the early part of the century. Reginald later staged opera as well as musical comedies at many European opera houses. With his eye on the big screen, he went to Hollywood to stage the operatic scenes in *One Night of Love* (1934) and *Love Me Forever* (1935). During the mid–30s, he continued to stage opera scenes for various studios.

    In 1937, Reginald not only became a U.S. citizen but also graduated to directing short subjects for several independent producers, including over 20 musical shorts for Universal. While in the Army during World War II, he directed informational and training films. Upon his discharge, he returned to Hollywood as a director. He quickly established himself in the horror genre by directing Lon Chaney, Jr., in *Calling Dr. Death* and *The Mummy's Ghost* in 1943 and *Weird Woman* and *Dead Man's Eyes* in 1944. By 1954, Reginald formed his own production company. He also directed many network television shows during the '50s.

    Reginald passed away on March 25, 1989, in Los Angeles of a heart attack.

Reginald Le Borg's Films Include:

1930s   *Swing Banditry, A Girls' Best Years.*

1940s   *Merry Madcaps, Serenade in Swing, Swingtime Blues, She's for Me, Calling Dr. Death, Weird Woman, Jungle Woman, The Mummy's Ghost, Dead Man's Eyes; San Diego, I Love You; Destiny; Joe Palooka, Champ; Philo Vance's Secret Mission, Adventures of Don Coyote, Fighting Fools, Hold That Baby!*

1950s   *Wyoming Male, Young Daniel Boone, G.I. Jane, Sins of Jezebel, The Great Jesse James Raid, The Black Sleep, Voodoo Island.*

1960s   *Diary of a Madman, House of the Black Death.*

1970s   *So Evil, My Sister.*

Leslie Goodwins

The Mummy's Curse—A former stuntman turned director, Leslie Goodwins began his career in show business by falling off motorcycles. Curiously, he didn't see the danger in it, only the comedy.

Leslie was born in London, England, on September 17, 1899. His father William Ernest Goodwins was a blind organist and a professor at London's Royal Academy of Music.

When World War I broke out, Leslie enlisted in the British Army, but was discharged when officers learned he was only 15. When he was old enough, he joined the RAF as a pilot.

After the war, Leslie entered the film business. In 1919 he became an assistant to his brother Fred, who was already a director (who died in 1924). Leslie came to the U.S. to study the American style of filmmaking. He decided to stay in the States and began directing American films in 1936.

During World War II, Leslie was drafted into the American Army but was discharged after a year of service, again due to his age (this time, he was too old). At the end of the war, he resumed directing features until the late '40s.

In the 50s, Leslie moved over to television. He directed various episodes of *The Cisco Kid*, *Topper*, *Maverick*, *77 Sunset Strip*, *My Favorite Martian*, *Gilligan's Island* and *F-Troop*.

In 1968, Leslie Goodwins contracted the Hong Kong Flu (pneumonia) and died on January 8, 1969, in Hollywood, California, at the age of 69.

Leslie Goodwins Films Include:

1930s *One Live Ghost, Morning Judge, Anything for a Thrill, Fugitives for a Night.*

1940s *Mexican Spitfire, Let's Make Music, Mexican Spitfire Sees a Ghost, Rookies in Burma; Gals, Incorporated; The Mummy's Curse, Murder in the Blue Room; Hi, Beautiful; Genius at Work, The Lone Wolf in London, Dragnet.*

1950s *Fireman Save My Children, Gold Fever, Fresh from Paris, The Go-Getter.*

1960s *Tammy and the Millionaire.*

The Music Makers

Frank Skinner

During the last century, scoring motion pictures with music has gone from one extreme to the other. In the days of Mary Pickford and Charlie Chaplin, a very primitive simulation and synchronization of music provided the atmosphere. Today, in many cases, massive special effects are presented on a bed of screeching electric guitars. Somewhere in the middle lies the genius of Frank Skinner.

In his career, Frank scored or helped score over 400 films, most of which was done during his 30–year stint with Universal. Despite this indelible record, it is only recently that his work has begun to achieve the recognition it so richly deserves.

Frank was born on New Year's Eve, 1897, in Meredosia, Illinois. Because he was the son of a noted musician, he began his musical training at a very early age. His formal education started at the Chicago Musical College. After he graduated, Frank moved to New York where he worked as a stock orchestrations arranger for many hit songs of that time.

Frank's talent and ambition led him to Hollywood. There he arranged music for 1936's *The Great Ziegfeld*. The same year he had an opportunity to debut his talent at Universal in Henry Koster's *Three Smart Girls* with Deanna Durbin. He could not have guessed at the time that this was where he would spend the rest of his career.

At Universal, Frank and his good friend and colleague Hans J. Salter created immortal film scores for every film genre. Frank and Hans continued to score music for Deanna Durbin films such as *Mad About Music* and *First Love*.

In 1938, Frank wrote one of his most spectacular scores. *Son of Frankenstein* not only ushered in the second horror cycle but the music Frank composed was so outstanding, cues from the film were reused numerous times in other Universal shockers.

Frank wrote music for W. C. Fields and Abbott and Costello comedies such as *My Little Chickadee*, *The Bank Dick*, *Buck Privates*, *In The Navy* and *Abbott and Costello Meet Frankenstein*. He also wrote with diversity for thrillers and action pictures, including *Saboteur* and *Pittsburgh*, the serials *Flash Gordon Conquers the Universe* and *Junior G-Men of the Air*, Westerns *Destry Rides Again* and *When the Daltons Rode*, the Maria Montez Technicolor epics *Arabian Nights* and *White Savage*, the mysteries *Sherlock Holmes and the Voice of Terror* and *Sherlock Holmes in Washington* and, of course, the horror films.

Although the scores from Universal's horror films are what Frank and Hans are best remembered for, the two simply regarded composing for those films as just another assignment. Understandably, there was no time to think otherwise. The pair would usually have to come up with complete scores in barely a week. In 1940 alone, Frank worked on scores for about 50 different films. That averages to about one a week!

After Universal merged with International Pictures in 1946, Frank was one of the few who remained on the lot. During the '50s and '60s, the frantic pace would begin to slow down. Bigger budgets and longer schedules allowed Frank to create his music at a far less hectic pace than he did during the war years. Frank continued to score larger budgeted features including *Harvey, Magnificent Obsession, Imitation of Life* and *Back Street*.

In 1966, Frank retired from composing for Hollywood. Like the absence of a great actor or great director, the void was noticed.

In the spring of 1968, Frank Skinner was diagnosed with cancer. He held on until October 9, when he passed away in the Valley Doctor's Hospital in North Hollywood, California, at the age of 70.

In many ways, Frank Skinner and Hans J. Salter were to Universal horror during the '40s, what Lugosi and Karloff were to the genre during the '30s. When we watch as Kharis slowly creeps up on his unsuspecting victim through the dark and gloomy shadows emanated by the full moon, all of our senses may not be focused on Tom Tyler. We are moved by what we hear—the suspenseful chords of Frank Skinner and Hans J. Salter.

The following is a list of the scores Frank Skinner has been credited for. It does not, however, begin to cover all of the films he has worked on throughout his career, as film credits rarely provide the whole story.

THE COMPLETE CREDITED SCORES OF FRANK SKINNER:

1937   *Some Blondes Are Dangerous.*

1938   *Outlaw Express; Swing, Sister, Swing; Youth Takes a Fling, Secrets of a Nurse, Exposed.*

1939   *Son of Frankenstein, Code of the Streets, Tropic Fury, First Love; Charlie McCarthy, Detective; Destry Rides Again, The Under-Pup, Two Bright Boys, The Sun Never Sets, The Spirit of Culver, Rio, One Hour to Live, Mutiny on the Blackhawk, The Forgotten Woman, Ex-Champ, Big Town Czar.*

1940   *Oh Johnny, How You Can Love; The House of the Seven Gables, My Little Chickadee, The Invisible Man Returns, Green Hell, Hot Steel, You're Not So Tough, If I Had My Way, Seven Sinners, One Night in the Tropics, Hired Wife, When the Daltons Rode, West of Carson City, La Conga Nights.*

1941   *The Man Who Lost Himself, The Lady from Cheyenne, The Flame of New Orleans, Buck Privates, Back Street, Never Give a Sucker an Even Break, South of Tahiti, Sing Another Chorus, Keep 'Em Flying, Flying Cadettes, Bachelor Daddy, Appointment for Love.*

1942   *Jail House Blues, Saboteur, Pardon My Sarong, Pittsburgh, Arabian Nights, You're Telling Me, Who Done It?, Sherlock Holmes and the Voice of Terror, Sherlock Holmes and the Secret Weapon, Ride 'Em Cowboy, Nightmare, Lady in a Jam, Junior G-Men of the Air* (serial), *Eagle Squadron, Boss of Hangtown Mesa.*

1943   *White Savage, All By Myself, Two Tickets to London, We've Never Been Licked, The Amazing Mrs. Holliday, Top Man, Gung Ho!, Fired Wife, Captive Wild Woman.*

1944   *Follow the Boys, The Suspect, Destiny.*

1945   *Pillow of Death, That Night with You, Strange Confession, See My Lawyer, Frontier Gal, Blonde Ransom.*

11. Behind the Scenes

1946 *The Runaround, Black Angel, Wild Beauty, She-Wolf of London, Rustler's Roundup, A Night in Paradise.*

1947 *The Egg and I, The Exile, Swell Guy; Smash-Up, the Story of a Woman; Ride the Pink Horse, I'll Be Yours.*

1948 *The Naked City, For the Love of Mary, Tap Roots, Hazard, Family Honeymoon, Black Bart, Abbott and Costello Meet Frankenstein.*

1949 *The Fighting O'Flynn, Tulsa, Bagdad, Sword in the Desert, The Life of Riley, The Lady Gambles, The Gal Who Took the West, Free for All.*

1950 *Woman in Hiding, Comanche Territory, The Sleeping City, Harvey, Wyoming Mail, One Way Street, Louisa, Francis, Double Crossbones, The Desert Hawk.*

1951 *Katie Did It, Francis Goes to the Races, Bright Victory, Bedtime for Bonzo, Week-End with Father, The Strange Door, Reunion in Rio, The Raging Tide, Mark of the Renegade, The Lady Pays Off.*

1952 *Steel Town, The World in His Arms, Sally and Saint Anne, No Room for the Groom, It Grows on Trees, Bronco Buster, Bonzo Goes to College, The Black Castle, Because of You.*

1953 *Desert Legion, Thunder Bay, The Mississippi Gambler, Wings of the Hawk, The Stand at Apache River, The Man from the Alamo, Forbidden, Back to God's Country.*

1954 *Magnificent Obsession; Taza, Son of Cochise; Ride Clear of Diablo, Destry.*

1955 *Sign of the Pagan, Six Bridges to Cross, Foxfire, One Desire, Chief Crazy Horse, Francis in the Navy, The Shrike, All That Heaven Allows, Ain't Misbehavin'.*

1956 *The Rawhide Years, Never Say Goodbye, Away All Boats, Behind the High Wall, Written on the Wind, Star in the Dust.*

1957 *The Tattered Dress, Battle Hymn, The Night Runner, Tammy and the Bachelor, Interlude, Man of a Thousand Faces, The Tarnished Angels, The Snow Queen, My Man Godfrey.*

1958 *Kathy O', This Happy Feeling, The Restless Years, The Perfect Furlough, Once Upon a Horse…, Monster on the Campus.*

1959 *Imitation of Life.*

1960 *Portrait in Black, Midnight Lace.*

1961 *Posse from Hell, Back Street.*

1963 *The Ugly American; Captain Newman, M.D.; Tammy and the Doctor.*

1964 *Bullet for a Bad Man.*

1965 *Shenandoah, The Sword of Ali Baba.*

1966 *Madame X, The Apaloosa.*

1967 *Ride to Hangman's Tree.*

Hans J. Salter

Remember the sorrowful score as Lon Chaney, Jr.'s, Dan McCormick walked the last mile in *Man Made Monster*? How about the angry villagers charging through the night with lighted torches, leading the way to blow up what was left of Frankenstein's castle in *The Ghost of Frankenstein*? Of course, there was the bed of mournful chanters for Princess Ananka's funeral in *The Mummy's Hand*. No self-respecting horror fan could deny knowing that the emotion and atmosphere they create are all the work of musical master Hans J. Salter.

On the Universal lot, Hans was known as "the master of terror and suspense," and those who knew him say he was one of nicest people ever to tickle the ivories. "He was a wonderful man, a very good friend of ours," said Peggy Moran during my interview with her.

Hans was born in Vienna in 1896. After graduating from the University of Vienna, he began his magnificent musical career in Berlin, Germany, conducting music for silent films at the UFA Studio. During the 30s, like so many talented artists, Hans fled Germany to escape the real-life terror of Nazi Fascism and the rise of Hitler. He migrated to Hollywood in 1937. The following year, he went to Universal to learn, but musical director Charles Previn approached him with what Previn called a "big chance." Hans was given the opportunity to score one scene in *The Rage of Paris* starring Douglas Fairbanks, Jr. The scene was nearly five minutes. Hans made the most of it, hitting every cue and impressing everyone in the orchestra, particularly Previn. The studio immediately realized the talent they had in their grasp, and not long after, Hans became a full-time member of the Universal music department.

Hans J. Salter

11. Behind the Scenes

Through the years, Hans and colleague Frank Skinner produced music scores at a frantic pace. Sometimes, one would write while the other napped in order to meet a deadline. Quite often, time would not allow for a completely original score, so music cues from previous films were re-used.

But Universal horror experts already know this. What they may not know was the unwritten law of the upbeat ending. Even if a film had an unhappy finale, the music over the closing titles had to contradict that.

Depending on the director and the amount of time allotted, Hans' work was rarely questioned. He was always praised and congratulated for his efforts. In 1944, he appeared in front of the camera as the conductor of Wagner's "Tristan and Isolde" in *Christmas Holiday* with Deanna Durbin and Gene Kelly, but he was not terribly fond of the makeup he had to wear.

During the '50s, as horror gave way to science fiction, Hans was right there tending to the needs of the *Creature from the Black Lagoon*, *The Mole People* and *The Incredible Shrinking Man*. With the demise of the assembly-line variety of filmmaking Universal was know for in the early '40s, Hans was now allotted more time and money to produce his scores.

During the 1970s, Citadel Records released "Horror Rhapsody," a suite comprised of some of Hans' best work from *The Mummy's Hand*, *Black Friday* and *Man Made Monster*. The disc has recently been reissued by Citadel with the soundtrack from *Maya*.

Hans' final film credit was *Return of the Gunfighter*, a 1967 made-for-TV movie. After he retired, he continued to compose music, but not for films. He felt that the business changed too much, and not for the better. He believed that most modern-day composers wanted only to get rich quick and that they were not really interested in contributing to quality filmmaking.

Hans was honored at the Hollywood Bowl in 1993 by the Society for the Preservation of Film Music. On this night, he joined the esteemed company of other honorees such as Henry Mancini, Jerry Goldsmith, John Williams and Miklos Rozsa, Hans' personal choice for best composer.

In February the following year, Hans lost his wife of many years, Mausi. Only a few months later, on July 27, he died in his Studio City home at the age of 98.

Today, Hans' music is reaching new audiences via home video, DVD and compact disc releases. In recent years, conductor William Stromberg paid homage to Hans J. Salter and his friend Frank Skinner by recreating many of their horror film scores from Universal during the forties. Marco Polo released "The Monster Music of Hans J. Salter and Frank Skinner" with cues from *Son of Frankenstein*, *The Invisible Man Returns* and *The Wolf Man*. Other discs include *The Ghost of Frankenstein*, *Sherlock Holmes and the Voice of Terror*, *Son of Dracula*, *Man Made Monster* and the entire score from *House of Frankenstein*.

In my own way, I too paid homage to these two maestros during my youth. While other teens were singing and tapping renditions of their favorite rock tunes, I was humming and whistling the melodies of Hans Salter and Frank Skinner.

THE HORROR AND SCIENCE FICTION SCORES OF HANS J. SALTER:

1939   *Tower of London.*
1940   *The Invisible Man Returns, Black Friday, The Mummy's Hand.*
1941   *The Wolf Man, Man Made Monster, Horror Island, The Black Cat, Hold That Ghost.*
1942   *The Ghost of Frankenstein, Invisible Agent, The Mad Doctor of Market Street, Mystery of Marie Roget, The Mummy's Tomb, Night Monster, The Strange Case of Dr. Rx, Sherlock Holmes and the Secret Weapon.*
1943   *Frankenstein Meets the Wolf Man, Son of Dracula, The Mad Ghoul, Sherlock Holmes Faces Death, Captive Wild Woman, Calling Dr. Death.*
1944   *House of Frankenstein, The Mummy's Ghost, The Spider Woman, The Invisible Man's Revenge, The Scarlet Claw, Weird Woman, The Pearl of Death, Jungle Woman.*
1945   *The House of Fear, The Jungle Captive, The Frozen Ghost, The Woman in Green, Pursuit to Algiers, House of Dracula.*
1946   *House of Horrors, Terror by Night, Dressed to Kill, The Brute Man.*
1951   *The Strange Door, Abbott and Costello Meet the Invisible Man.*
1952   *The Black Castle.*
1953   *Abbott and Costello Meet Dr. Jekyll and Mr. Hyde, The 5,000 Fingers of Dr. T.*
1954   *Creature from the Black Lagoon.*
1955   *This Island Earth, Abbott and Costello Meet the Mummy.*
1956   *The Mole People, The Creature Walks Among Us.*
1957   *The Incredible Shrinking Man, The Land Unknown.*

Remembering

JACK P. PIERCE

It is impossible to unmask the entire career of a man whose genius created the iconoclastic images of Frankenstein, the Mummy, and The Wolf Man. However, I would be remiss to sweep the name of Jack Pierce under the rug, as many people before me have.

Jack was born in New York City on May 5, 1889. An immigrant from Athens, Greece, he began his career in the film industry as a stage actor and, later, a stuntman. At Universal, Jack had a meticulous work ethic and dedication to perfection. At this time, Universal's President, "Uncle" Carl Laemmle and his son Carl Jr., were about to make the decision to delve into the world of the supernatural, a decision that would forever link the words *Universal* and *horror*. Actors Karloff and Lugosi and directors Whale and Browning will forever be associated with the success of the first great horror cycle, but makeup man Jack Pierce's role was just as significant.

After Karloff was cast for the role of the Monster in *Frankenstein* (1931), he and Jack worked together for weeks, experimenting with multiple tests and attempting to perfect the final makeup. During a typical hot southern California summer, Jack applied layers of makeup, putty, grease paint and strips of highly flammable collodion-soaked cotton to Karloff, who sat motionless for upwards of four to six hours. Jack also strapped braces to Karloff's legs. This prevented the actor from bending his knees, which created the Monster's now famous shuffle.

In 1936, Jack survived the Laemmles' ousting and was a significant factor in aiding the studio as they plunged into the second horror cycle. During the '40s, Jack put the same amount of care into his forthcoming creations. In 1941, he created *The Wolf Man*, who ironically was made up not of wolf, but imported yak hair. The transformation scenes were grueling. Actor Lon Chaney, Jr., had to remain absolutely motionless while Jack made facial applications. The camera would shoot a few seconds of film, then stop. Jack would add more yak hair, the camera would shoot again, and so on. All the while, Chaney would have to lie perfectly still. This tedious process sometimes would take an entire day. Of course this was a walk in the park compared to the torturous head-to-toe make up Chaney would have to endure for his three outings as the Mummy.

When Universal merged with International Pictures in 1946, Jack was shown the door. With all of Universal-International's new policies, there was no place for horror. Jack did what many who were cut loose did — he freelanced. He moved from studio to studio for a while, but it was clear that Jack's true niche was in the creation of monsters.

Jack eventually gave way to the more modern methods of makeup and retired in 1962. By the time he died on July 19, 1968, at the age of 79, Jack was nearly forgotten.

Hollywood has a long history of mistreatment of its own. Someone new comes along, the changing of the guard takes place and before you know it, you can't make the trade papers if you robbed a bank. What makes the case of Jack Pierce so painful is that Jack was the personification of "old school." He had a passion for his craft and a dedication that is seldom, if ever, seen nowadays. He was a true genius. So for all his meticulous efforts in creating my favorite figures of fright, I say *thank you* to Jack Pierce.

Appendix: More Mummies

For those truly obsessed with Egypt's living dead, here is a list of Mummy films other than the '40s Universal series.

The Mummy (1912) A silent comedy.

Vengeance of Egypt (1912) A stolen mummy brings death to all who possess it.

The Egyptian Mummy (1914) A silly comedy.

The Mummy and the Hummingbird (1915) Based on a play of the same name by Isaac Henderson. No Mummy.

The Eyes of the Mummy (1918) Directed by Ernst Lubitsch. This doesn't help much considering there's no Mummy.

The Mummy (1932) An early Karloff, Pierce and Freund Universal masterpiece. Don't miss it!

Mummy's Boys (1936) Comedians Wheeler and Woolsey with a fake Mummy.

We Want Our Mummy (1939) Fake mummies are all that is needed to frighten the wits out of the Three Stooges.

The author and a couple of rare one-sheet posters at the home of Ron Borst/Hollywood Movie Posters.

Abbott and Costello Meet the Mummy (1955) Why not, they met everyone else.

The Aztec Mummy (1957) A Mummy stands guard in his pyramid.

Pharaoh's Curse (1957) An Egyptian transforms into a Mummy and drinks the blood of the other defilers after a cursed tomb is opened. The film includes Kurt Katch from *The Mummy's Curse*.

Curse of the Faceless Man (1958) A mummified man buried for 2,000 years near a volcano is revived and seeks out the girl whom he believes is his reincarnated love.

The Mummy (1959) Good Hammer remake has touches of several of the Universal Mummy films of the '40s. Good cast headed by horror greats Christopher Lee as the Mummy, with Peter Cushing.

Curse of the Aztec Mummy (1959) A master criminal has his eye on an Aztec treasure guarded by a living Mummy.

The Robot vs. the Aztec Mummy (1959) The Mummy does battle with a robot.

The Curse of the Mummy's Tomb (1964) Get-rich-quick schemer intends to tour the world with the Mummy of King Ra. But things don't quite work as planned.

Attack of the Mayan Mummy (1964) Reincarnated ancient Mayan Princess and her warrior lover are reunited after centuries.

Face of the Screaming Werewolf (1964) A Mummy and a werewolf are worth checking out only to see Chaney don the Wolf Man makeup for the last time.

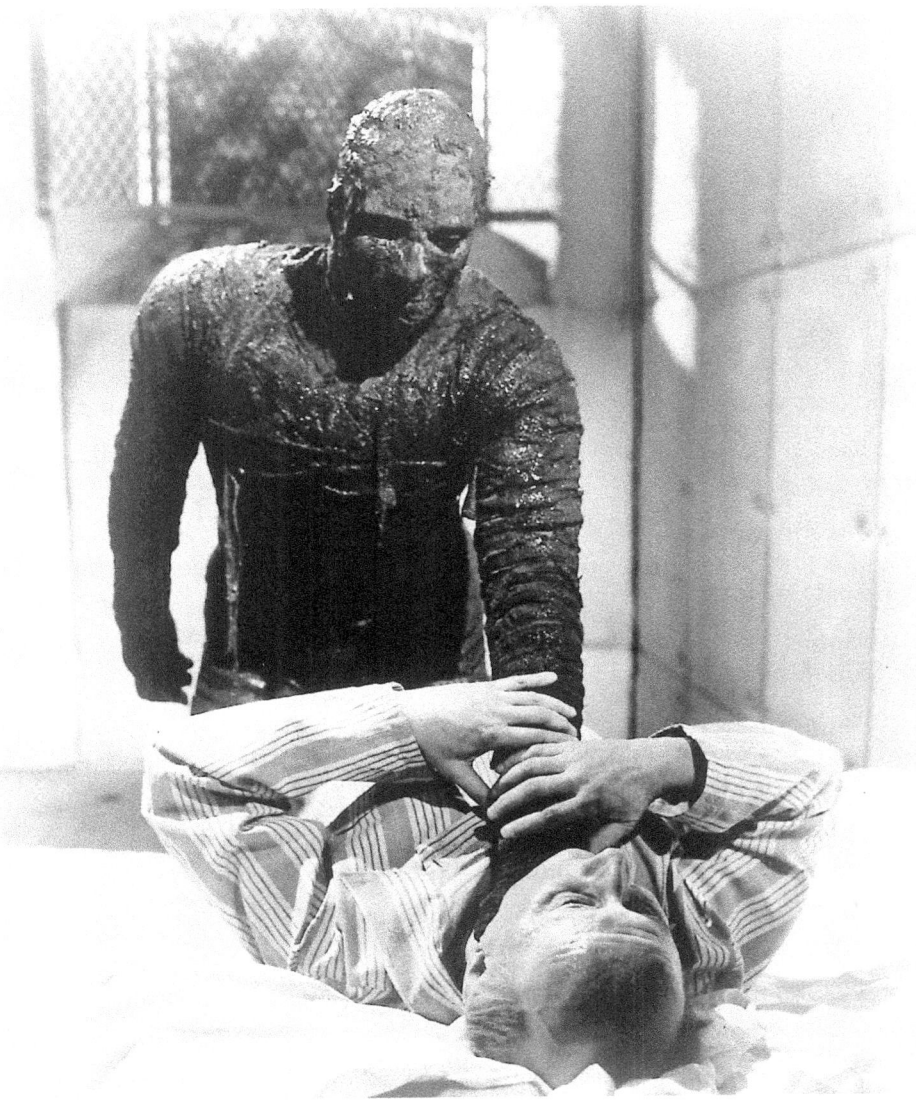

Kharis (Christopher Lee) begins his murder spree by killing Stephen Banning (Felix Aylmer) in England's Hammer Films' effective remake *The Mummy* (Hammer, 1959). It all goes to prove, it doesn't matter what country you hide in, the Mummy will get you!

The Wrestling Women vs. the Aztec Mummy (1965) A Mummy flick from Mexico. What's next, the Mummy vs. the bean burrito?

Orgy of the Dead (1965) A talking Mummy and a talking werewolf! Good luck.

The Mummy's Shroud (1967) After being shipped off to a museum, a Mummy rises to seek revenge on those who ruined his nap.

Mad Monster Party? (1968) A real animated bash with a lot more than the Mummy, Boris Karloff and Phyllis Diller too.

The Mummy and the Curse of the Jackals (1969) "Werejackal" and Mummy in Las Vegas. A loser.

Assignment Terror (a.k.a. ***Dracula vs. Frankenstein***) (1969) Michael Rennie, obviously slumming, attempts world domination with the help of Dracula, the Frankenstein Monster, the Wolf Man and, you guessed it, the Mummy.

Blood from the Mummy's Tomb (1972) The Mummy of an Egyptian queen extends a mystical influence. Based on Bram Stoker's *Jewel of the Seven Stars*.

The Mummy's Revenge (1973) Spanish horror star Paul Naschy stars as the Mummy of a sadistic Pharaoh, revived after centuries to continue killing.

Voodoo Black Exorcist (1975) A Mummy of an African voodoo priest searches for his reincarnated love.

The Awakening (1980) This time it's Charlton Heston who invades the tomb of an Egyptian queen just as his daughter is born. Years later — well, you could figure out the rest. Remake of ***Blood from the Mummy's Tomb***.

Sphinx (1980) A lost royal tomb, a curse and plenty of treachery, but where's the Mummy? Adapted from a Robin Cook novel. With Frank Langella.

Dawn of the Mummy (1981) A fashion photographer and his models disturb the tomb of an ancient Egyptian king. The king comes back to life accompanied by his slaves, who are now zombies. Things get ugly.

The National Mummy (1981) Horror-comedy from Spain involves an Egyptian princess who becomes a genuine bimbo when unwrapped.

The Time Walker (1982) A Mummy from another world, discovered in King Tut's tomb yet, is revived after his sarcophagus is X-rayed.

Secret of the Mummy (1982) Comedy-horror from Brazil with all the gratuitous sex to satisfy anyone with poor taste.

The Outing (1987) An evil genie revives a Mummy and sends him after a group of teens that broke into the museum.

The Monster Squad (1987) Dracula summons the Frankenstein Monster, the Wolf Man, the Creature from the Black Lagoon and, of course, the Mummy to try to find an occult amulet. Homage to the Universal monsters, but strictly for kids.

Waxwork (1988) A unique museum features many different horror exhibits, one of which is the Mummy. But don't get too close!

Tales from the Darkside: The Movie (1990) A student revives a Mummy and sends him out to take care of his enemies. Based on a short story by Sir Arthur Conan Doyle.

The Mummy Lives (1993) Imagine Tony Curtis in a Mummy film.

Tale of the Mummy (1999) Poor attempt at a living Mummy; not scary either.

Bram Stoker's The Mummy (1997) More warnings of curses, but at least there's a Mummy.

The Mummy (1999) Fun for seekers of special effects and lots of action, but if you're waiting for a genuine Mummy, forget it. A poor man's *Raiders of the Lost Ark*. With Brendan Fraser.

The Mummy Returns (2001) The Mummy of Imhotep is back, this time in England. A sequel, with Brendan Fraser.

Bibliography

Screenplays

The Mummy's Curse. By Bernard Schubert. Copyright 1944, Universal Pictures Co., Inc.
The Mummy's Ghost. By Griffin Jay, Henry Sucher and Brenda Weisberg. Copyright 1943, Universal Pictures Co., Inc.
The Mummy's Hand. By Griffin Jay and Maxwell Shane. Copyright 1940, Universal Pictures Co., Inc.
"The Mummy's Return" (treatment). By Leon Abrams.
The Mummy's Tomb. By Griffin Jay and Henry Sucher. Copyright 1942, Universal Pictures Co., Inc.

Books

Fitzgerald, Michael G. *Universal Pictures.* New Rochelle, N.Y.: Arlington House, 1977.
Hirschhorn, Clive. *The Universal Story.* New York: Crown, 1983.
Katz, Ephram. *The Film Encyclopedia.* New York: Thomas Y. Crowell, 1979.
Mank, Gregory William. *The Hollywood Hissables.* Metuchen, NJ, & London: Scarecrow, 1989.
Zinman, David. *Saturday Afternoon at the Bijou.* New Rochelle, NY: Castle Books, Arlington House, 1973.

Articles

Bojarski, Richard. "Remember Peter Coe?" *Hollywood Studio Magazine,* August 1985.
Jones, Preston Neal. "The Ghost of Hans J. Salter: The Man Who Brought Harmony to the House of Frankenstein." *Cinefantastique,* vol. 7, no. 2.

Leifert, Don. "An Actress Brimming with Talent, Virginia Christine." *Filmfax*, no. 21.
Mank, Gregory. "The True Life and Death Story of George Zucco." *Filmfax*, no. 31.
McCallum, Lawrence. "The Dark Charisma of Turhan Bey." *Filmfax*, no. 33.
Taylor, Frank. "Jack Pierce — Forgotten Make-up Artist." *American Cinematographer*, January 1985.

Letters

Knox, Elyse. Letter to author, 2000.
Kosleck, Martin. Letter to author, 1991.

Production Notes

Green Hell, "Vital statistics."
The Mummy's Curse.

Studio Biographies

Disney	Dick Foran
Paramount	Eduardo Ciannelli, July 1942.
	Dick Foran, 1949
	Holmes Herbert, 1931
	Martin Kosleck, 1940
	Frank Reicher
RKO Radio	Ramsay Ames
	Wallace Ford
Republic	Dennis Moore, April 1941
	Tom Tyler, 1943
20th Century–Fox	Elyse Knox, October 1940.
	Robert Lowery
Universal	Ramsay Ames, February 1944
	Lon Chaney, May 1945
	Leslie Goodwins, June 1944
	Mary Gordon, December 1945
	Elyse Knox, March 1942
	Kay Harding, February 1944
Warner Bros.	Dick Foran, 1958

Newspapers and Trade Papers

Films in Review Letters, April 1968
Hollywood Citizen News 1946, 1951, 1954, 1968
The Hollywood Reporter 1968
"Keyhole Portraits"
L.A. Herald Examiner 1947, 1969, 1988

The Los Angeles Times, 1937, 1944, 1953, 1954, 1956, 1961, 1965, 1969, 1973, 1979, 1981, 1985, 1988, 1993, 1994, 1996
MCA INK, January 1984
The New York Times 1988
People, 1979
RTS Music Gazette, 1977
The Society for the Preservation of Film Music; Tribute to Hans J. Salter. Program, 1993
T.V. Radio Mirror, 1971
Variety, 1963, 1968, 1969, 1972, 1988, 1989

Additional Thanks

American Film Institute Catalog, 1931-1940 and 1941–1950
The Internet Movie Database
USC Film and Television Archives
My good buddy Oliver Kapp
The entire *cast* at the Larry Edmunds Bookshop, Hollywood, CA
Dan and Scott Schwartz of Baseball Cards—Movie Collectibles, Westlake Village, CA
Buddy Barnett of Cinema Collectors, Hollywood, CA, and Chris Ortiz of Cinema Collectors, Las Vegas, NV
Jerry Ohlinger's Movie Material Store, New York, NY
The late Bob Coleman of the Hollywood Poster Exchange, Los Angeles CA
Backlot Books, Hollywood CA
Donovan, Heidi and Clair at Eddie Brandt's Saturday Matinee, North Hollywood, CA

Index

Abbott and Costello 34, 96, 135, 150, 191, 209
Abbott and Costello Meet Frankenstein (movie) 201, 209
Abbott and Costello Meet the Mummy (movie) 29, 218
Abdo, Eddie 99
Abie's Irish Rose 138
Abraham Lincoln 138
Abrams, Leon 85, 95, 99–100
Adam-12 136, 141
Adams, Jane 59
The Adventures of Captain Marvel (movie) 196
The Adventures of Sherlock Holmes (movie) 165
Ali Baba and the Forty Thieves (movie) 156, 168, 194
Allbritton, Louise 59
The Amazing Mr. X (movie) 168
Ameche, Don 153
American-International 202
Ames, Ramsay 55–56, 58, 62, 82, 154–156
Andrews Sisters 135, 182
Ankers, Evelyn 167–168
Arabian Nights (movie) 168, 209
Arno, Sigfried 5, 6
Arnold, Jack 35
Assignment Terror (movie) 220
Astaire, Fred 193

Attack of the Mayan Mummy (movie) 218
Atwill, Lionel 70, 97, 192, 201
The Awakening (movie) 220
Aylmer, Felix 219
The Aztec Mummy (movie) 218

Babcock, Dwight V. 99
Babylon Five (movie) 168
Back Street (1961 movie) 209
Bacon, Lloyd 186
Bad Girl 138
Bancroft, George 31–32, 170
The Bank Dick (movie) 209
Bara, Nina 99
Barclay, Stephen 55
Barefoot in the Park (movie) 185
Barry, Gene 193
Barrymore, Ethel 187
Barrymore, Lionel 181
Beach, Rex 190
Beery, Noah, Jr. 135
Belasco, Leon 5, 7, 182–183
Ben Hur 190
Bennett, Joan 31, 32, 33
The Best People (movie) 182
Bey, Turhan 35–36, 38, 43, 52–53, 82, 167–169
Big Jim McLain (movie) 141
Bird of Paradise (movie) 200
The Black Castle (movie) 202
The Black Cat (1934 movie) 170

Black Friday (movie) 2, 213
Bloch, Robert 136
Blonde Venus (movie) 186
Blood and Sand (movie) 171
Blood from the Mummy's Tomb (movie) 220
Bluebeard (movie) 171
Bogart, Humphrey 135, 189, 193
Bonanza 136, 171
Boot Hill (movie) 162
Bram Stoker's The Mummy (movie) 221
Brando, Marlon 175
Bredell, Elwood 5
Brent, George 168
The Bride of Frankenstein (movie) 36, 112, 170, 186
Brighty of the Grand Canyon (movie) 136
Brissac, Virginia 35, 37
Broadway 138
Broder, Jack 131
Brown, Bernard B. 5, 35, 55, 99
Brown, Lew 134
Browning, Todd 138, 214
Bruce, David 55, 165, 168
Bruce, Nigel 160, 192
Buck Privates (movie) 209
Burnett, Carol 158
Burns, Paul E. 35, 54, 185
Burton, Richard 151
Bushman, Frances X. 205

227

INDEX

Buster, Bud 99
Butch Minds the Baby 135
Byron, Walter 35

Cabanne, Christy 5, 13–14, 205–206
Cagney, James 143, 186, 189, 193
Cahn, Philip 5
Calling Dr. Death (movie) 155, 207
Captains Courageous (movie) 172, 189
Captive Wild Woman (movie) 168
Carradine, Bruce 170
Carradine, Christopher 171
Carradine, David 170
Carradine, John 55–56, 59–60, 71, 82, 96, 169–174, 190
Carradine, Keith 171
Carradine, Robert 171
Carrillo, Leo 135, 150
Carroll, Charles 5
Carruth, Milton 35
Carson, Johnny 158
Case, Eddie 99
Chaney, Lon, Jr. 35, 38, 43, 53, 55–56, 59, 71–72, 97, 99, 101–102, 135, 151, 155, 178, 189, 192, 199–204, 207, 212, 215, 218
Chaney, Lon, Sr. 199–200
Change of Heart (movie) 134
Chaplin, Charlie 208
Chicago Hope 154
Christine, Virginia 97, 99, 101, 104, 156
Christmas Holiday (movie) 213
Ciannelli, Eduardo 5, 161–163
The Cisco Kid 208
Clark, Cliff 35, 43
The Clock (movie) 193
Cobra Woman (movie) 34
Codee, Ann 99–100, 104, 193
Coe, Peter 97, 99–100, 174–176
Columbia Pictures 155, 170
Columbo, Russ 182
Come and Get It (movie) 143
Conan Doyle, Sir Arthur 220
Confessions of a Nazi Spy (movie) 178
The Connecticut Yankee 136
Conrad, Joseph 136
Cook, Robin 220
Cooke, Caroline 55
Cording, Harry 35
Corman, Roger 175
Coward, Noel 162
Cowl, Jane 187
Craig's Wife (movie) 181

Crawford, Broderick 135
Crawford, Joan 181
Crazy House (movie) 156
The Creature from the Black Lagoon (movie) 213
Crosby, Bing 175
Cugat, Xaviar 155
Cummings, Robert 150
Cunard, Grace 35
Curse of the Aztec Mummy (movie) 218
Curse of the Faceless Man (movie) 218
The Curse of the Mummy's Tomb (movie) 18, 131, 218
Curtis, Tony 193, 221
Cushing, Peter 131, 218

Daddy Long Legs (movie) 193
Danger in the Pacific (movie) 168
Dark Streets of Cairo (movie) 165
Darrian, Frank 35
Daughter of the Mind (movie) 158
David and Bathsheba (movie) 192
David Copperfield 159
Davis, Bette 135, 178, 193
Dawn of the Mummy (movie) 220
Dead End Kids 206
Dead Man's Eyes (movie) 207
DeLacy, Ralph M. 5, 35
DeMille, Cecil B. 191
The Desert Fox (movie) 165
Destry Rides Again (movie) 209
Devine, Andy 135, 170
Dickens, Charles 165
Dietrich, Marlene 175, 177–178, 186
Diller, Phyllis 158, 220
Dr. Jekyll and Mr. Hyde (1932 movie) 192
Doctor X (movie) 70
Dodds, William 99
Don Winslow of the Navy (movie) 194
Don't Call Me Charlie 141
Douglas, Lloyd C. 160
Dracula (movie) 1, 2, 22–23, 39
Dracula (movie, Spanish) 188
Dracula vs. Frankenstein (movie) 202, 220
Dracula's Daughter (movie) 39
Drake, Oliver 99
Drums Along the Mohawk (movie) 170

Drums of the Congo (movie) 150
Durbin, Deanna 150, 209, 213

Eagle-Lion 168
Edge of Darkness (movie) 157
The Egyptian Mummy (movie) 217
Elliott, Heenan 99
Emmett, Fern 35
The Eyes of the Mummy (movie) 217

F-Troop 208
Face of the Screaming Werewolf (movie) 218
Fairbanks, Douglas, Jr. 31–33, 212
Fairbanks, Douglas, Sr. 205
Family Affair 141
Farnum, William 99, 101, 113, 190–191
Faye, Alice 153
FBO Studios 196, 205
Feitshans, Fred R., Jr. 99
Feld, Fritz 157
Feldman, Charles K. 174
Ferguson, Al 99
Field, Betty 189
Fields, W.C. 135, 209
Fighting Mad (movie) 140–141
Film Classics 39
The Firefly (movie) 165
First Love (movie) 150, 209
Flash Gordon Conquers the Universe (movie) 209
Flower Drum Song (movie) 151
Flowers, Bess 55
Flynn, Errol 149–150, 157, 168, 175
Follow the Boys (movie) 156, 175
Fonda, Henry 153
Foolscap 162
Footsteps in the Dark (movie) 168
For Whom the Bell Tolls (movie) 162
Foran, Dick 5–6, 8,13, 29, 35–36, 38, 54, 133–137, 150, 152, 184, 201
Ford, John 170, 172
Ford, Wallace 5–6, 8,13, 35, 37–38, 134, 138–140, 187, 200
Foreign Correspondent (movie) 162, 178
Foster, Eddie 5
Foster, Susanna 34
Fowler, Gene 136
Fox Studios 134–135
Foy, Bryan 135

Index

Frankenstein (movie) 1–2, 39, 50, 215
Frankenstein Meets the Wolf Man (movie) 97, 201
Fraser, Brendan 85, 221
Freaks (movie) 138
Freund, Karl 217
The Front Page 162
The Frozen Ghost (movie) 178
Frye, Dwight 23
The Fugitive 157
Fulton, John P. 99
Furneaux, Yvonne 97

Gable, Clark 143
Gangelin, Victor A. 99
Garland, Judy 193
Gausman, Russell A. 5, 35, 55, 99
Gershenson, Joseph 55
The Ghost of Frankenstein (movie) 104, 192, 201, 212–213
Gilligan's Island 208
Gilmore, J. Andrew 35
Gish, Lillian 205
Gleason, Jackie 158
Goetz, William 131
Goldsmith, Jerry 213
Goldwyn, Samuel 143
Goodkind, Saul 55
Goodman, John B. 55, 99
Goodwins, Fred 208
Goodwins, Leslie 99, 208
Gordon, Mary 35, 37, 185
The Gorgeous Hussy (movie) 181
Gould, Charles 35
The Grapes of Wrath (movie) 169, 170–171
Gray, Zane 136
Great Guy (movie) 143
The Great Ziegfeld (movie) 209
The Greatest of Ease (movie) 175
Green Acres 141
Green Hell (movie) 31–34, 111
Green Stockings 159
Greene, Lorne 158
Griffith, D.W. 205
Grossman, Abraham 55
Guess Who's Coming to Dinner? (movie) 156
Gung Ho! (movie) 174–175
Gunga Din (movie) 162
Gunsmoke 141, 171
Gwynne, Anne 135, 175
Gypsy 138

Hale, Alan 31
Hall, Jon 168, 171, 192
Hammer Studio 97, 131, 218–219
Harding, Kay 97, 99–100, 102, 146, 159–160
Harmon, Mark 154
Harold Young Productions 206
Harvey (movie) 151, 209
Hatton, Rondo 178
The Haunted Palace (movie) 202
Have Gun, Will Travel 202
Hedda Gabler 157–158
Henderson, Isaac 217
Hepburn, Katharine 172
Herbert, Holmes 97, 99, 102, 191–193
Heston, Charlton 220
Hey Mulligan 141
Heywood, Herbert 99
High Noon (movie) 202
Hit the Ice (movie) 153
Hitchcock, Alfred 138, 178, 185
Hoffman, Otto 35
Hogan, Dick 35
Hold 'Em Navy 140
Holt, Tim 188
Hope, Bob 158, 175, 202
Horror Island (movie) xi, 135, 150, 201
The Hound of the Baskervilles (movie) 169
House of Dracula (movie) 59, 171, 201
The House of Fear (1939 movie) 2
House of Frankenstein (movie) 59, 83, 96, 171, 175, 201, 213
House of Horrors (movie) 178
The House of the Seven Gables (movie) 135
Hubbard, John 35–36, 38, 43, 140–142
The Hunchback of Notre Dame (movie) 165

I Remember Mama 194
Imitation of Life (1959 movie) 209
In the Navy (movie) 135, 209
Ince, Thomas 192
The Incredible Shrinking Man (movie) 213
International Pictures 168, 202, 209, 215
Invisible Agent (movie) 192
The Invisible Man (movie) 1, 170
The Invisible Man Returns (movie) 2, 213
The Invisible Man's Revenge (movie) 171
The Invisible Ray (movie) 201
Irish in Us (movie) 186
It Started with Eve (movie) 150

Jack and the Beanstalk (movie) 191
Jay, Griffin 5, 21–22, 29, 35, 42, 55, 82
Jesse James (movie) 169
Joe Palooka 154
Johann, Zita 82
Jones, Buck 135, 146, 201
Journey's End 165
Judgment at Nuremberg (movie) 156
Junior G-Men of the Air (movie) 168, 209

Karloff, Boris 2, 96, 125, 170, 192, 199, 201–202, 210, 214–215, 217, 220
Katch, Kurt 97, 99–100, 194, 218
Keep 'Em Flying 135
Kellaway, Cecil 5–6, 13
Kelly, Gene 213
Kelly, Lew 35
King 55, 114
King Kong (movie) 188
Kings Go Forth (movie) 193
Kitty Foyle (movie) 162
Knight, Fuzzy 150
Knowles, Patric 153
Knox, Elyse 35, 37–38, 45, 53, 82, 153–154
Korda, Alexander 206
Kosleck, Martin 97, 99, 101, 177–179, 194
Koster, Henry 150, 209

Lackteen, Frank 5, 183–184
Laemmle, Carl, Jr. 214
Laemmle, Carl, Sr. 214–215
The Lamb (movie) 205
Langella, Frank 220
Lassie 136
Lease, Rex 35
Le Borg, Reginald 55, 72, 207
Lee, Christopher 97, 131, 218–219
Less Than the Dust (movie) 183
Letters to Lucerne 159
Lillian Russell (movie) 153
Linda Be Good (movie) 140
Little Tough Guy (movie) 206
Litvak, Anatole 178
Lloyd, Frank 191
Loftin, Carey 99
London, Jack 136, 188
Lorre, Peter 189, 192

INDEX

Lottery Lover (movie) 134
Love Me Forever (movie) 207
Lowery, Robert 55, 57, 142–145, 155
Lubin, Arthur 159
Lubitsch, Ernst 217
Luck of the Irish (movie) 150–151
Lugosi, Bela 22, 96, 146, 192, 199, 201, 210, 214

MacLane, Barton 55, 57
MacMurray, Fred 158
MacQuarrie, Murdock 5, 19, 184
MacVicar, Martha 55
Mad About Music (movie) 209
The Mad Doctor (movie) 178
The Mad Doctor of Market Street (movie) 70
The Mad Ghoul (movie) 165, 168
Mad Monster Party? (movie) 220
Magnificent Obsession (movie) 209
The Male Animal 159
A Man in the Shadow (movie) 174
Man Made Monster (movie) 97, 201, 212, 213
Man Who Fights Alone (movie) 190
The Man Without a Country (movie) 191
Mancini, Henry 213
Mangean, Teddy 99
Manners, David 59
Mantell, Robert 169
March, Frederick 192
Margin for Error (movie) 194
Marie Antoinette (movie) 165
Mark, Michael 5
Mark of the Vampire (movie) 192
Marsh, Charles 35
Martel, Jeannie 196
Mary Had a Little 141
Mary, Mary, Bloody Mary (movie) 169
Maverick 208
Maya 213
Mayo, Virginia 168
McKinney, Mira 35, 55, 64
McVey, Pat 35
Meek, Donald 170
Melford, George 188
Mendelssohn, Eleanor von 178
The Merchant of Venice 169, 178
MGM 134, 138, 165, 171

A Midsummer Night's Dream 165
Milestone, Lewis 157
Milland, Ray 146
Miller, Virgil 99
Mind the Paint Girl 191
Mr. Skeffington (movie) 193
M'Liss 159
The Mole People (movie) 213
The Monkees 202
Monogram 154
The Monster Squad (movie) 220
Montez, Maria 34, 156, 168, 194, 209
Moore, Dennis 97, 99–100, 145–147
Moran, Peggy xi, 5, 13, 31, 32, 33, 38, 53, 82, 135, 149–152, 165, 212
Moulin, Jess 55
The Mummy (1912 movie) 217
The Mummy (1932 movie) 8, 10, 22, 24, 30–31, 58, 82, 217
The Mummy (1959 movie) 97, 131, 218, 219
The Mummy (1999 movie) 221
The Mummy and the Curse of the Jackals (movie) 220
The Mummy and the Hummingbird (movie) 217
The Mummy Lives (movie) 221
The Mummy Returns (movie) 85, 221
Mummy's Boys (movie) 217
The Mummy's Curse (movie) 3, 85, 96, 97, 99–132, 145, 156, 159, 174–175, 177, 190–191, 193–194, 199, 201, 208, 218
The Mummy's Ghost (movie) 42, 53, 55–83, 96, 104, 106, 114, 142, 154, 164, 169, 171, 187–190, 199, 201, 207
The Mummy's Hand (movie) xi, 3, 5–34, 36, 38–39, 42, 53–54, 56, 82, 96, 108, 112–113, 133, 135, 138, 149, 152, 161, 164–165, 181–184, 195–196, 205, 212–213
"The Mummy's Return" (treatment) 85–97, 100
The Mummy's Revenge (movie) 220
The Mummy's Shroud (movie) 219
The Mummy's Tomb (movie) 35–54, 56, 58–59, 61–62, 82, 113, 120, 133, 135, 138, 140, 153, 164, 167, 184–185, 187, 199, 201, 206

The Munsters 141, 171
My Favorite Brunette 202
My Favorite Martian 208
My Little Chickadee (movie) 135, 209
Mystery of the Wax Museum (movie) 192

Naish, J. Carrol 83, 202
Nancy's Birthright (movie) 184
Naschy, Paul 220
The National Mummy (movie) 220
Neal, Paul 99
Neuman, Harry 35
Never Wave at a Wac (movie) 165
A Night in Paradise (movie) 168
Night Key (movie) 2
The Night of January 16 159
Obzina, Martin 99
O'Driscoll, Martha 59
Of Mice and Men 138, 200
Of Mice and Men (1940 movie) 189
O'Hara, Maureen 165
Olsen and Johnson 156
Once More, with Feeling 182
One More Spring (movie) 134
One Night in the Tropics (movie) 150
One Night of Love (movie) 207
Only the Valiant (movie) 202
Orgy of the Dead (movie) 219
Orth, Frank 99
O'Shea, Oscar 55, 57, 71, 189–190
Otterson, Jack 5, 35
Out of the Blue (movie) 168
The Outing (movie) 220
The Ozzie and Harriet Show 154

Paige, Robert 59
Paramount 134, 140, 192, 200, 202, 206
Pardon My Sarong (movie) 34
Parker, Eddie 35, 99
Parker, Jean 143
Pastell, George 97
Pasternak, Joe 150
Pathé 205
Peanuts 55, 75, 114
Pepper, Bob 99
Perry Mason 136
Phantom Lady (movie) 159
Phantom of the Opera (1943 movie) 34, 159, 202
The Pharaoh's Curse (movie) 218

Index

Pickford, Mary 183, 208
Pierce, Jack P. 5, 31, 35, 55, 99, 214–215, 217
Pigs 138
Pittsburgh (movie) 209
Pivar, Ben 5, 35, 55, 99
Power, Tyrone 151
Previn, Charles 212
Price, Vincent 31–32, 135, 202
Prichard, Robert 99
Private Buckaroo (movie) 135
Psycho 136
Puppets 162
Pursuit to Algiers (movie) 178

Raft, George 175
The Rage of Paris (movie) 212
Raiders of the Lost Ark (movie) 221
The Rainmaker 136
Rains, Claude 34, 159, 193, 201
Randall, Slats 143
Rathbone, Basil 160, 165, 178, 185, 192, 199
Rawhide 202
Realart Pictures 39, 131
Reicher, Frank 35, 37, 55–56, 187–188
Reid, Wallace 205
Rennie, Michael 220
Republic Pictures 188, 196–197
The Return of Frank James (movie) 171
Return of the Gunfighter (movie) 213
Reunion in Vienna 162
Rich, Doris 171
Richards, Addison 97, 99–100
Richmond, Ted 99
Ride 'Em Cowboy (movie) 135
Riders of Death Valley (movie) 135, 201
The Rifleman 202
RKO Studios 131, 139, 145, 165, 186, 200
Roach, Hal 140
Road to Bali (movie) 175
The Roaring Twenties (movie) 189, 193
The Robe (movie) 151
Robertson-Cole Studios 186
Robinson, Ann 193
Robinson, George 35
The Robot vs. the Aztec Mummy (movie) 218
Rockwell, Jack 55
Rocky Mountain (movie) 175
Rogell, Al 135
Rogers, Ginger 146
Rogers, John 35, 37
Romeo and Juliet 187

Rooney, Mickey 141
Rose Marie 162
Route 66 202
Rozsa, Miklos 213
Ruhl, Bill 35, 45
Runyon, Damon 135

Sabatini, Rafael 136
Saboteur (movie) 185, 209
St. Elsewhere 154
Salter, Hans J. 5, 20, 35, 42, 55, 209, 210, 212–214
San Antonio Rose (movie) 201
Sanders, George 31–32, 135
Sangster, Jimmy 97
Santchi, Tom 190
Santoro, Tony 99
Savage, Henry, W. 162
Sawtell, Paul 99
Scared to Death (movie) 205
The Scarlet Claw (movie) 160
The Scarlet Pimpernel (movie) 206
Schubert, Bernard 99
Schwartz, William 35
Scorsese, Martin 151
Scott, Randolph 174
The Scoundrel (movie) 162
The Sea Wolf (1941 movie) 188
The Secret Invasion (movie) 175
Secret of the Mummy (movie) 220
Seventeen 138
77 Sunset Strip 208
Shadow of a Doubt (movie) 138
Shakespeare, William 190
Shane, Maxwell 5, 21–22, 29
Shannon, Harry 55
Sharpe, Lester 55, 57
Shaw, Janet 35
She Done Him Wrong (movie) 186
Sheehan, Winfield 134
Sheridan, Ann 157
Sherlock Holmes and the Voice of Terror (movie) 209, 213
Sherlock Holmes in Washington (movie) 165, 209
Shyer, Melville 55
Sickner, William 55
Silk Stockings 182
Simpson, Napoleon 99–100
Sinatra, Frank 193
Siodmak, Curt 201
Siodmak, Robert 159
Skinner, Frank 14, 20, 25, 208–211, 213
Smith, Ernie 99

Smith, Jack C. 55
Smith, L.R. 55
Smith, Thorne 136
Soldier in the Rain (movie) 141
Son of Dracula (1943 movie) 59, 201, 213
Son of Frankenstein (movie) 2, 209, 213
The Son of Kong (movie) 2
Sorel, Sonia 171
Sosso, Pietro 55
Sphinx (movie) 220
Spitz, Leo 131
The Spoilers (1942 movie) 190
Spring Parade (movie) 150
Stagecoach (movie) 170, 172
Stand Up and Cheer (movie) 134
Starsky and Hutch 171
Steinbeck, John 138, 200
Stevens, Charles 99–100
Stevens, Onslow 59
Stewart, James 151, 181
Stoker, Bram 220
Stolen Identity (movie) 168
The Story of Louis Pasteur (movie) 188
Stranded in Paris (movie) 193
Strange, Glenn 35, 59, 83
Stranger on the Third Floor (movie) 189
A Streetcar Named Desire (movie) 175
Stromberg, William 213
Stubbs, Harry 5
Sucher, Henry 35, 55, 82
The Suffragette 164

Tale of the Mummy (movie) 221
Tales from the Darkside: The Movie (movie) 220
Tales of Wells Fargo 158
The Taming of the Shrew 165
Tartar, Mara 5
Taylor, Elizabeth 206
Taylor, Robert 181
Temple, Shirley 134
There's One Born Every Minute (movie) 206
Three Comrades (movie) 165
Three Smart Girls (movie) 209
The Three Stooges 217
Three Weeks (movie) 196
Thriller 171
Tiffany-Stahl 205
The Time Walker (movie) 220
Tol'able David (movie) 170
Tone, Franchot 150
Top Secret (movie) 165
Topper 208

Tower of London (1939 movie) 2, 192
Tracy, Spencer 172
Trail of the Vigilantes (movie) 150
Trevor, Claire 170
Triesault, Ivan 55
Trowbridge, Charles 5–6, 181–182
20th Century–Fox 131, 142–143, 153, 165, 170–171, 192
Twilight Zone 157, 171
Two Senoritas from Chicago (movie) 155
Tyler, Tom xi, 5, 7, 19, 29, 31, 32, 33, 151, 195–199, 210

UFA Studio 212
United Artists 201–202
Universal International 215
Universal Pictures 1–3, 8–9, 14, 21–22, 31–34, 37, 39, 43, 55, 59, 71–72, 83, 85, 96–97, 100, 102, 125, 131, 135–136, 138, 149–150, 155–156, 158–160, 165, 168, 170–171, 174–175, 181, 186, 196, 201–202, 206–207, 209–210, 212–215, 217–218
Usher, Guy 35

The Vampire Hookers (movie) 169
Varnick, Neil P. 35
Vaughan, Dorothy 55, 72, 155
Vengeance of Egypt (movie) 217
Verdugo, Elena 59
Vernell, Carl 55
Victoria Regina 165
Vogan, Emmett 35, 43, 55, 57
Voodoo Black Exorcist (movie) 220

Waggner, George 201
Wagon Train 202
Walker, Robert 193
Waller, Eddy C. 35, 43, 55, 57, 64, 188–189
War of the Worlds (movie) 193
Warde, Anthony 55
Warner Bros. 134–135, 149–150, 157, 168, 171, 193, 202
Waxwork (movie) 220
Wayne, John 136, 170, 195
We Want Our Mummy (movie) 217
Weird Woman (movie) 207
Weisberg, Brenda 55, 82
Weissmuller, Johnny 174
Wells, Orson 175
West, Mae 135, 186
West, Vera 5, 35, 55, 99
Western Union (movie) 169, 171
Wetzell, Edwin L. 99
Whale, James 31, 33, 111, 186, 214
What Happened to Jones 164
Wheeler and Woolsey 217
When the Daltons Rode (movie) 209
Where Brains Are Needed (movie) 184
White Savage (movie) 209
Whitney, Claire 55
Wilder, Billy 151
Williams, John 213
Williams, Tennessee 175
Winners of the West (movie) 135
The Wolf Man (movie) 104, 194, 201, 213, 215
Woman of the Year (movie) 158
World's Fair (movie) 174
The Wresting Women vs. the Aztec Mummy (movie) 219
Wright, Mac 99

You Are There 158
Young, Harold 35, 206
Young Sinners 138

Zanuck, Darryl F. 153
Zucco, Frances 165
Zucco, George 5, 13–14, 19, 31, 32, 33, 35–36, 38, 55–56, 60–63, 82, 164–166, 168

www.ingramcontent.com/pod-product-compliance
Ingram Content Group UK Ltd.
Pitfield, Milton Keynes, MK11 3LW, UK
UKHW050532150426
5217IPUK00026B/1905